Bookplay

Books by Margaret Read MacDonald

Booksharing: 101 Programs to Use with Preschoolers
Celebrate the World: Twenty Tellable Folktales for Multicultural Festivals
The Folklore of World Holidays
Look Back and See: Twenty Lively Tales for Gentle Tellers
A Parent's Guide to Storytelling
Peace Tales: World Folktales to Talk About
The Old Woman Who Lived in a Vinegar Bottle
The Skit Book: 101 Skits from Kids
*The Storyteller's Sourcebook: A Subject, Title, and Motif-Index to Folklore
    Collections for Children.*
*The Storyteller's Start-up Book: Finding, Learning, Performing and Using
    Folktales*
Thai Tales: Folktales of Thailand (with Supaporn Vathanaprida)
*Twenty Tellable Tales: Audience Participation Folktales for the Beginning
    Storyteller.*
Tom Thumb (Oryx Multicultural Folktale Series)
When the Lights Go Out: Twenty Scary Tales to Tell

❧ *Bookplay* ❧

101 Creative Themes
to Share with
Young Children

by Margaret Read MacDonald

with drawings by Julie Liana MacDonald

Library Professional Publications • 1995

First published 1995 as a
Library Professional Publication, an imprint of
The Shoe String Press, Inc.
North Haven, Connecticut 06473.

Library of Congress Cataloging-in-Publication Data

MacDonald, Margaret Read, 1940–
    Bookplay: 101 creative themes to share
with young children/by Margaret Read MacDonald;
with drawings by Julie Liana MacDonald.
        p.   cm.
    Includes bibliographical references and index.
    ISBN 0-208-02280-5
    1. Storytelling.   2. Children—Books and reading.
3. Education, Primary—Activity programs.
I. MacDonald, Julie Liana, ill.   II. Title.
LB1042.M22   1995
372.64′2—dc20   94-25146

The paper used in this publication meets the minimum
requirements of American National Standard
for Information Sciences—Permanence of Paper
for Printed Library Materials,
ANSI Z39.48–1984. ⊗

Printed in the United States of America

To my father, Murray Read

> *Who built with his hands a retreat where I can write these books,*
> *and builds with his thoughts a place where my ideas can grow.*
> *Thanks for being there for us for ninety-two years.*

Contents

Fall

Winter

Those starred can be used for celebrations other than Christmas

What Can You Do with . . . ?

Just Me!

Concepts

What If You Were a Goose?

Music

Acknowledgments

The children's librarians of the King County Library System in Seattle, Washington are a creative and generous lot. Thanks to all who have shared program ideas over the years!

Thanks to Jennifer MacDonald for typing and to Julie MacDonald for her sketches.

Thanks to the staff of the Bothell Library for their smiling faces under repeated onsets of roaring preschoolers.

Thanks to all of the parents, grandparents, and daycare providers who bring their children to our library storytimes. And thanks, most of all, to the children who make it happen!

Introduction

A few years ago a delightful young Hungarian woman, Veronica Cohn, began bringing her daughter Ilona to my storytimes. Veronica always stayed in the story room long after everyone else was gone, reading to Ilona and discussing the day's activities with her. Each day, as Veronica and Ilona left the room, Veronica would turn and call, "Thank you, Dr. MacDonald, for a good time." The thanks for a "good time" surprised me. Over the years Veronica continued to bring Ilona to my storytimes, and she continued to thank me each day for a "good time." Gradually I began to look at my storytimes in a slightly new light. They were packed with educational activities and reading promotion, certainly. But they were also, importantly, a chance for children and parents to share a "good time."

While preparing story programs for this book, I have asked myself each week, "If I were four what would be a really FUN thing to do?" I have kept, of course, my emphasis on the sharing of really fine picture books. But I have tried to imagine activities to accompany the picture book-sharing which would be great fun for myself and the children. And since I am only one librarian preparing for three storytime classes each week, I had to keep preparation for this fun activity very simple.

I hope you enjoy these suggestions for mixing story, poetry, musical games, dramatic play, and simple art projects in a program of BOOKPLAY.

To the Preschool Teacher

These programs take about forty-five minutes to execute, including the craft period. In your preschool setting, you may wish to break these units into mini-units and spread the thematic activities over two or three days.

You will find reference to adult involvement throughout these programs. If you do not have parents on hand, the programs can all be executed solo. I have used them with a class of fifteen 4- to 6-year-olds without any other adult in the room. However, if you work with a parent co-op, I hope you will include your parent helpers in these units. So often I see parents "hanging out" and chatting on the fringes while the children are engaged in their creative activities. The parents need to have *their* creativity spiced a bit, too. Please get them involved.

To the Librarian Offering Preschool Storytimes

In my earlier programming collection, *Booksharing,* I spoke of the importance of including parents in the preschool storytime. Sadly, I see few public librarians inviting adults into their inner sanctums. Years of working behind closed doors have made us wary of the critical adult. I ask you to examine your attitudes on this matter.

The parents, grandparents, and daycare providers who bring the children to the library need your storytimes as much as do their children. By including them you double the audience you serve. Through attending storytime with their children, parents become familiar with good books and learn techniques for reading aloud. They learn fingerplays, songs, and activities to share. You are demonstrating good booksharing techniques to the adults as you perform your storytime.

Perhaps even more important is the warm adult-child relationship which takes place during storytime. The child and parent sit close together, usually touching, as they share this experience. The child sees the *parent* modeling enjoyment of books and creative activities. And in the creative drama and singing games, the child sees the adult in a playful mode. In addition to the knowledge of booksharing and creative activities gained, the parent has a chance to interact with other adults—a contact much needed in those years of early childhood parenting.

The inclusion of the parent in storytime programs means that the story theme can be continued in the home. Picture books can be re-read. Songs and fingerplays can be repeated. The story event can be remembered and the take-home craft shared with other family members. And the bits of information gained in the story program can be reinforced in other areas of the child's life.

Not least of the reasons to include the adults is the wonderful helping hand they offer during storytime. Circle games are easy with adults to hold hands. Crafts projects are simple with an adult to help each child. And a sharing adult can whisper explanations into the ears of listening children, helping them make better sense of the story images they are seeing and hearing.

To make this story-sharing experience available to more parents, plan special "Sharing Time" programs in early evening or on weekends. Find times when parents and children can come together to enjoy books. I urge you to try this and *double* your storytime impact.

Programming for Primary Age Children

These programs have been used with 2½- to 5-year-old classes, and with 4- to 6-year-old classes. Some have been used as library programs for grades K through 3. They work well as programming for kindergarten groups. To use them with primary children, provide time for a decorative element in your craft period, letting the older children embellish the simple craft according to their own artistic talents.

To the Primary Teacher

Though these programs were developed for use in library preschool storytimes, response to my earlier collection, *Booksharing,* has shown that these are useful in the primary classroom. Teachers generally pick a few items from each theme, using the craft, music, and drama ideas to extend enjoyment of picture books. In the classroom it often works best to select a variety of these elements and spread their use over several days. Most of us have been mixing our genres in this fruitful way for years, but now that we have the term "whole language" we are more aware of the extensions we are making. These programs may suggest some simple extensions for the picture books you already love to share with your children, and they may also introduce you to some exciting new materials. By grouping several books and activities on a single theme, you create an energy which makes the materials more memorable to the children. And as the books and activities bounce off each other, each is enhanced by its relationship to the rest.

Preparing a Book Program

When preparing a program of books and book-related activities, think in terms of the entire event. You need a rational flow from beginning to end. My books and activities are selected to enhance each other and to carry my theme forward through the entire program. The programs in this book take forty-five to fifty minutes.

Opening

I like to open and close with special "hello" and "goodbye" songs. The musical notation for the songs I use are in the appendix to this book. You will probably have favorite welcoming songs of your own. I recommend using the same songs from week to week, as the children love these familiar opening and closing times. During the opening songs I take time to sing to each child by name, welcoming them to the storytime ("Jenny, Jenny, are you here?," p. 163). This singing time quiets the children, allows latecomers to enter the group unobtrusively, acknowledges the importance of each child as he or she is named, and melds the children and parents into a unit ready to listen.

First set of books

The children now are ready to hear two, perhaps three picture books. A fingerplay or short poem can be used between the picture books, or you can engage in brief conversation about the books.

Active time

Now the children need a wiggle time. I move the group into a standing circle and we engage in a singing activity. I usually have prepared a singing activity which extends the theme of the storytime. Or I may substitute a creative drama replay of one of our stories at this slot. The point is to extend the story through an activity incorporating movement.

Second set of stories

After our energetic singing/drama activity, the children are ready to sit and listen to two more stories.

A craft or other activity

To unwind at storytime's end we move to tables and work on a simple craft, which again extends the storytime theme.

Closing songs

In order to keep the sense of programming, I call the children back to the story circle at the program's end to sing closing songs. I draw the children to the story circle gradually, examining each child's craft project as they come to me from the tables, and then settling them down to sing. Often some children will continue working at their craft while we sing. We sing "Goodbye" to each book used during that storytime, and then sing "Goodbye" to our craft project. The storytime ends with "Our storytime is over," a song which enables me to wave goodbye to each child as I look around the room. (See page 164 for these songs.)

Use this book as a map to create your own programs. These program models worked well at my branch library in Seattle. You will want to adapt them to meet your own needs. If the suggested books are not available to you, substitute other titles. And keep an eye out for strong new books on these themes which should be added to your programs.

It is important to treat the storytime for young listeners with the same critical responsibility you apply to program preparation for adults. I put the same kind of energy and thought into my weekly preschool storytimes that I put into my workshops for adults. Never take your responsibility to these children lightly. Plan creatively, execute energetically. Give them your best.

Artwork in the storytime

I resisted adding art activities to my storytimes for years. The preparation necessary seemed excessive and it seemed an unnecessary addition to my literary emphasis. However, after a weekend class with art educator Hazel Koenig, I had so many projects I was eager to try that I rushed to add an art element to my storytimes. I liked the addition so much that I have included a simple project with each storytime ever since. But be warned: Once you start providing an art activity with your storytime, parents and children will come to expect it every week. So be sure you want to do this before you jump in.

Here are a few good reasons to include an artwork period in your story program.

1. It allows the adults and children a time to chat and move about within the bounds of the group. Good parent-to-parent and parent-to-child interaction takes place here. This is especially important for the homebound adult raising preschoolers.

2. Your art project can introduce new ideas to parents for use with the children at home.

3. The children have a brief time to explore creatively with materials. One disadvantage of having parents on hand is that they tend to do the artwork *for* the child. One way to avoid this is to provide each parent with materials to do their own art project. This keeps them out of the child's way and lets the child see the adult in creative artplay.

4. Your art project can extend the theme of the story program. Working on this project, the children think again about the story theme. Taking it home, showing it to other family members, and hanging it on the refrigerator reminds them again of this storytime. Thus the story theme is reinforced.

5. The addition of a ten-minute art break at the end of the story program turns the preschool storytime into a forty-five to fifty-five minute program. The full program, with singing, action songs or games, picture books, poetry, and an art project makes a hearty event which parents value. It is a time they don't like to miss, and attendance runs high.

Tricks of the trade

Here are some shortcuts I take to save time in storytime preparation.

1. When preparing craft pieces always free-cut the pieces. Do not strive for neat, symmetrical cut-outs. Learn to love the look of freeform art. NEVER trace patterns and cut precisely. Just cut an approximate shape using only your eye as guide. By using freeform cutting and by cutting through several sheets of paper at a time, you can cut out ninety hearts in under fifteen minutes. Free-cut EVERYTHING—Christmas trees, moons, chickens. Such free-cut pieces have their own distinctive look and work just fine for storytime.

2. If you have followed my advice and are including adults in your storytime, let *them* cut out any photocopied pictures or pictures from book jackets and magazines, if these are required for your craft. Children too young to succeed at cutting can point out the pictures they choose to use in their art projects and the parents can do the cutting. However you need to monitor this, as some parents will cut for older children who would prefer to do their own cutting.

3. To make a very simple craft look good, pre-select the colors of paper, crayons, paints, and other materials which the children will work with. If you provide them with complementary colors, anything they create will have an artistic flair. Of course you don't want always to limit their range in this way, but it does enable them to produce attractive theme-related artwork.

Provide the children with specialty items to use in their artwork at times. Glitter, sequins, shiny stickers, tiny pom-poms and feathers are fun additions. These are expensive, so I provide them only occasionally.

Song and dance

Don't forget to sing and dance! Children need music. They need movement. Young children, who are being trained in the art of sitting still, need to learn also the joy of expressing themselves physically and verbally. Dancing interludes and singing games at mid-storytime provide expressive outlets.

Opening and closing songs draw the group together. They provide the children with a tradition which runs through all of the storytimes. This opening and closing song tradition makes the storytime feel like a programmed *event*. It provides an easy entry into story and a satisfying closure.

Dramatic play

Provide opportunities within the storytime for children to stretch their imaginations *and* their bodies through dramatic play. Assign parts, spread out around the room, under and over tables and chairs, and *act out* the story you just heard. You retell the story while the children provide the actions and the simplest of lines—often barks, growls, and roars. This activity never fails to please.

Film/video

Introduce fine pieces of cinema into your storytimes. Children and parents need to see quality cinema and to begin developing their own critical skills in judging the images they choose to view. It is important that you introduce parents and children to good books *and* good videos. This is an important part of your collection *and* your work.

Audio cassettes/CDs

Storytime is also an excellent place to introduce fine audio. Play music as the children enter the room and during craft period. Many storytime leaders enjoy using audio as background for singing games. I prefer the freedom of *acappella* singing, which allows me to respond to the children's suggestions and build song around the group. Try it both ways. You may want to use both techniques.

Poetry

Insert a poem or two into each storytime. Begin with a poem, use poetry breaks between stories, or plan a poetry basket tradition. Put a poem and an accompanying object in a covered basket before each storytime. When the group settles down after their mid-storytime song/dance break, produce the basket and share the poem.

Fingerplays also make enjoyable between-story breaks and introduce children to rhythm and rhyme. Jeff Defty's *Creative Fingerplays and Action Rhymes: An Index and Guide to Their Use* provides an index to fingerplay collections along with a good selection of fingerplays and intelligent comments about their use.

I have used all of these programs at my King County Library System branch in Bothell, Washington. I hope you enjoy them as much as we did. Use only those which excite you and give you a sense of joy. And, of course, adapt them all to suit yourself.

❧ *Magical Environments* ❧

1. A Walk in the Moonlight

Opening songs.

Read: *Salt Hands* by Jane Chelsea Aragon; illus. by Ted Rand. A young girl quietly offers salt to a backyard deer.

Read: *Owl Moon* by Jane Yolen; illus. by John Schoenherr. A silent moonlight walk to spot an owl.

Read: *Come Out to Play* by Jeanette Winter. Children follow a wee dwarf out into a magical moonlight party.

Circle song:

> I see the moon up over my head.
> (*look at sky*)
> I don't want to go to bed.
> (*shake head*)
> I want to dance in the bright moonlight.
> (*dance*)
> I don't want to go to bed tonight!
> (*stamp feet and shake head*)

Music: See the music on page 165.

·Read: *Raccoons and Ripe Corn* by Jim Arnosky. Raccoons party in the moonlit cornfield.

Read: *When the Sky Is Like Lace* by Elinor Lander Horwitz; illus. by Barbara Cooney. Fantasy dancing and partying in the moonlight. Take time to let older children talk about which presents they want, which activities they would like to do . . . within the story.

1

Make a moonlight picture: Give out sheets of pale blue paper and provide
photocopied cut-outs of deer, raccoons, or owls for the children to paste
on. Use blue crayons to color the dark sky. Paste on a yellow paper
moon. Use yellow watercolor to paint on a glow of moonlight if you like.

Closing songs.

More books to share:

In the Moonlight, Waiting by Carol Carrick; illus. by Donald Carrick. Quietly waiting to see.

Mamma Don't Allow by Thacher Hurd. Dancing in the swamp till dawn.

The Moon Jumpers by Janice May Udry; illus. by Maurice Sendak. Playing
outside in the moonlight.

The Tomten and the Fox by Astrid Lindgren; illus. by Harald Wiberg. The
tomten makes his rounds at night.

White Bear, Ice Bear by Joanne Ryder; illus. by Michael Rothman. A bear
in the polar night.

Follow-up activities for home or school:

•Take a moonlight walk.

•Go on a moonlight picnic.

•On a calendar paste a stick-on dot on the full moon night of each month
for several months. Plan a moonlight activity for these evenings.

•Make a list of animals and birds near your home that move about at
night. Watch for them.

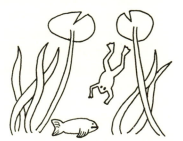

2. *At the Bottom of the Pond*

Opening songs.

Read: *In the Pond* by Ermanno Cristini and Luigi Puricelli. No words. A close
look at life above and within a pond.

Read: *Come Out, Muskrats* by Jim Arnosky. Muskrats swim and feed.

Read: "Bullhead in Winter," "Bullhead in Spring," "Bullhead in Summer," and
"Bullhead in Autumn" from *Turtle in July* by Marilyn Singer; illus. by Jerry
Pinkney. Stress the "belly down in the shallows" line to tie the four poems
together. Also read "Turtle in July," "Dragonfly," and "Beaver in November" from the same collection. Let the children recite the chorus of "Bea-

ver in November" with you as you all pretend to be beavers and push sticks and mud into place.

Form a circle and sing:
    All the ducks are diving in the pond,
    Diving in the pond,
    Diving in the pond.
    All the ducks are diving in the pond.
    Heigh-ho, rowly rowly day.

Sing of all the animals who live in the pond, one by one: All the snakes are swimming in the pond; all the dragonflies are darting over the pond; all the muskrats are surfing in the pond; all the frogs are jumping in the pond, etc.

Music: See the music on page 165.

Read: *Fishing at Long Pond* by William T. George; illus. by Lindsay Barrett George. A look at pond life from a rowboat.

Film: *A Boy, a Dog, and a Frog.* 9 min. Video or 16 mm film. Great underwater shots of a sassy frog. From the book *A Boy, a Dog, and a Frog* by Mercer Mayer.

Read: *Tuesday* by David Wiesner. Pond life gone berserk.

Make a frog-on-flying-lily-pad picture: Photocopy picture of frog on lily pad from *Tuesday.* I used the frog on the fourth page. Have these ready and give to each child along with one green crayon, one glue stick, several strips of green paper (tapered at the top to serve as pond weeds), and one piece of paper on which a blue line has been drawn to signify the top of the pond. The frog can be pasted floating on the pond, under the pond, flying above the pond, diving into the pond, hiding in the weeds, etc.

Closing songs.

More books to share:
    At the Edge of the Pond by Jennifer Owings Dewey. Too much detail for storytime, but good to share with older children and clear illustrations for the younger ones.
    Beaver at Long Pond by William T. George and Lindsay Barrett George. Lovely illustrations of beavers' pond life.
    Box Turtle at Long Pond by William T. George and Lindsay Barrett George. More Long Pond wildlife.
    In the Small, Small Pond by Denise Fleming. Big, bright illustrations of pond activity.

Lily Pad Pond by Bianca Lavies. Photos of pond life arranged into a narrative that begins with tadpole and ends with frog. Could be read aloud in storytime.

Follow-up activities for home or school:

> •Visit a pond. Make a list of the things you see there. Sit very still for a few minutes. Do you see things you didn't see before?

> •Visit the pond in spring and collect some frog eggs and pond water in a glass jar. Care for the eggs in your home or classroom and watch them grow into baby frogs.

3. A Winter Wonderland

Opening songs.

Read: *Owl Moon* by Jane Yolen; illus. by John Schoenherr. The wonder of a walk in the night woods in search of an owl.

Read: *Stopping By Woods on a Snowy Evening* by Robert Frost; illus. by Susan Jeffers. A late afternoon ride through the snowy woods.

Read: *Midnight Snowman* by Caroline Feller Bauer; illus. by Catherine Stock. Neighborhood snowplay at midnight.

Sing or chant and act out:

> Walk-ing, walk-ing, walk-ing in the woods.
> Walk-ing, walk-ing, walk-ing in the woods.
> (*Walk, pretending to take big steps in the snow*)

Sing again and walk sliding in the snow.

Sing again and walk very quietly looking for owls.

Alter the words to:

> Build-ing, build-ing, a snowman in the woods.

Let the children suggest snow activities and invent more verses.

Music: See the music on page 166.

Read: *The Tomten and the Fox* by Astrid Lindgren; illus. by Harald Wiberg. A tomten, household elf of Swedish farms, feeds a hungry fox one snowy night.

Read: *The Snowy Day* by Ezra Jack Keats. Many things to do in a snowy landscape.

Make a stencil snow picture: Show the endpapers of *The Snowy Day*. Make your own snowflake picture by patting blue tempera paint over snowflake stencils using small sponges. Pre-cut the stencils, one for each child. To make these, fold a square of paper over three or four times and cut small wedges from the sides of the piece you have folded. Open and you will have a snowflake.

Mix the tempera to a very stiff consistency and spread it in a thin coating on a plate, saucer, or other flat surface. Give each child a small flat sponge. Dip the flat side of the sponge in the paint, then tap it over the stencil, which the child holds against the sheet of paper. I let each child stencil several pictures and select one to leave in the library for our bulletin board. I backed the bulletin board with blue paper and gave the children dark blue paint to stencil onto white or pale blue paper. I added a simple sign announcing the next session of preschool storytimes and had a ready-made display.

Closing songs.

More books to share:

Snow by Isao Sasaki. A train station in winter. Wordless.

The Tomten by Astrid Lindgren. Tomten guards the farm on a snowy Swedish night.

White Bear, Ice Bear by Joanne Ryder; illus. by Michael Rothman. A polar bear in a white wilderness.

Follow-up activities for home or school:

•Go for a walk in a snow-covered landscape.

•Make your own path through the snow.

•Notice the way snow covers tree branches, grasses.

•Walk under a snow-covered tree and shake its branches.

•Lie down on your back and make angels in the snow by swishing your arms and legs up and down.

•Go outside during a snowfall and catch falling flakes on a black slate or a piece of black paper. Observe the varying forms of the snowflake crystals.

•If you live in an area where there is no snow, prepare a basin full of finely crushed ice, dump it on a chilled platter, and let the children play snow games with tiny dolls in the ice slush. This soon begins to simulate the spring thaw of snowbound areas, where everything turns to mud and slush . . . no longer a winter wonderland.

4. Into the Rain Forest

Opening songs.

Read: *The Camel Who Took a Walk* by Jack Tworkov; illus. by Roger Duvoisin.
The tiger hiding in the forest plans to pounce on the camel walking
slowly down the road.

Read: *Who Is the Beast?* by Keith Baker. Animals flee from a prowling tiger,
but he doesn't consider himself a scary beast.

Act out: "Walking Through the Forest." Form a ring and follow each other,
walking stealthily around in a circle as you pretend to walk through the
dangerous forest, chanting:

Walking through the forest,
What did I see?
A big, tawny lion was ROARING at me!

Turn and roar at the person behind you. Then turn forward again and continue walking through the forest. Let the children suggest which animals,
reptiles, or birds you might encounter and chant about them. "A huge
grey elephant was TRUMPETING at me!" I end with something gentle
such as "A funny little monkey was CHATTERING at me!" or "A little
yellow bird was SINGING just for me!"

Read: *A Nice Walk in the Jungle* by Nan Bodsworth. Children on a field trip
are swallowed one by one by a giant pink-and-chartreuse boa constrictor.

Read: *Where the Forest Meets the Sea* by Jeannie Baker. A young boy explores
the rain forest, imagining inhabitants of the past . . . and future.

Make a rain forest diorama: Use a piece of cardboard four inches square. Fold
this in half for a diorama. Using plasticine, form vines, trees, and flowers
to create your rain forest.

Closing songs.

More books to share:

Amazon Boy by Ted Lewin. Life along the river, as Paulo travels to town
with his father.

Rain Forest by Helen Cowicher. The rain forest's creatures are threatened
by man's bulldozers.

Rain Forest Secrets by Arthur Dorros. Information about rain forests, with
address to write for more information.

The Zabajaba Jungle by William Steig. Leonard's bizarre adventure in an
imaginary jungle.

Follow-up activities for home or school:
- •Visit a zoo to see animals who live in a rain forest.
- •Take care of a plant that might live in the rain forest.
- •Adopt a philodendron, orchid, or other tropical plant. What does it need to survive? Look after its needs for a few months.

⚓ Sillies ⚓

5. Here Comes the Babysitter!

Opening songs.

Read: *The Goodbye Book* by Judith Viorst; illus. by Kay Chorao. Excuses to keep parents from going out for the evening.

Read: *My Babysitter* by Anne and Harlow Rockwell. Simple look at a baby-sitter.

Read: "Mitzi Takes a Taxi" from *Tell Me a Mitzi* by Lore Segal; illus. by Harriet Pincus. Mitzi takes care of little brother while her parents sleep in.

Singing game:

> I wish I were a babysitter.
> A babysitter, a babysitter.
> If I were a babysitter,
> This is what I'd do . . .

Let the children suggest things a babysitter does and act them out. Example: "If I were a babysitter . . . I'd make peanut butter sandwiches for the kids."

Music: See the music on page 166. Adapt the words to fit the tune.

Read: *The Napping House* by Audrey Wood; illus. by Don Wood. Cumulative rhyme of napping granny and kids. In a hushed tone, all join in on phrase, "Where everyone is sleeping."

Read: *The Lady with the Alligator Purse* by Nadine Bernard Westcott. Bouncy rhyme of humorous disasters. All chant on the phrase, "In comes the lady with the alligator purse."

Reprise: Read it again and let all join in.

Activity: Make a picture book to share with your own babysitter. Let kids cut up old book jackets or magazines. Paste the pictures onto folded sheets of paper to form a picture book. Two folded sheets will give you a four-page booklet. Fasten the pages together by punching holes in the spine and tying with yarn or a ribbon. Or simply staple them at the spine.

Closing songs.

More books to share:

Be Good, Harry by Mary Chalmers. Shy kitten, Harry, and his sitter.

Bear and Mrs. Duck by Elizabeth Winthrop; illus. by Patience Brewster. Bear gradually accepts his sitter, Mrs. Duck.

The Best Little Monkey in the World by Natalie Standiford; illus. by Hilary Knight. Naughty monkeys.

Eleanor and the Babysitter by Susan Hellard. Eleanor doesn't want to have anything to do with the teenage sitter . . . until Eleanor gets a fright.

George the Babysitter by Shirley Hughes. A male sitter delights the family.

The Lemonade Babysitter by Karen Waggoner; illus. by Dorothy Donohue. Molly tries to frustrate her elderly sitter, Mr. Herbert, but he wins her over.

M & M and the Bad News Babies by Pat Ross; illus. by Marilyn Hafner. Mandy and Mimi babysit unruly twins.

Mr. and Mrs. Pig's Evening Out by Mary Raynor. A wolf at the door?

Shy Charles by Rosemary Wells. Shy Charles saves the sitter!

Stay Up Late by David Byrne; illus. by Maria Kalmar. From the song "Stay Up Late" on the Talking Heads' recording *Little Creatures*. Silliness about keeping a baby up all night to carouse.

Follow-up activities for home or school:

•Draw a picture of your favorite babysitter.

•If you were a babysitter, what would you do?

•Draw a picture of yourself, babysitting.

6. *Kitchen! Kitchen!*

Opening songs.

Read: *In the Night Kitchen* by Maurice Sendak. Kids should chant "milk in the batter" with you. Keep it rhythmic and playful. Talk about the fact that bakers do bake while we sleep.

Read: *The Wedding Procession of the Rag Doll and the Broom Handle and Who Was in It* by Carl Sandburg; illus. by Harriet Pincus. Let the kids lick imaginary spoons, eat imaginary chocolate bars, as you read. I stop after each page and we all mime the action and repeat the book's phrase.

Sing a kitchen song:

Kitchen! Kitchen! I'm in the kitchen.
When I'm in the kitchen, this is what I do.

Let the kids tell what you do . . . then act it out: bake a cake, fry pancakes, wash dishes, etc. Sing the song, ask for the suggested action, stop and act it out. Then repeat.

Music: See the music on page 167.

Make a kitchen band: Display chopsticks, aluminum foil pie plates, cake pans, wooden spoons, etc. Let each child choose two items to bang together and form a kitchen band. March and play to a jouncy recording.

Read: *If You Give a Mouse a Cookie* by Laura Joffe Numeroff; illus. by Felicia Bond. Babysitting a mouse can be quite a chore.

Read: *Benny Bakes a Cake* by Eve Rice. Benny helps Mom bake a cake. Sing happy birthday to Benny at the book's end.

Make a spoon puppet: Paste stick-on dots on the back of a plastic spoon for eyes. Use a smaller dot for a nose/ mouth. Place a dab of glue in the tip of the spoon's bowl and stick on four inch-long pieces of yarn for hair. Wrap one pipe cleaner around neck of spoon for arms.

Closing songs: Using your spoon puppets, sing the "Kitchen! Kitchen!" song again. Act out things a spoon does in the kitchen: it stirs, it scoops, it eats ice cream, etc. My spoon also danced at night after everyone was in bed.

See also: Holiday Cake Tales, program 66; Bakers at Work, program 44.

More books to share:

    Love from Aunt Betty by Nancy Winslow Parker. Aunt Betty cooks up a gift.

    Pots and Pans by Anne Rockwell; illus. by Lizzy Rockwell. Close up of the kitchen's pots.

    Teddy Bear's Cookbook by Suzanna Gretz and Alison Sage; illus. by Suzanna Gretz. Teddy bears in the kitchen.

Follow-up activities for home or school:

- Take a guided tour of your kitchen.
- Point out the use of each cabinet, the function of each appliance. After learning all you can about the kitchen, let the children take turns leading kitchen tours.
- Make a kitchen collage using an assortment of things you find in your kitchen. Try incorporating macaroni, spaghetti, toothpicks, bits of wax paper, foil, plastic wrap, etc.

7. *Greedy Gluttons*

Opening songs.

Read: *The Very Hungry Caterpillar* by Eric Carle. A tiny caterpillar eats and eats.

Read: *There Was an Old Woman Who Swallowed a Fly*. Sing along with this old folk song. The cut-out pages show the lady's innards.

Poem: "Eat-It-All-Elaine" by Kaye Starbird in *Poem Stew* by William Cole; illus. by Karen Ann Weinhaus, p. 27.

Show: *The Greedy Cat*. In this Sign-a-Language video Billy Seago signs the story and Ted Hinkey provides a voiceover. Lively and engaging. The Greedy Cat eats up everyone he meets. Discuss a few of the signs to be used beforehand. You will have previewed the video to learn signs for *cat, fat, elephant,* and *stomp*. If this video is not available to you, a picture book may be substituted in this slot. *The Fat Cat* by Jack Kent tells the same story in picture book format.

Sing: A Fat Cat Song and sign along if you have watched the video; otherwise mime the actions:

I will eat eat eat eat eat,
(*sign "slurp"*)
Till I'm fat fat fat fat fat.
(*sign "fat, fatter, fattest"*)
I will eat eat eat eat eat.
I'm a fat fat fat fat CAT!
(*sign "cat" with very fat signs*)

Talk about what you want to eat.
Sing the song again, then EAT. Mime eating and getting fatter and fatter, then
EXPLODING!
I'll eat
and I'll eat
and I'll EAT
and I'll EAT!!!
and KAPLOIEEE!!!

Music: See the music on page 167.
Make a Fat Cat paper bag puppet: pre-cut eyes, round nose, six strips for
whiskers, and ears. Children paste these on paper bag.
Closing songs.
More books to share:
The Eye of the Needle retold and illus. by Teri Sloat; based on a Yupik tale
as told by Betty Huffman.
The Fat Cat trans. from the Danish and illus. by Jack Kent. The Fat Cat
eats everyone he meets.
Follow-up activities for home or school:
•Talk about the concept of "too much."
•Blow up a balloon until it pops.
•Stuff a paper bag until it is as full as you can fill it.

8. Bad Babies

Opening songs.
Read: *The Elephant and the Bad Baby* by Elfrida Vipont; illus. by Raymond
Briggs. Encourage adults to hold children on their laps during this reading. They should all bounce kids on knees as you "rump-ita, rump-ita"
down the road with each refrain.
Read: *Eat Up, Gemma* by Sarah Hayes; illus. by Jan Ormerod. Baby sister
won't eat.

Read: *Poor Carl* by Nancy Carlstrom. A baby and a put-upon watch dog.

Action song: Form a circle and sing
    I wish I were a baby, a baby, a baby.
    If I were a baby, this is what I'd do . . .

Let children suggest actions for the bad baby . . . throw food on floor, cry,
    smash bananas, etc.
Music: See the music on page 166.
Film: *Tin Toy*. 4 min. Video/16 mm film. Baby terrorizes a wind-up toy.
Poem: "Brother" by Mary Ann Hoberman in *Sunflakes: Poems for Children* by
    Lillian Moore; illus. by Jan Ormerod, p. 65.
Read: *What a Good Lunch* by Shigeo Watanabe; illus. by Yasuo Ohtomo.
Make a dribble bib: Free-cut bibs from paper before the children arrive. Pro-
    vide runny poster paints and aprons. Let the children dribble paints on
    their bibs. The bibs lie on the table for painting, *not* on the children.
Closing circle: Ask children what foods the baby spilled on the bib. I pro-
    vided green and yellow paints, so peas, spinach, eggs, bananas might
    have been spilt.
Closing songs.
See also: Oh No, Baby!, program 30.
More books to share:
    Go and Hush the Baby by Betsy Byars; illus. by Emily Arnold McCully.
    Baby will not hush.
    Nobody Asked Me If I Wanted a Baby Sister by Martha Alexander. A new
    baby brings problems . . . and pleasures.
    101 Things to Do with a Baby by Jan Ormerod. 101 illustrations of fun
    things to do with a baby.
    Silly Billy by Pat Hutchins. Monster Baby wrecks all of Hazel's toys, until
    he falls asleep.
    The Wild Baby Goes to Sea by Barbro Lindgren and Eva Eriksson; adapted
    from the Swedish by Jack Prelutsky. Fun rhyme tells of bad baby's adven-
    tures.
Follow-up activities for home or school:
    •Invite a baby to visit. Entertain the baby, feed the baby, observe its dia-
    per-changing.
    •Talk about crazy things *you* did as a baby.
    •Make a gallery of your baby pictures.

9. Upside-Down Day

Opening songs.

Read: *Silly Sally* by Audrey Wood. Sally bounces along, walking on her hands and joining up with a pig, a loon, and a sheep.

Read: *You Think It's Fun to Be a Clown?* by David A. Adler; illus. by Ray Cruz. The clown, upside down *and* right side up, is someone's *mom*.

Act out *Silly Sally*: Read the book again and this time act it out.

    1. Moms hold kids by their feet and let them walk on their hands backwards.

    2. We all dance a jig with the pig.

    3. We sing like a loon.

    4. We lie on the floor and fall asleep.

    5. We tickle the pig, loon, sheep, Sally.

    6. We walk to town on our hands again.

Read: *Little Duck's Bicycle Ride* by Dorothy Stott. Duck is upside down *and* sideways, riding his bike.

Poem: "Whenever" by Mary Ann Hoberman in *Sunflakes: Poems for Children* by Lillian Moore; illus. by Jan Ormerod, p. 39.

Read: *Inside, Outside, Upside Down* by Stan and Jan Berenstain. After reading this once with fervor, read it again. This time let the children repeat each phrase after you.

Activity: Photocopy the scene from *Silly Sally* showing her leaping to town, and photocopy the bear on the fly leaf of *Inside, Outside, Upside Down*. Each child can paste two bears onto the picture of Sally leaping. The bears could be pasted on right-side up . . . upside down . . . sideways. Color the picture.

Closing songs.

More books to share:

    Round Trip by Ann Jonas. A book to turn upside down.

The Turnaround Wind by Arnold Lobel. Turn the book upside down and the faces change.

Follow-up activities for home or school:
- •Turn things upside down in your room and have an upside-down party.
- •Bend over and lean your head on the floor. Look around at the world. How do things look from this upside-down perspective?

10. Parrot Parties

Opening songs.

Read: *The Horrendous Hullabaloo* by Margaret Mahy; illus. by Patricia MacCarthy. The pirate's auntie parties with parrots.

Read: *But Where Is the Green Parrot?* by Thomas and Wanda Zacharias. Find the green parrot on each page. An easy find for younger listeners.

Read: *Cockatoos* by Quentin Blake. "Good morning, my fine feathered friends," booms Professor Dupont, and his cockatoos flee at the sound. Let the children spread their arms like cockatoo wings and repeat the phrase with you. Each time you say it, add a few "Good Mornings" to the text.

Act it out: You, or a mature child, take the role of Professor Dupont. The birds run off and hide. When Professor Dupont looks for them, they must sit absolutely still so that he won't see them. I send them to hide on one side of the room (the "kitchen"), then they move to the other side of the room (the "bathroom"). Finally, they return to the story circle (the "conservatory"). Professor Dupont turns his back and goes to sleep while they move; then he wakes up and hunts again. Everytime he wakes, he goes to the conservatory and calls, "Good morning, my Fine Feathered Friends."

Form a circle, holding hands and sing:
Green Parrot, Green Parrot fly through my window.
Green Parrot, Green Parrot fly through my window.

Green Parrot, Green Parrot fly through my window,
Early in the morning.

One child flies in and out the "windows" made by raising your clasped hands.
I lead the younger children. Older ones can fly alone, flapping their
wings. Or, you can form a line of children all holding hands and weave
in and out.

Music: See the music on page 168. Adapt the words to fit the tune.

Read: *Papagayo the Mischief Maker* by Gerald McDermott. Papagayo, the parrot, helps the birds make a raucous sound to scare off the moon-eating
sky-dog.

Make tail feathers: Pre-cut three long tail feathers from
construction paper for each child. Let the children
roll them up to make them curl. Staple the feathers
to a construction paper waistband and fasten this
around the child's waist with masking tape.

Play: "Green Parrot, Green Parrot, Fly Through My
Window" again. Shake your tail feathers as
you fly.

Closing songs.

See also: Where Is the Green Parrot?, program 16.

More books to share:

Hey, Al by Arthur Yorinks and Richard Egielski. Al and dog Eddie are
happy in bird paradise until they discover they are turning into birds.

Tuntuni the Tailor Bird by Betsy Bang; adapted and translated from a Bengali tale by Betsy Bang; illus. by Molly Bang. Spunky bird tricks everyone.

Follow-up activities for home or school:

•Invite a friend with a parrot to bring their bird for a visit. Watch how
the bird moves. Look carefully at its coloration.

•Give a parrot party. Look at a book with photos of parrots and cockatoos. Decide what bird you will dress as, then make a parrot tail using
the appropriate colors for your paper feathers. Let everyone at the party
costume themselves and show off their feathers.

•Practice walking like a parrot and do a parrot dance.

❧ Motor Mania ❧

11. Toothgnasher Superflash

Opening songs.

Read: *Uncle Wizzmo's New Used Car* by Rodney A. Greenblat. Gaudy trip to the city to buy a new used car.

Read: *Toothgnasher Superflash* by Daniel Pinkwater. A new car does wild things on its test run. It turns into a chicken and better!

Talk about: What do you think their previous car, the old green THUNDER-CLAP, could do?

Film: *Susie the Little Blue Coupe.* 8 min. Susie grows old, but there is a lot of spunk in her yet. A Disney animated classic.

Make a Toothgnasher Superflash:

Fold a cardboard sheet in half and free-cut cars for the children. The fold becomes the top of your car. The folded cardboard car will stand up on your table top. Let kids paste on wings, feelers, and other weird shapes. These can be pre-cut and strewn on table. Stick-on dots make good wheels.

Closing circle: Let each child explain what strange things his/her car can do.

Closing songs.

More books to share:

The Magic Auto by Janosch, trans. from *Das Regenauto*. A magical car.

Maxi, the Hero by Debra and Sal Barracca; illus. by Mark Buehner. A day in the life of a taxi dog.

William the Vehicle King by Laura P. Newton; illus. by Jacqueline Rogers. A boy's toy car collection.

Follow-up activities for home or school:
- •From a large cardboard box, create a super-car you can sit in. Discuss the car and decide what its attributes will be and what objects to attach to it.
- •Draw your own super-car. Explain it to someone else.
- •Watch: *Alexander and the Car with the Missing Headlight*. 16 min. Video or 16mm film. A magical car carries a child to adventures.

12. On the Road

Opening songs.

Talk about: Taking trips. Who has taken a trip by plane? Train? Car? Hiking?

Read: *Mr. Gumpy's Motor Car* by John Burningham. Mr. Gumpy's animal friends all join him for a ride. Mr. Gumpy takes a dirt road shortcut and a rainstorm plagues him.

Read: *Trucksong* by Diane Siebert; illus. by Byron Barton. Bright pictures illustrate a poem about cross-country trucking. Keep it fast and rhythmic.

Truck driving play: Pretend to drive a truck. Start the engine, release the brake, pull out into traffic . . . turn corners, go up hills slowly and down hills fast. Stop for stop lights. Pull up to a restaurant and STOP for lunch.

Read: *Freight Train* by Donald Crews. Brief. Keep it rhythmic. I add a gentle *chug chug chug chug* after reading each page. This allows time to look at the pictures. Some children join me on the chugs.

Take a train/car ride: Form a line and drive or chug over an obstacle course. Pass between bookcarts (a canyon), under tables (tunnels), over a row of stools (a bridge), etc. End up back in your story circle and chug to a halt.

Go for a motorboat ride: Holding hands, the group circles faster and faster as they chant.

Motorboat, motorboat, go so slow.
(chant and move slowly)
Motorboat, motorboat, go so fast.
(speed the chant up and move faster)
Motorboat, motorboat, run out of gas!
(move even faster and end by collapsing on the floor)

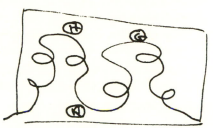

Make a map and play a trip game: Give each child a large piece of paper and a felt-tip pen. The idea is to make a squiggly line across the paper with loops in it that can serve as a highway map. Explain to the children that the felt-tip pen must not leave the paper while they are drawing the map. Demonstrate drawing such a map first.

1. Ask everyone to start drawing from one side of the paper when they hear the command, "GO!"
2. They should squiggle the line all over the paper any way they want, not stopping or lifting the pen until you give the command.
3. They will "drive" the pen off the other side of the paper on the command, "STOP!"
4. Now give each child three stick-on dots. You have drawn a letter onto each dot. H = hotel; R = restaurant; G = gas. Use a different color for each. They may stick these on the map anywhere along the road they have drawn.
5. Pass out beans or macaroni for toy cars.
6. Say "Chug . . . chug . . . chug" and tell the children to drive their cars along the road wherever they want to go as long as you are making chugging noises.
7. Call "OUT OF GAS!" Now everyone must drive the car to a gas station as quickly as possible, while staying on the lines. Fill up with gas. Then drive on.
8. Make chugging noises again while the children drive around.
9. Call, "Lunch Time!" Drive to the restaurant.
10. Drive on. "Chug . . . chug."
11. Call. "It's getting dark. Time for bed!" Drive to the hotel.
12. Next morning drive on to the end of the trip and off the opposite side of the paper from where you entered. At the end I call, "Grandma's House!"

Closing songs.

See also: Out the Train Window, program 14; The Relatives Came, program
   26.

More books to share:

   How Georgina Drove the Car Very Carefully from Boston to New York by
   Lucy Bate; illus. by Tamar Taylor. A child imagines driving her family on
   a road trip.

   I Had Trouble in Getting to Solla Sollew by Dr. Seuss. Silliness.

   Night Ride by Michel Gay. A nighttime car trip.

Follow-up activities for home or school:

   •Make a "road" from your room to the kitchen by laying down newspapers. "Drive" to the kitchen and back on your road. Make a map of the
   road you have laid out.

   •Make a crazy map picture. Give each child a photocopy of a road map
   (or an expendable road map). Explain that the black lines show where
   the roads go. Instruct the child to place the tip of a colored marker down
   on a road line. Now follow the line as far as possible without taking the
   pen from the paper. Choose another colored marker, start at a different
   spot and repeat. Keep this up until you have a crazy colored map.

13. Safe Biker!

Opening songs.

Read: *Delphine* by Molly Bang. A tongue-in-cheek fantasy, as a wild child
   learns to ride her first bike.

Read: *The Bear's Bicycle* by Emilie Warren McLeod; illus. by David McPhail.
   Boy follows all biking rules, but his bear companion *does not.*

Read: *The Bike Lesson* by Stan and Jan Berenstain. Biking disasters to avoid!

Play: Set up an obstacle course for a trike or Big Wheel. Have one trike or Big
   Wheel available and let each child navigate the course in turn, or let all
   bring their own vehicles from home to ride. Have a wagon available to
   pull younger children through the course.

Make a set of nylon handlebar streamers: Fasten them to your own bike,
   trike, scooter, wagon, doll carriage, or just wave them in the wind. Pre-
   cut nylon strips in bright colors, 2 feet long by 1 inch wide. Children
   select three colors and staple their strips together at the mid-point to
   form a streamer. They should make two identical streamers. Show the
   children how to cut into the streamer ends to fray them. With masking
   tape, fasten one streamer set to each handlebar of the child's vehicle.

Closing songs.

Note: For fives and up, add or substitute the book *Lucky Chuck* by Beverly Cleary; illus. by J. Winslow Higginbottom. A humorous introduction to motorcycle safety.

More books to share:

Bicycle Race by Donald Crews. A chance to read numbers, as each biker wears a number on helmet.

Bikes by Anne Rockwell. A look at several kinds of bikes.

Curious George Rides a Bike by H. A. Rey. George has a newspaper route.

Miffy's Bicycle by Dick Bruna. Very simple words and illustrations depict bunny Miffy and her bike.

Follow-up activities for home or school:

•Look at a trike or bike carefully to see how the pedals move the chain, which moves the wheels.

•Decorate your tricycle wheels with day-glo stick-ons and watch the effect when you spin them.

•Watch: *The Remarkable Riderless Runaway Tricycle.* 16 min. Video or 16 mm film. A trike runs away and has adventures of its own.

•Plan a trike and Big Wheel parade. Those who don't have vehicles can direct the traffic. Decorate the trikes and make flags for the "traffic police."

14. *Out the Train Window*

Opening songs.

Read: *The Train to Lulu's* by Elizabeth Fitzgerald Howard; illus. by Robert Casilla. Big sister Beppy is in charge of little sister Babs on the nine-hour trip from Boston to Baltimore.

Talk about: Things the girls saw from the train window. Look again at the pages which show the girls looking out the window at trees, bridges, and New York buildings.

Read: *Country Crossing* by Jim Aylesworth; illus. by Ted Rand. The excitement of a train rushing by in the night.

Talk about: What did the people in the caboose see when they looked out the window?

Form a circle and sing:
> Take me riding on the train train,
> Take me riding on the train train,
> Take me riding on the train train,
> Take me riding on the train.

Now clench your fists and move your arms in a chugging motion as you march in place and chug in time to this tune. Ask the children where they want to go on the train. Form a line by putting each child's hands on the shoulders of the child in front, and chug around the room. Sing: "Going to the zoo on my train train" or sing of whatever destination your children have suggested. Take time to repeat the song with each child's suggested destination. Last of all sing a verse of "Take me home on the train train." Chug to a halt and all sit back down.

Music: This is sung to the tune of Woody Guthrie's "Car Song." It can be found in *Making Music Your Own* by Mary Tinnen Jaye, p. 157.

Read: *The Polar Express* by Chris Van Allsburg. A magical train carries children through frozen woods to the North Pole.

Talk about: Things the children saw from their train windows on the trip to the North Pole.

Make a train window picture: This activity requires a bit of preparation as windows, scenes, and train seats must be prepared in advance. Cut photos of scenery from old magazines. Cut these to a size about 4½ inches high by 5½ inches wide. Children paste these on an 8½ × 11-inch sheet of black paper. A sheet of colored paper 5½ × 8½ inches will be the inside wall of your train compartment. Free-cut a window in the center of this wall; don't bother poking a hole in the paper and cutting tidily, just slice in from the bottom of the page and cut out a hole. When the paper is pasted down, the cut at the bottom won't show anyway. A window about 3 inches high by 3½ inches wide is about the right size. Fold in half a piece of constrasting colored paper approximately 5½ inches high by 4½ inches wide. Free-cut from this paper a train seat. (See diagram). This actually gives you *two* seats since you have folded the paper in half.

1. Children select a scene from those you have cut out of magazines. (Older children could cut out their own pictures). They paste this scene in the center of their black 8½ × 11-inch paper.

2. The children paste the colored rectangle representing the inside of the train coach OVER the scene in such a way that the scene shows through the cut-out window.
3. The children paste a train seat on each side of the window. Demonstrate the proper placement of these.

Closing songs.

More books to share:

Adrienne and the Magic Clockwork Train by Tannis Vernon. A toy steam train is fired up by dolls, then carries them away while the little girl owner watches.

Black and White by David Macaulay. An intricate tale of trains and cows. Four stories in one. Requires careful scrutiny for full enjoyment.

The Christmas Train by Ivan Gantschev. A child burns her Christmas tree to save the train. The fire stops the train and saves it from disaster.

The Owl Who Became the Moon by Jonathan London; illus. by Ted Rand. A night train ride through a snowy landscape.

Teddy Bears Take the Train by Susanna Gretz. Teddies on the train.

There's a Train Going by My Window by Wendy Kesselman; illus. by Tony Chen. Bouncy rhyme as we travel around the world in an imaginary train.

Time Train by Paul Fleischman; illus. by Claire Ewart. A train carries us back to the time of dinosaurs.

The Train by David McPhail. A toy train carries a boy away for a magical adventure in the night.

Follow-up activities for home or school:

•Collect pictures of trains from magazines and make a gallery of trains.

•Cut a train car out of construction paper for every child in the class. Write names on the cars and form them into a train on the wall after the children decorate them. Count the train cars on the wall.

❧ *Flights of Fancy* ❧

15. Ride Away!

Opening songs.

Read: *All the Pretty Horses;* illus. by Susan Jeffers. Sing it if you know the melody!

Read: *Ride with the Wind* by Liz Damrell; illus. by Stephen Marchesi. The feeling of riding on horseback is strikingly portrayed. In the last frame we see that the child moves about in a wheelchair when not riding.

Action song:

    Trot trot trot trot,
    Trot trot trot trot,
    Trot trot in a ring.

    Trot trot trot trot,
    Trot trot trot trot,
    Stop . . . and shake your mane.

Form a circle and trot around the circle as you sing. Repeat the action using "canter," "walk," "dance," "gallop," etc. Trot quietly back to your sitting spot on the final chorus.

Music: See the music on page 168.

Read: *Beautiful My Mane in the Wind* by Catherine Petroski; illus. by Robert Andrew Parker. Poetic horse loving.

Read: *Carmina, Come Dance!* by Mary K. Whittington; illus. by Michael McDermott. As a young girl sits under the grand piano while her grandmother plays, the music stirs her imagination.

24

It is possible to read this book to the accompaniment of piano music. This takes a bit of rehearsal ahead of time, but is worth the effort. Mary Whittington conceived this book while listening to Ravel's *Gaspard de la Nuit*, Part 1, *Ondine* (a recording of this work is listed in the bibliography). Here is how I use the music *with* the book.

•I explain to the children that the girl is going to be imagining things as her grandmother plays the piano.

•I begin playing the recording and draw their attention to the sound of the piano playing, then I begin reading.

•When the grandmother in the book begins to play the piano, I pause and let them listen for a moment to the recorded piano music which is still playing in our background.

•If you read slowly, matching your voice to the mood of the music and practice a time or two, you will be able to hear the horse approaching when you reach that part of the story. I usually end up with a quiet playing when I reach the stormy scenes, but that works fine because the illustrations are misty anyway.

•I pace my reading so that I reach a spot where the music pauses just as I read "The music stops." Then I stop the recording and read the rest in silence.

Activity: Play a short selection of stirring piano music and listen with closed eyes. Ask the children to imagine what the music is telling them. Can they imagine castles? horses? stormy weather as the music plays?

Paste ribbons on a horse's mane: photocopy pages 8–9 of *Carmina, Come Dance!* This is the picture of the girl on the horse's back, grasping the mane. Cut paper ribbon and curl it with scissors to make little ribbon curls. Strew these on the table and let the children paste little curls of ribbon all along the mane of the horse in the picture.

Closing songs. Take time to let the children hold up their horses and sing "Goodbye to the Horses." See music p. 164.

More books to share:

Charlotte and the White Horse by Ruth Krauss; illus. by Maurice Sendak. Girl, horse. Easy-to-read.

The Girl Who Loved Wild Horses by Paul Goble. A Native American girl and a herd of wild horses.

The Silver Pony by Lynd Ward. Lengthy wordless fantasy.

Stopping by Woods on a Snowy Evening by Robert Frost; illus. by Susan Jeffers. An old man has a playful moment alone in a snowy woods.

Suho and the White Horse by Yuzo Otsuka; trans. by Ann Herring; illus. by Suekichi Akaba. Mongolian legend of the steppes.

Follow-up activities for home or school:
- •Listen to any selection of classical piano.
- •Watch *Dream of the Wild Horses* by Albert Lamorisse. 16 mm film.
- •Clip photos of horses from magazines and paste a horse collage.
- •Close your eyes and listen to a piece of music by Ravel. Pretend horses are standing in a field as the music begins. Imagine what the horses are doing as the music plays.

16. Where Is the Green Parrot?

Opening songs.

Read: *The Baby Beebee Bird* by Diane Redfield Massie. The baby beebee bird wakes all the animals in the zoo.

Read: *The Good Bird* by Peter Wezel. A wordless picture book. Let the children tell YOU what happens. A good bird shares a worm with a goldfish.

Read: *Hey, Al* by Arthur Yorinks; illus. by Richard Egielski. Al and dog Eddie are carried off to a jungly paradise by a huge bird. The paradise is too good to be true. They sprout wings.

Make: Wings! Make brightly colored feathers from paper strips which are 18 inches long and 3 inches wide. Taper them at the ends to resemble feathers. Give each child two of these paper strips and show them how to cut slits into the sides of the strips to make them look like feathers. Small ones will need adult assistance with this, but the children enjoy using scissors. Using masking tape, fasten one wing to each wrist of the child.

Activity: Fly around the room flapping your wings. Help the children climb onto a bench or low table and let an adult fly them off the other end. They should flap their wings as the adult soars them through the air. Heavier children may need to fly piggyback. Caution the children not to try to fly without a grownup's assistance.

Sing and play: "Green parrot, green parrot, fly through my window."

Music: See the music on page 168. Adapt the words to fit the music. See directions for game on page 16.

Read: *Parrot Cat* by Nicola Bayley. A cat imagines how it would feel to be a parrot.

Read: *But Where Is the Green Parrot?* by Thomas and Wanda Zacharias. Find the green parrot on each page. Simple text.

Closing songs. Take time to flap your wings a few more times and sing "Goodbye to the parrots." See music page 164.

See also: Parrot Parties, program 10.

More books to share:

Papagayo the Mischief Maker by Gerald McDermott. The parrot, Papagayo, scares off the moon-eating sky-dog.

Two Can Toucan by David McKee. A sassy toucan.

Follow-up activities for home or school:

•Look at a photo of a real parrot. What color does it have on its feathers? List these colors, then select matching crayons and create a parrot-colored picture.

•Hide a toy parrot, or a parrot picture. Play "Where is the Green Parrot?" and search for the parrot. Hide a box of crackers with the parrot. When the parrot is found ask, "Polly want a cracker?" and eat the crackers.

17. Dance-a-Path

Opening songs.

Read: *The Camel Who Took a Walk* by Jack Tworkov; illus. by Roger Duvoisin. The beautiful camel comes down the jungle path, while the tiger lies waiting.

Read: *Bears in the Night* by Stan and Jan Berenstain. The bear kids follow the path into the woods one dark night. Read the book. Then read it again, letting the audience repeat each phrase after you.

Poem: "Three Bears Walking" in *The Three Bears Rhyme Book* by Jane Yolen; illus. by Jane Dyer, p. 9. Stand in a circle and recite the poem again as you act it out.

Make a dance path: Tear up a large piece of paper and place the pieces on the floor like stones in a pathway. This is your choreography guide for the dance. Small pieces mean tiny steps, large pieces equal big jumps, etc. The path can be interpreted in any way you want. Turn on a lively musical selection and demonstrate dancing on the path. Let kids volunteer to dance their interpretation of the path.

Now give each adult a large piece of paper to tear up with the assistance of
the children he or she accompanies. Assign each child/adult group a
section of the room in which to lay out their path. After all are finished,
you connect their paths with a few additional strips, making one continu-
ous pathway.

Line up and dance the pathway to some jazzy music. We used Bobby McFerrin's "Don't Worry, Be Happy" from his album *Simple Pleasures*. This piece
is lengthy enough to dance around all of the pathways several times. We
then picked up the pieces and threw them in the wastebasket—still moving to the rhythm, and returned to sitting position—listening until the
music ended.

Read: *Where Are You Going, Emma?* by Jeanne Titherington. Emma leaves the
path to explore.

Read: *Little Red Ridinghood* by Trina Schart Hyman. A little girl leaves the
path . . . and you know what happens. This version has a lovely "path"
illustration, but the text is lengthy. If the wolf consuming Red bothers
you, substitute *The Gunniwolf* by Wilhelmina Harper.

Make a pathway through the forest: Give each child a piece of cardboard to
use as gameboard. Pre-cut triangles for trees from green paper and fold
over the bottom edge of each to use as a tab to paste the tree onto the
gameboard. Litter the table with pre-cut trees and show the children how
to put paste on the tabs and fasten
the trees to their gameboards. Encourage each child to paste on
three or more trees. Demonstrate
drawing a pathway from one edge
of the board to the other. Make it
curl around and between the trees
on its way across the board. After
the children have drawn on their

paths, give each a brown stick-on dot to hide behind one tree. This is
the wolf. Play at following the path with your index finger. Run quickly
past the wolf. Older children can draw a house for Red Riding Hood and
a house for Grandma at either end of their path.

Closing songs.

More books to share:
> *A Road Might Lead to Anywhere* by Rachel Field; illus. by Giles Laroche. To Mexico or Maine. Interesting collage illustrations.

Follow-up activities for home or school:
> •Go for a walk and follow a path. Let each child have a turn at being path leader. Talk about safety in following paths.

18. *Dress Up*

Opening songs.

Read: *Dandelion* by Don Freeman. Dandelion the lion overdresses.

Read: *Song and Dance Man* by Karen Ackerman; illus. by Stephen Gammell. Grandpa dresses up in a dance outfit from his youth and performs.

Action song:
> I'll dress up,
> I'll dress up,
> Here's what I'll wear
> When I dress up!
>
> My new shoes,
> My new shoes,
> I'll wear my new shoes
> When I dress up!

Music: See the music on page 169.

Read: *Come Out to Play* by Jeanette Winter. A full moon and the children venture out, dress up, and party.

Make party hats: Provide construction paper headbands. Kids paste or tape on stars, feathers, rolled paper coils, etc.

Closing circle: Wear your headbands and show them to each other.

Closing songs.

More books to share:
> *Nini at Carnival* by Errol Lloyd. Nini dresses up for Jamaican Carnival.
> *The Philharmonic Gets Dressed* by Karla Kushkin. We watch as each member of the orchestra dresses at home.

Follow-up activities for home or school:
> •Plan a dress-up event. Create outlandish costumes and have a parade to show them off.

19. If a Forest Grew in Your Room

Opening songs.

Read: *The Salamander Room* by Anne Mazer; illus. by Steve Johnson. A boy brings a salamander home and constructs an indoor forest to keep it happy.

Read: *Where the Wild Things Are* by Maurice Sendak. "That night in Max's room a forest grew . . . ."

Act out: *Where the Wild Things Are*. Ask for a Max volunteer. Put him to bed. Gather the other children around Max as trees. Let them wave their branches and whoosh. Wake Max up and sail him away. When he comes sailing around again, the trees have changed to wild things. Act out the entire story.

Read: *The Plant Sitter* by Gene Zion; illus. by Margaret Bloy Graham. An overwhelming proliferation of house plants.

Make a "forest growing in my room" picture: Pre-cut colored rectangles to be used as beds, and small squares for pillows. The children paste these on their papers. Litter the table with long green strips cut to serve as grasses or trees. The children paste these over the bed picture to make a forest grow in the bedroom.

Closing songs. Take time in your closing circle to have the children hold up their pictures as you remind them, "That night in Max's room a forest grew . . . and grew . . . until the ceiling hung with vines . . . and the walls became the world . . . all around."

More books to share:

Elizabite, Adventures of a Carnivorous Plant by H. A. Rey.

In silly verse, a Venus flytrap-like plant devours everything in sight, and finally becomes a heroine.

Follow-up activities for home or school:

•Watch *Where the Wild Things Are*. 8 min. Video or 16 mm film.

•Bring in a collection of house plants with luxurious foliage and create a forest in your room.

20. Freaky Frog Day

Opening songs.

Read: *Seven Froggies Went to School* by Kate Duke. Frogs learn to dive, swim, and avoid cats, all in bouncy rhyme.

Read: *Tuesday* by David Wiesner. Frogs sail about on lily pads all night. Brief text. Let the children discuss the magical illustrations as you turn the pages.

Read: *The Wide-Mouthed Frog* by Rex Schneider. Based on the joke about the frog who talks with a wide mouth until he meets an animal who EATS wide-mouth frogs.

Sing and act out:

> I'm a little green frog,
> Sitting on the water.
> A little green frog,
> Doing what he oughter.
> Took a bite of a lily pad.
> Made a jump!
> And I said, "I'm glad,
> I'm a little green frog,
> Sitting on the water.
> Croak! Croak! Croak!

Litter the floor with pieces of green paper as lily pads. On "Jump!" all jump to another lily pad. After each verse jump to a new lily pad and sing it over again. Sing to the tune of "The Little White Duck" in *Burl Ives Sings Little White Duck.*

Read: *Frog Went A-Courtin'* by John Langstaff; illus. by Feodor Rojankovsky. The old folk song about Mr. Frog courting and marrying Miss Mouse. Sing along with this book if you know the tune. If you sing, encourage the children to join you on the "um-hums" at the end of each verse. Since the book becomes very lengthy as several wedding guests arrive, just sing one line per guest rather than repeating the entire chorus. Finish the book by singing the full chorus for the last two-page spread in which the cat arrives.

Film: *The Foolish Frog*. 8 min. Video or 16 mm film. Sing along if you like, or rerun the film and sing the whole thing with the film on the second run through. If the film is unavailable, read the picture book *The Foolish Frog* by Pete Seeger and Charles Seeger.

Make a clay frog: From a small dab of green clay make a frog. Pinch two bits off for eyes. Roll them into tiny balls and set aside. Roll the big bit into a ball. Squish it onto a pre-cut green cardboard lily pad. Add the eyes. Use a thumbnail to indent the mouth and pupil slots in the eyes.

Play with the frog: Call out "Tuesday night! All frogs fly!" and fly your frogs around in the air. Call "Wednesday morning! All frogs land!" and put them on the ground. Count off "Thursday, Friday, Saturday, Sunday, Monday, Tuesday!" Repeat.

Closing songs. Take time to fly your frogs through the air as you sing "Goodbye to the frogs."

More books to share:

Captain Toad and the Motorbikes by David McPhail. A toad's infatuation with a motorcycle.

Frog Medicine by Mark Teague. The boy, Elmo, gains empathy with the frog's life by visiting a frog doctor down in Frogtown.

Gorky Rises by William Steig. A remarkable longer fantasy about a frog who levitates.

I'm Taggarty Toad by Peter Pavey. A bouncy, rhyming Mr. Toad.

Tale of Mr. Jeremy Fisher by Beatrix Potter. A frog nearly has a bad end.

Follow-up activities for home or school:

•Reproduce a frog picture and cut it out. Give each child a frog. Play a piece of classical music and let each child fly his or her frog around the room. When you stop the music it is daybreak and the frogs fall from the air. Each child drops a frog and watches it drift to the floor. Look to see where all of the frogs have landed. Then pick them up and play again.

•Watch the Jeremy Fisher scene from *Tales of Beatrix Potter*. 86 min. video. Stunning Royal Ballet of London performance. Cue up just the Jeremy Fisher scene, about 5 minutes in length.

21. Space Place

Opening songs.

Read: "Little Bear Goes to the Moon" from *Little Bear* by Else Holmelund Minarik; illus. by Maurice Sendak. Little Bear's pretend flight to the moon doesn't get far off the ground.

Read: *Guys from Space* by Daniel Pinkwater. Guys from space carry our hero off for a root beer float on another planet.

Act out *Guys from Space:* We chose a kid, a mom, a big ugly space thing to sell root beer, and a talking rock. The rest of us were the guys from space. The guys from space held hands to form a circle and swirled around the room beeping until we landed, picked up the kid, and swirled off to the root-beer planet.

Read: *A Trip to Mars* by Ruth Young; illus. by Maryann Cocca-Leffler. Preparing for a pretend trip to Mars.

Poem: "Message from a Mouse Ascending in a Rocket" by Patricia Hubbell in *Mice Are Nice,* compiled by Nancy Larrick; illus. by Ed Young, p. 10.

Read: *I Want to Be an Astronaut* by Byron Barton. An astronaut's trip through space.

For older children read also: *Moog-Moog, Space Barber* by Mark Teague. A trip to space for a rotten haircut.

Make a space-scape: Kids create a space-scape by tearing colored tissue paper into blobs and pasting them onto a sheet of construction paper. Provide tissue paper in complementary colors. I used pinks, magentas, dark blues, and purples . . . colors similar to those in *A Trip to Mars*. Into this space-scape each child can paste one spaceship shape pre-cut by you from silver paper.

Closing songs.

More books to share:

Alistair in Outer Space by Marilyn Sadler; illus. by Roger Bollen. Alistair is carried off on a space trip by Goots.

Regards to the Man in the Moon by Ezra Jack Keats. An imaginary trip in space.

UFO Diary by Satoshi Kitamura. A visit to Earth from a UFO's perspective.

My Place in Space by Robin and Sally Hirst; illus. by Roland Harvey with Joe Levine. Technical but fun look at an Australian child's address, beginning with street and expanding to include planet, galaxy, and solar system.

Follow-up activities for home or school:

•Draw a communal picture of a space guy. Teacher or parent can draw the outline, then ask children to suggest the space guy's features.

22. *If I Were a Painter*

Opening songs.

Read: *Benjamin's Portrait* by Alan Baker. Benjamin's attempt at a self-portrait becomes a mess and so does he.

Read: *Benjamin's Book* by Alan Baker. Benjamin's attempts to write in his blank book turn into a mess!

Read: *The Art Lesson* by Tomie de Paola. Young Tommy learns to draw with his new crayons. An autobiographical picture book. Provide a display of Tomie de Paola's other books for children to check out later.

Form a circle and sing and act out:

If I were an artist,
An artist, an artist,
If I were an artist,
I'd draw big blue circles like this!

Let the children suggest the color of paint and the strokes . . . circles, up-and-down stripes, side-to-side stripes, zig-zags, squares, etc. Sing the song several times, drawing various colored shapes in the air with large imaginary brushes.

Music: See the music on page 166. Adapt the tune to fit your words.

Read: *Diego* by Jeanette Winter. Text by Jonah Winter. In English and Spanish. A charming biography of the Mexican muralist Diego Rivera, which reads aloud well. The bright illustrations are small, so this can be used best when children crowd close to look at the pictures. Some of the illustrations may disturb you, so read this before using.

For older groups read also: *Emma* by Wendy Kesselman; illus. by Barbara Cooney. Seventy-two-year-old Emma takes up painting.

Activity: Tape large sheets of paper to the wall (3 × 2 feet or larger). Let the children draw or paint on them using broad strokes similar to those we practiced in our song. Make large circles, stripes, zig-zags, etc.

Closing songs.

More books to share:

Artists' Helpers Enjoy the Evening by M. B. Goffstein. Artists' pastels at play.

Bear's Picture by Daniel Pinkwater. Two fine proper gentlemen criticize Bear's abstract picture, but Bear loves his own drawing.

John's Picture by Elizabeth MacDonald; illus. by David McTaggart. John's drawing of a little man comes to life and draws up a family and a life for himself.

Little Mouse's Painting by Diane Wolkstein; illus. by Maryjane Begin. Mouse's friends see themselves in his landscapes, so he lets them each enjoy his painting in their own way.

The Little Painter of Sabana Grande by Patricia Maloney Markun; illus. by Robert Casilla. Fernando likes to paint but has no paper . . . solution? He paints the houses in his village.

Mary's Tiger by Rex Harley; illus. by Sue Porter. A girl's tiger drawing comes down off the page and becomes her friend.

Matthew's Dream by Leo Lionni. Matthew the mouse visits an art gallery and dreams of becoming a painter.

A Painter by Douglas Florian. Simple, evocative text shows a painter at work.

Regina's Big Mistake by Marissa Moss. Regina worries about making a mistake in her picture until she learns to use the "mistake" as an idea to improve her picture.

Tye May and the Magic Brush by Molly Garrett Bang. Chinese folktale about a girl whose drawing becomes real.

❧ Build It Once, Use It Twice ❧

23. Good Wood

Opening songs.

Read: "Beaver in November" from *Turtle in July* by Marilyn Singer; illus. by Jerry Pinkney. Read the poem first. Repeat, letting the children chant the chorus with you, adding motions of a beaver building his dam: "This stick here . . . that stick there . . . Mud . . . more mud . . . add mud . . . good mud."

Read: *Good Wood Bear* by Bijou Le Tord. Bear builds a birdhouse.

Talk about woodworking sounds: Talk about the sounds Bear makes as he works. Demonstrate how they might sound by using rhythm instruments such as serrated rhythm sticks, wood blocks, and sand blocks.

Read the story again with sound effects: Hand out instruments so that one group has sticks; one, sand blocks; one, wood blocks. Let each group add proper sound effects as Bear saws, hammers, planes, and sands.

Sing:

> Aserin, aseran,
> Los maderos de San Juan
> Aserin, aseran,
> Los maderos de San Juan.
>
> See them saw, see them saw,
> The woodcutters of San Juan.
> See them saw, see them saw,
> The woodcutters of San Juan.

Ask what else woodworkers could do. Sing about it.: "See them hammer. See them hammer. The woodworkers of San Juan."

Music: See the music on page 169.

Read: *At Taylor's Place* by Sharon Phillips Denslow; illus. by Nancy Carpenter. A visit to an elderly woodworker who makes animal weathervanes.

Read: *A Carpenter* by Douglas Florian. A carpenter and his tools. Simple text.

Make a saw: Provide the children with an isosceles triangle of stiff poster board, approximately 3 inches on the longest side by 2 inches high. Provide a small piece of poster board in a contrasting color as the board to saw on. Both boards and saws must be of a thick poster board. The children can draw teeth on the saw and knotholes on the board. Now saw on the "board" with the "saw." A wonderful squeaking, sawing sound should ensue.

Sing the woodcutter's song again: Saw on your boards as you sing.

Closing songs.

More books to share:

> *Albert's Alphabet* by Leslie Tyron. Albert the goose builds an alphabet of wood.
>
> *Good Times on Grandfather Mountain* by Jacqueline Briggs Martin; illus. by Susan Gaber. Old Washburn can whittle something out of anything.
>
> *The Grandpa Days* by Joan W. Blos; illus. by Emily Arnold McCully. Grandpa shows Philip his tools and the kinds of wood he has to work with. Philip designs a project they can build.
>
> *The Heart of Wood* by Marguerite W. David; illus. by Sheila Hamanaka. A fiddle made from the heart of a tree.
>
> *Winter Wood* by David Spohn. A father and son chop wood.

Follow-up activities for home or school:

> •Ask a woodworker to show you how he or she saws and hammers. Perhaps the woodworker could make a simple object while you watch.
>
> •Make a sawdust picture. Draw a design on paper with glue and sprinkle the design with sawdust.
>
> •Saw into three different kinds of wood. Pass them around and smell them. Look at their color and grain. Talk about their differences.

24. Use It Again!

Opening songs.

Read: *Just My Size* by May Garelick; illus. by William Pène du Bois. An outgrown coat is put to good use.

Read: *Dear Garbage Man* by Gene Zion; illus. by Margaret Bloy Graham. Stan the garbage man tries to save *everything*.

Read: *Aunt Ippy's Museum of Junk* by Rodney A. Greenblat. Aunt Ippy saves everything!

Sing a recycling song:

> What shall we do with a piece of paper?
> What shall we do with a piece of paper?
> What shall we do with a piece of paper?
> How can we re-cycle?

Let the children suggest things to do with it: Write on the back of it . . . fold it into an origami bird . . . recycle it.

Sing about whatever the group suggests doing with the paper.

> Turn it over and draw on the back.
> Turn it over and draw on the back.
> Turn it over and draw on the back.
> Early in the morning.

Music: See the music on page 170.

You could present the group with other recyclable objects and let the children create more verses for their song. "What shall we do with a peanut shell?" "What shall we do with an aluminum can?" I ended my singing by showing a piece of foil from a candy and singing: "What do we do with a piece of foil?" My group suggested: "Wad it up in a little ball," "Fold it into a tiny boat," and "Save it and recycle it." I added the verse, "Paste it on a paper and make a picture." This was to be our craft for the day.

Read: *The Winter Bear* by Ruth Craft and Erik Blegvad. An old toy bear found in a tree is revived.

Read: *Jamaica's Find* by Juanita Havill; illus. by Anne Sibley O'Brien. Sometimes a lost toy needs to be returned to its owner.

Make a picture: Paste the foil and strips of tissue paper from three candy kisses onto a sheet of paper to make a design. At Christmas and Easter,

chocolate candy kisses are packaged in multi-colored foils. My students
made flowers, boats, and random designs, and everyone loved the candy!
Closing songs: Give each child a piece of discarded paper. I asked my group
to take off their name tags and discard them.

Sing the recycling song again and toss your papers into a recycling bin:
Toss it in the recycling bin.
Toss it in the recycling bin.
Toss it in the recycling bin.
That's how we re-cycle.

More books to share:
Fix-It by David McPhail. A broken TV is finally fixed.
Good as New by Barbara Douglass; illus. by Patience Brewster. A visiting
cousin ruins a teddy bear, but grandpa washes it, re-stuffs it, and re-sews
it.
The Old Red Rocking Chair by Phyllis Root; illus. by John Sandford. A
tossed-out chair is recycled and recycled.
The Paper Bag Prince by Colin Thompson. The old man who spends his
days at the dump moves in when the dump closes, and watches nature
reclaim the dump. Detailed illustrations that older listeners will enjoy
examining.
Something from Nothing by Phoebe Gilman. Adapted from a Jewish folktale. Baby Joseph's blanket is re-made into a jacket, vest, tie, handker-
chief, button. And finally into this story.
Stay Away from the Junkyard! by Tricia Tusa. Theo discovers a *treasure*—
the junkyard, it's owner, and the pet pig, Clarissa.
Tiffky Doofky by William Steig. Elaborate tale of a garbage collector in
pursuit of love. For older listeners.
What's Wrong with a Van? by Franz Brandenberg; illus. by Aliki. The old
van proves best after all.
Follow-up activities for home or school:
•Make a trash collage with discarded objects.
•Collect toys you don't want to keep anymore and give them to a charity
that reuses them.

❧ *Families Together* ❧

25. *Dinner at Grandma's House*

Opening songs.

Talk about: What do you eat when you go to a grandmother's house?

Read: *At Grammy's House* by Eve Rice; illus. by Nancy Winslow Parker. A visit to a French-American grammy's farm. Roast for dinner.

Read: *Staying with Grandma* by Eileen Roe; illus. Jacqueline Rogers. An overnight visit with Grandma. Jam and toast for breakfast!

Sing:

> When I go to Grandma's house,
> To Grandma's house,
> To Grandma's house.
> When I go to Grandma's house,
> I have good things to eat!

Children suggest things they eat at Grandma's house and the group sings about each of them while acting out the eating.

> Toast and jam at Grandma's house,
> At Grandma's house,
> At Grandma's house.
> Toast and jam at Grandma's house,
> That is what I eat!

Music: See the music on page 170.

Read: *Eat Up, Gemma* by Sarah Hayes; illus. by Jan Ormerod. Baby Gemma won't eat anything. Not Grandma's dinner, not the pizza, until. . . .

Read and sing: *Over the River and Through the Woods* by Lydia Maria Child; illus. by Brinton Turkle. Hurray for the pumpkin pie!

For older classes add: *A Visit to Grandma's* by Nancy Carlson. Grandma moves to St. Petersburg, Florida, and stops cooking!

Make a feast table: Give each child a piece of paper to serve as a table. You have pre-cut circles from colored paper to represent mashed potatoes, a turkey, green beans, pumpkin pie. Children paste these in the center of their paper (the table) and draw plates around the edges of the paper. Draw a plate for each person coming to the feast. A plate for Mom, Dad, Grandma, Aunt Sally.

Closing songs.

More books to share:

Grandma Gets Grumpy by Anna Grossnickle Hines. Macaroni, hot dogs, and ice cream from this grandma.

My Grandma Leoni by Bijou Le Tord. Simple text. Loving, elderly grandma comes to stay and is missed when she is gone.

The Grandma Mix-up by Emily Arnold McCully. Two grandmas, two menus. An "I-Can-Read" format.

Grandma's Promise by Elaine Moore; illus. by Elise Primavera. Oatmeal with peaches and an adventure when the power fails.

Green Beans by Elizabeth Thomas; illus. by Vicki Jo Redenbaugh. Guess what's for dinner at this gardening granny's house?

Just Listen by Winifred Morris; illus. by Patricia Cullen-Clark. Memories of freshly baked bread at grandmother's country cabin.

Me & Nana by Leslie Kimmelman; illus. by Marilee Robin Burton. Orange juice and cereal boxes, hot chocolate and marshmallows, and lots of fun shared with this grandma.

Tales of a Gambling Grandma by Dayal Kaur Khalsa. A Russian emigrant cardplaying grandma. Sweet, sad, and funny.

Follow-up activities for home or school:

•Make a list of foods your grandmother or an older friend prepares. Which are your favorites?

•Write a letter to your grandma or older friend telling them which food they prepare that you especially like.

•Make a "Grandmas Gallery" bulletin board in your classroom with photos of grandmothers.

For older children:

•Create a grandmother collage. Paste a photo of your grandmother or other favorite relative on a piece of paper. Clip photos from magazines that remind you of this person (foods, flowers, scenes, furniture, etc.), or draw pictures of things that remind you of her or him and paste them around the photograph.

26. The Relatives Came

Opening songs.

Talk about: Visits from relatives; visits to relatives.

Read: *The Relatives Came* by Cynthia Rylant; illus. by Stephen Gammell. A passel of relatives drive up from Virginia and fill our house and our hearts.

Fingerplay:

> Everyday when we eat our dinner
> Our table is just this small.
> (*hold hands close together to show size*)
> There's room for father, and mother, and brother,
> And sister, and me, that's all.
> (*point to fingers to count*)
> But every time that company comes,
> You'd scarcely believe your eyes.
> (*point to eyes*)
> For our little table grows bigger and bigger,
> (*spread hands*)
> Until it is just this size!
> (*arms spread wide apart*)

Talk about: Extending tables and how we make room for lots of relatives or friends to eat together.

Read: *Night Ride* by Bernie and Mati Karlin; illus. by Bernie Karlin. A ride through the night to reach Grandma's house at dawn.

Act out: Driving to Grandma's house. Start the car, turn corners, go through stop lights, drive over hills, around curves, cross a bridge, take a ferry, jump out of the car and give Grandma (Mom can substitute for Grandma in this part of the play) a hug when you get there.

Read: *I Go with My Family to Grandma's* by Riki Levinson; illus. by Diane Goode. Travel by bike, trolley, ferry to Grandma's house. Pause before you turn the page and let the children chime in on the phrase "I went to . . . (turn page) . . . Grandma's house!"

Read: *Roger Loses His Marbles* by Susanna Gretz. Aunt Lulu takes over Roger's bed and necessitates a room-cleaning when she comes to visit. But she turns out to be a great aunt in the end.

Make a family picture: Provide pieces of paper and stick-on dots in various sizes and colors. Children select dots to represent each family member.

They stick these onto their paper as heads, draw on faces, and add stick bodies. I provided each child with an 8 ½ by 11 inch paper with a frame already drawn around the edge, and they arranged their family portrait within the frame. To draw a frame, simply cut a piece of cardboard one inch smaller on each side than your paper, put it in the middle of your paper, and draw around it.

Closing songs.

More books to share:

The Doorbell Rang by Pat Hutchins. Sharing with unexpected guests.

The Family Reunion by Tricia Tusa. A large, wacky family arrives for the reunion, but nobody knows who they are!

Katie Morag and the Big Boy Cousins by Mairi Hedderwick. Spunky Kate encounters her cousins.

Follow-up activities for home or school:

•Make a photo album of family and relatives. Use the album to talk to your child about his/her relations.

•Make a "Relative Stories Book." Write down family anecdotes about each relative. Paste the story on a page with that relative's photo. Read the stories to your child.

•OR, ask relatives to tell a story about, "When I was a child. . . ." Write these down and make a "Childhood Stories" book to share with *your* children.

27. *Picnic!*

Opening songs.

Talk about picnics.

Read: *Having a Picnic* by Sarah Garland. A windy day picnic is taken over by ducks.

Read: *This Is the Bear and the Picnic Lunch* by Sarah Hayes; illus. by Helen Craig. After dog, bear, and rain wreak havoc, boy packs an indoor lunch.

Form a circle and sing:

We're going on a picnic,

A picnic, a picnic,

We're going on a picnic,
And this is what we'll bring.

Let the children suggest what to bring and sing of each item as you mime
eating it or playing with it.

We'll bring along some hot dogs,
Some hot dogs, some hot dogs,
We'll bring along some hot dogs,
That is what we'll bring!

Sing of beach balls, frisbees, grape juice, apples, etc.
Music: See music on page 166.
Read: *Ernest and Celestine's Picnic* by Gabrielle Vincent. A picnic in the rain.
Read: *A Winter Picnic* by Robert Welber; illus. by Deborah Ray. A picnic in
the snow.
Pack a picnic lunch: Give each child a small paper bag and a paper cup. Let
each make one peanut-butter-on-cracker sandwich. Wrap the sandwich
in wax paper and place it in the sack. Select and wrap one carrot stick,
one cookie. Select five grapes (or raisins) and wrap. Stow all of these
items in the paper sack along with the cup. Go on a picnic. Bring blankets
or beach mats to sit on. You need not go far. If necessary, you can just
walk around the library and arrive back in the storytime room for the
picnic. Bring along a jug of juice to fill their cups.
Closing songs.
More books to share:
Before the Picnic by Yoriki Tsutsui; illus. by Akiko Hayashi. Sashi makes
quite a mess before Mother gets the picnic ready.
Marmalade's Picnic by Cindy Wheeler. Marmalade the cat stows away and
consumes the picnic basket contents.
Picnic with Piggins by Jane Yolen; illus. by Jane Dyer.
The Picnic by Jean Claverie. Rain drives the family to a fastfood stand.
Pig William by Arlene Dubanevich. A pig family on an outing.
A Ripping Day for a Picnic by Keith Du Quette. Four strange animals set
off through imaginative lands seeking a picnic spot.
Sophie and Jack by Judy Taylor; illus. by Susan Gantner. Two hippo
friends on a picnic.
Follow-up activities for home or school:
•Plan a picnic! Make a list of the things you will need to take. Let the
child help you prepare, wrap, and pack the items. Invite a friend. Go on
a picnic!

•Have a Lunch Bunch storytime. King County (Washington) librarian Sue Mooseker holds brown bag lunch storytimes each Wednesday during the summer in her library courtyard. She reads to the children while they eat the lunches they have brought.

28. Grandpa and Me

Opening songs.

Read: *Where Are You Going, Emma?* by Jeanne Titherington. Emma goes apple-picking with Grandpa. Very brief text.

Poem: "Grandpa in March" by Arnold Adoff in *Sunflakes: Poems for Children* by Lillian Moore; illus. by Jan Ormerod.

Read: *William and Grandpa* by Alice Schertle; illus. by Lydia Dabcovich. When William goes to Grandpa's to visit, they share supper, stargazing on the roof, and hot chocolate. Spunky writing. A bit lengthy, but even younger children can follow and are intrigued by the "climbing on the roof" scene. We sang a chorus of "I Went to the Animal Fair" with Grandpa and William on page 2 and again at the book's end.

Form a circle and sing: "I Went to the Animal Fair."

Act out the song as you sing. Sing the song twice. The first time through, act the part of the elephant. Lumber in on: "I went to the animal fair, the birds and the beasts were there." Comb your hair with the big baboon: "The big baboon by the light of the moon was combing her auburn hair." Hold out your trunk for the monkey to jump on: "You ought to have seen the monk. He jumped on the elephant's trunk." Fall on your knees and sneeze: "The elephant sneezed and fell on his knees." Shrug your shoulders and wonder what happened to the monkey: "And what became of the monk, the monk, the monk?"

Now sing and act this out again. This time be the monkey. Let the children jump into their mother's arms when you sing, "He jumped on the elephant's trunk". After each chorus ask the children, "So what did become of the monk?" Let them make up answers: He ran away, he fell off the trunk, etc.

For the complete text and tune see: *The Fireside Book of Children's Songs* by Marie Winn, p. 152.

Read: *A Balloon for Grandad* by Nigel Gray; illus. by Jane Ray. A boy's Grandad lives far away in another country.

Talk about: Grandpas who live far away.

For older groups add: *When I Was Young in the Mountains* by Cynthia Rylant; illus. by Diane Goode. Two children live with their grandparents.

Talk about: Grandfathers and what we think of when we think of them.

Make a "Grandfather Book" for your grandpa: Fold a sheet of paper in half. On the front, write: "These things remind me of my grandpa." Draw a line at the top of each page and ask the child to provide one word that reminds of the grandfather. Ask the adults to talk with their children and then write the words they select. If you are the only adult working with the group, take time to do this for each child. Adults can help the children select an appropriate color to accompany each word. Older children will want to draw cars, lawnmowers, etc. For younger children, simply covering the page with a significant color is evocative. Example: My grandfather always grew petunias, so I wrote "petunias" on one page. I colored the whole page pink. He raised bees and ate honey, so I wrote "honey" on a page and colored the page yellow.

Closing songs.

More books to share:

Crack-of-Dawn Walkers by Amy Hest; illus. by Amy Schwartz. Sadie and Grandfather go for an early morning walk through the neighborhood.

Grandad's Magic by Bob Graham. Grandad performs magic tricks with disastrous results.

Grandpa's Face by Eloise Greenfield; illus. by Floyd Cooper. Tamika sees Grandpa practicing mean faces for a part in a play and begins to fear him, until Grandpa reassures her of his love.

Grandpa's Song by Tony Johnston; illus. by Brad Snead. A singing grandpa delights his grandchildren, but gradually begins to forget the words.

My Grandson Lew by Charlotte Zolotow; illus. by William Pène du Bois. Gentle memories of a grandfather no longer living. Reads aloud well, but illustrations are tiny for storytime use.

The Purple Coat by Amy Hest; illus. by Amy Schwartz. Amy's tailor grandfather conspires with her for a new purple coat.

Song and Dance Man by Karen Ackerman; illus. by Stephen Gammell. Grandpa revives his old vaudeville act in the attic.

Tom by Tomie de Paola. This grandpa teaches Tommy a trick that gets him into trouble.

When Grandpa Came to Stay by Judith Casely. A borscht-eating Grandpa comes to stay when Grandma dies. A visit to the cemetery with his grandson consoles him.

Follow-up activities for home or school:

•Make a "Grandpa Collage": Paste a photo of your grandpa or older friend onto a blank page. Surround it with clippings from magazines or drawings of things that remind you of him or her.

•Make a book of "Grandpa Stories": Let the child dictate a story about something he or she did at Grandpa's house. Put this and other episodes together in a booklet. Read it aloud from time to time.

29. Quilts to Remember

Opening songs.

Show quilts: Talk about the use of various fabrics in the quilts. Talk about quilt patterns, the quilting process. I talk about the quilt as a tool for remembering clothing once worn, as a trigger for memories.

Read: *The Quilt Story* by Tony Johnston; illus. by Tomie de Paola. A pioneer girl draws comfort from the quilt her mother made as she settles into her new log cabin. Generations later, another little girl finds the quilt and takes comfort from it during a move to her new home.

Read: *Ernest and Celestine's Patchwork Quilt* by Gabrielle Vincent. This is a wordless book. Gather the children close and let them tell you what is happening in the pictures. Ernest makes a quilt for himself. Celestine wants one, too. The children might tell you how Celestine feels as she sits on Ernest's new quilt and what she says to Ernest.

Singing game: "The Old Brass Wagon."
    Circle to the left,
    The old brass wagon.
    Circle to the left,
    The old brass wagon.
    Circle to the left,
    The old brass wagon.
    You're the one, my darling.

Hold hands in a circle and do whatever the words suggest. Change the words on subsequent choruses: jump up and down, go into the center, go back out again, etc.

Music: See the music on page 171.

Read: *The Patchwork Quilt* by Valerie Flournoy; illus. by Jerry Pinkney. Tanya's grandmother makes a quilt using fabrics from each member of the household. Condense this for younger listeners by telling what happens and showing the pictures. Children age four and up can listen to the complete text.

Talk about: Show a memory quilt if you have one and talk about the origins of the various fabrics. I let the children gather around the quilt, which I spread on the floor. My grandmother made it from dress scraps. I ask the children to guess what kinds of dresses she had once had. They point out blue squares (a blue dress), red polka dots, and so on. Make a patchwork picture: Pre-cut small squares of fabric. Color coordinate them for best effect. Draw a rectangle on a sheet of paper and let the children paste fabric squares in the rectangle to form a patchwork quilt picture. You can coat the entire rectangle with rubber cement and let the children just stick the patches on. Rubber cement remains adhesive even if it dries as they work.

Closing songs.

More books to share:

The Berenstain Bears and Mama's New Job by Stan and Jan Berenstain. Mama Bear starts up a new business selling her quilts.

The Josefina Storyquilt by Eleanor Coerr; illus. by Bruce Degen. A quilt comforts a little girl on the long wagon train west.

The Keeping Quilt by Patricia Polacco. A quilt's many uses through time in the life of a Russian-Jewish emigré family.

Luka's Quilt by Georgina Guback. Luka is disappointed to find that the Hawaiian quilt her *tutu* makes for her has no bright flowers on it.

The Quilt by Ann Jonas. A quilt to snuggle under.

Texas Star by Barbara Hancock Cole; illus. by Barbara Minton. The quilters come to work on Mama's Texas Star quilt.

Follow-up activities for home or school:

•Share quilts from your own family. If you don't have any at home, ask an aunt or grandmother to bring hers out for the children to examine. Talk about the quiltmaker. Think about the time and caring which went into each quilt.

•Look at pictures of quilts in books. Talk about the varying patterns, the use of different fabrics.

•Make a patchwork keepsake picture using squares of fabric from discarded clothing, or scraps of cloth left over from sewing projects. Save this to help the child remember clothing the family once wore.

•Tell: "Grandmother's Apron" from *The Family Storytelling Handbook* by Anne Pellowski, p. 113.

•Visit a fabric store and examine the fabrics there. Feel them, talk about their textures and their colors. Buy a few small pieces to use in making a patchwork picture.

30. *Oh No, Baby!*

Opening songs.

Read: *Oh My Baby Bear!* by Audrey Wood. Baby makes a mess of dressing, eating, bathing.

Read: *Catch the Baby!* by Lee Kingman; illus. by Susanna Natti. Big brother and sister can't keep up with baby.

Read: *Eat Up, Gemma* by Sarah Hayes; illus. by Jan Ormerod. Big brother finally finds a way to get Baby Gemma to eat.

Poem: "Baby's Drinking Song" by James Kirkup in *Sunflakes: Poems for Children* by Lillian Moore; illus. by Jan Ormerod, p. 26.

Form a circle and sing:
>   If I were a babysitter,
>   A babysitter, a babysitter,
>   If I were a babysitter,
>   The baby would act like this!

Let the children suggest how the baby might behave, and act this out after each verse. Sing it over and over until each child has had a chance to suggest a bad-baby antic. Baby might throw food on the floor, cry, run away, tear up books, etc.

For example, you might sing:
>   Baby would throw food on the floor,
>   Throw food on the floor,
>   Throw food on the floor.
>   Baby would throw food on the floor.
>   That's what baby would do!

Music: See the music on page 166.

Read: *Big Brother Blues* by Maria Polushkin; illus. by Ellen Weiss. There are lots of things wrong with baby, but sister likes him anyway.

Read a poem: "African Lullaby," a traditional lullaby in *Pass It On: African-American Poetry for Children*. Selected by Wade Hudson, illus. by Floyd Cooper, p. 6. A baby is loved by its mother.

Read: *Where's the Baby?* by Pat Hutchins. A monster baby creates a mess through the entire house.

Make a picture card for a baby: Let the children cut pictures from magazines or old book jackets and paste one on each side of a 5 by 5-inch piece of colored tagboard. Then help each child cover the card with clear plastic shelf liner.

Closing songs.

See also: Bad Babies, program 8.

More books to share:

New Baby by Emily Arnold McCully. Wordless. Little mouse feels left out when a new baby arrives.

Oh, No! by Sarah Garland. Baby gets into *everything*.

Follow-up activities for home or school:

•Arrange for a baby to visit your class. Let the children tell you what they observe about the baby. Can they find ways to please the baby?

•Make a display of photos of your class as babies.

•Create a "baby book" for your child. Write down simple remembrances: "When you were a baby, you _____." Staple several of these into a booklet. Illustrate with drawn pictures or photographs.

•Have a baby-food tasting. Place samples of four different baby foods on each child's plate. Vote on which tastes best.

31. Families, Families, and More Families

Opening songs.

Read: *More, More, More Said the Baby!* by Vera B. Williams. Three babies, three families, three bouncy rhymes.

Talk about the three families: For our purposes, let's assume each child lives with the adult shown in the book. On a poster board or flannel board put up a baby and father (Little Guy), a baby and grandmother (Little Pumpkin), and a baby and mother (Little Bird). Three families. To make the figures for your poster board, simply photocopy family members from the picture book. Cut these out and stick them to the poster board with a loop of tape behind the figure.

Read: *Charlie Anderson* by Barbara Abercrombie; illus. by Mark Graham. A stray cat makes a home with Sarah and Elizabeth and their mom. It turns out he spends *nights* with them and *days* with another family.

Talk about these families: On your poster board put up a cat, Sarah and Elizabeth, and their mother. Put up also the man and woman in the cat's *other* family, and the father and stepmother in Sarah and Elizabeth's other family.

Read: *Mommy, Buy Me a China Doll* by Harve Zemach; illus. by Margot Zemach. Sing this if you can. The song is a bit too complicated for most preschoolers, but they can chime in on "do Daddy do" and "Eliza Lou" at the refrain's end.

Talk about this family: On your poster board put up Eliza Lou, Momma, Grandma, Daddy, Sister, and Baby. Add cats, chickens, pigs, and horses if you like.

Sing and play: "The Farmer in the Dell." Let the brother take the sister, the sister take the baby, the baby take the grandma . . . etc.

Read: *When I Was Young in the Mountains* by Cynthia Rylant; illus. by Diane Goode. Living with grandma and grandpa in the country circa 1940.

Talk about this family: Put up a grandma, grandpa, brother, and sister on your poster board.

Paste a picture of your own family: I photocopy adults, grandparents, children, teenagers, babies and toddlers from various children's books. I make a photocopy sheet for each child with an assortment of such family members. They cut out those they need for their own family picture, paste them on a paper, and color them. You can pre-cut these and make piles of mothers, grandfathers, babies, and siblings for the children to select, if their cutting skills are not developed. Since there is an adult with each child in my younger storytimes, the adults help with the cutting. A good source for family member pictures to use in making a photocopy sheet is *Peter's Pocket* by Judi Brown; illus. by Julia Noonan.

More books to share:

Baby-O by Nancy White Carlstrom; illus. by Sucie Stevenson. A Caribbean family in bouncy rhyme: "Sing a song of Family-O."

Follow-up activities for home or school:

•Make a poster portraying each child's immediate family.

•Look at a family photo album.

32. *Gone Fishing*

Opening songs.

Read: *Just Like Daddy* by Frank Asch. Little Bear wakes up, dresses, and goes fishing, "just like Daddy," but he catches a fish—"just like Mommy!"

Read: *River Parade* by Alexandra Day. A child's toys fall into the river and float along. Then the child falls in and floats along, too.

Form a circle and sing:

> Did you ever go a-fishin' on a hot summer day?
> Sittin' on a log, and the log rolls away.
> Alligator bites you by the seat of the pants.
> And all the little fishes do the hoochy-koochy dance.

Sing this several times and act it out. Ask what other disasters might happen when fishing besides rolling off a log. Sing of them. Example:

> Did you ever go a-fishin' on a hot summer day?
> *Caught a big fish and it pulled you in the water.*
> Alligator bites you by the seat of the pants.
> And all the little fishes do the hoochy-koochy dance.

Simply replace the second line with the disaster the children suggest. Don't worry about making it rhyme, but try to edit it for rhythm. Our group suggested: "Caught three fish and they were too small to keep"; "Sat on a log and it floated to the ocean"; and "Put my foot in the water and the fish bit my toes."

Music: See the music on page 171.

Read: *Dark and Full of Secrets* by Carol Carrick; illus. by Donald Carrick. Boy is afraid of murky pond waters until he snorkels and explores its depths.

Read: *Dawn* by Uri Shulevitz. A boy and his grandfather wake at dawn and row out onto the lake. This can be rendered especially lovely by reading it over a tape of the first few moments of Richard Strauss's *Blue Danube* waltz. Listen to the opening of the musical piece several times and fit the words to it. Read slowly. Try to time your reading so that the crescendos come with the rising of the sun.

Catch a fish: Make several fishing poles from thin wooden dowels about 3 feet long. Tie a string to one end. Stick a loop of masking tape, looped with the sticky side out, to the end of the string as your hook. This loop will stick to your string easily.

Cut out 2 inch-long fish from colored typing paper or other lightweight paper and litter the floor with paper fish. I put down three large sheets of blue paper as the pond. Four children can fish at a time. Once they have caught their fish, each child hands the pole over to another and goes to the craft table to decorate the catch. Later they return to catch another fish. Everyone has time to catch several fish and decorate them.

Closing songs.

More books to share:

Fishing at Long Pond by William T. George; illus. by Lindsay Barrett George. Grandpa and Katie explore the pond.

Liam's Catch by Dorothy D. Parker; illus by. Robert Andrew Parker. A slow-paced and descriptive look at a family net-fishing a river in Ireland.

Tobias Catches a Trout by Ole Hertz. A family in Greenland goes camping and catches a load of fish to sell.

Tobias Goes Ice Fishing by Ole Hertz. A child in Greenland goes ice fishing.

Follow-up activities for home or school:

•Go fishing.

•Clean and fry a fish.

•Look at a fish identification handbook and decorate paper fish to match specific species.

•Make a fish print: Roll out ink (tempera will work; you will need an ink roller). Lay a real fish on its side in the ink. Then pick up the fish and press its side onto a sheet of paper.

33. *Lullaby*

Opening songs.

Read: *Hush Little Baby* by Aliki. Sing or read this lullaby.

Read: *The Sun's Asleep Behind the Hill* by Mirra Ginsburg; illus. by Paul O. Zelinsky. Armenian lullaby. Sun, breeze, leaves, bird, squirrel, and child go to sleep. Moon rises to shine through the night. Book unfortunately does not include the music.

Read: *Goodnight Moon* by Margaret Wise Brown; illus. by Clement Hurd. Little bunny says goodnight to every object in the room. I like to let the children repeat each "goodnight."

Act out:

Rock-a-bye baby,
In the tree top.
When the wind blows,
The cradle will rock.

When the bough breaks,
The cradle will fall.
And down will come baby,
Cradle and all.

Ask the adults to rock the children on their laps as they sing and gently drop
them between their knees when the bough breaks.

Music: See the music on page 172.

Read a poem: "Poppa Bear's Hum" from *The Three Bears Rhyme Book* by Jane
Yolen; illus. by Jane Dyer. Make up a tune and sing Poppa Bear's hum.
Let the children help you make up a lullaby for other animals using this
same format. Poppa Bear sings of honey. What would a papa cat sing of?
A papa canary?

Read: *On Mother's Lap* by Ann Herbert Scott; illus. by Glo Coalson. Have
adults hold children on their laps and rock them "back and forth . . .
back and forth" as you read. This early edition has black-on-beige illustrations. A 1992 edition of this same book has color illustrations by the
same illustrator. I prefer the earlier work, but it is interesting to show
both and compare.

Make a sleeping bunny in bed: Hold an index
card with one short side at the top. Fold the
bottom third of the card up to form a bed.
Put paste just along the edges of this flap
and glue shut, leaving the top open so you
can slip in a bunny cut-out later. Paste two
pink strips (ears) to the top of one pink or
white rectangle (bunny). Draw on sleeping
eyes. Stick your bunny into its bed. Sing a
lullaby to put it to sleep.

Closing songs.

More books to share:

Once: A Lullaby by bp Nichol; illus. by Anita Lobel. Animals in fancy
beds fall asleep one by one.

The Star Rocker by Joseph Slote; illus. by Dirk Zimmer. An old, old
woman on a houseboat in a pond sings the pond animals to sleep.

When the Dark Comes Dancing: A Bedtime Poetry Book. Compiled by
Nancy Larrick; illus. by John Wallner. Selection of bedtime poems.
Follow-up activities for home or school:
- •Show the film *Lullaby*, 4 min., 16 mm. The narrator sings good night to
each animated object in the child's room.
- •Learn a special lullaby and sing it to a baby or a teddybear.
- •Make up your own lullaby. Ask the child to think about what to tell the
baby and sing that. It need not be an elaborate song, just singing "Go to
sleep" over and over is fine.

❧ Feelings ❧

34. Whoops!

Opening songs.

Talk about: Accidental happenings. Falling down, spilling things, bumping into things, etc.

Read: *Where Is My Friend?* by Betsy & Giulio Maestro. Harriet falls off a chair while looking for a friend. I alert children to call out "WHOOPS!" if Harriet has an accident, and pause briefly in the story to discuss her fall.

Read: *It Hurts!* by Anne Sibley O'Brien. Jessica scrapes her knee. Ask if anyone has had this happen to them.

Read: *Sam's Wagon* by Barbro Lindgren; illus. by Eva Eriksson. Sam overloads his wagon and things keep falling out. We all say "WHOOPS!" when something falls out.

Song:
> When I was playing yesterday,
> When I was playing yesterday,
> When I was playing yesterday,
> Something happened to me!

Ask for ideas about what accidents could have happened, such as:
> I fell off my bed yesterday,
> I fell off my bed yesterday,
> I fell off my bed yesterday,
> That's what happened to me.

Ask what they did about this, for example:
> I got back in bed,
> In bed,
> In bed,
> I got back in bed.
> That is what I did.

Music: See the music on page 172.

Read: *Mr. Gumpy's Outing* by John Burningham. Mr. Gumpy's animals fail to sit and their boat is upset.

Read: *The Circus Baby* by Maud and Mishka Petersham. Baby Elephant spills his beans and breaks the stool. Mamma Elephant walks off with the tent!

Film: *Luxo, Jr.,* directed and animated by John Lasseter. 12 min. Baby Lamp breaks his ball.

Talk about accidents: Give each child a worksheet with photocopied pictures of children having minor accidents. I use pages 12–13 from *I Can Ride* by Shigeo Watanabe; illus. by Yasuo Ohtomo, in which Bear falls off his skateboard. Any disaster from *Poofy Loves Company* by Nancy Winslow Parker will do. See also *The True Francine* by Mark Brown, in which Francine falls off her chair, and p. 15 in *The Silly Mother Goose* by Leonard Kessler, in which Mother Goose's grocery bag breaks. Provide stick-on dots with both happy and sad faces. Let children paste a happy or sad face on each picture to show whether the character is laughing or crying over the accident.

More books to share:

Bad Egg: The True Story of Humpty Dumpty by Sarah Hayes; illus. by Charlotte Voak. Humpty Dumpty laughs when everyone falls off his wall until *he* falls off.

Dinosaurs, Beware! A Safety Guide by Marc Brown and Stephen Krensky. Safety tips for the primary level.

Lucky Chuck by Beverly Cleary; illus. by J. Winslow Higginbottom. Chuck rides his motorcycle into disaster.

Messy Baby by Jan Ormerod. Baby undoes all of Dad's house cleaning.

Oh, No! by Sarah Garland. Baby causes many disasters. Four words per page—"Getting dressed . . . Oh No!"—and so on.

Ooops! by Suzy Kline; illus. by Dora Leder. Not only children meet with minor disasters. Teachers and parents make mistakes, too.

Follow-up activities for home or school:

• Talk about accidents in the home or school. Make a list of potential dangers. Talk about how to avoid them.

35. I'm Proud to Be Me!

Opening songs.

Read: *I Can Build a House!* by Shigeo Watanabe; illus. by Yasuo Ohtomo. Baby bear builds a house of blocks, cushions, and a cardboard box. He's proud.

Read: *The Carrot Seed* by Ruth Krauss; illus. by Crockett Johnson. A boy grows a huge carrot. He's proud.

Read: *How Do I Put It On?* by Shigeo Watanabe; illus. by Yasuo Ohtomo. Baby bear dresses himself and is proud.

Make a circle and sing:
Look what I can do.
Look what I can do.
I can do most anything!
Look what I can do!

Let the children suggest things they can do—tie shoes, dress themselves, brush teeth, build with blocks, ride a trike, paint a picture, etc. Decide what *you* can do and then act it out as you sing. End each verse by exclaiming for the group, "I can ride a trike!" or whatever applies.

Music: See music on page 173.

Read: *The Hare and the Tortoise* by Jean de la Fontaine; illus. by Brian Wildsmith. Sometimes you can be TOO proud. Hare is proud of his fast running, but loses the race.

Read: *Who's Mouse Are You?* by Robert Kraus; illus. by Jose Aruego. A little mouse is proud of his family.

Talk about: Being proud of yourself, your family, your city. . . .

Do a cheer with pom-poms: Pass out a few pom-poms or crepe paper streamers and let two or three lead the group in cheers for the library:

YEAAAH, LIBRARY!
YEAAAH, LIBRARY!
YEAAAAAAAHHHHHH, LIBRARY!

Give everyone a chance to lead the cheers for the group.
Make a pom-pom to take home: Paste crepe paper streamers to the edge of a
    small paper plate. Wave these to lead your cheers.
Lead your own cheer: Let each child lead the group in a cheer for him/
    herself—"YEAAAH, JENNY!"
More books to share:
    Chrysanthemum by Kevin Henkes. Chrysanthemum takes much teasing
    about her name but ends up adoring it.
    Hooray for Me! by Remy Charlip and Lilian Moore; illus. by Vera B. Wil-
    liams. A song in praise of oneself.
    I'm Terrific! by Marjorie Weinman Sharmat; illus. by Vera B. Williams.
    More reasons to like oneself.
Follow-up activities for home or school:
    •Make a list of things you or your school can be proud of.
    •Make your own proud-to-be-me flag and wave it around. Draw pictures
    on the flag of things that make you proud.

36. *Too Proud to Ask for Help!*

Opening songs.
Talk about: How to ask for help when you need it.
Read: *Jim Flying High* by Mari Evans; illus. by Ashley Bryan.
    Jim Flying Fish is stuck in a tree and too proud to ask for help. Just read
    the story boldly and don't worry about the dialect. Let the kids "shew,
    shew, shew" with Jim as he stews around in the tree.
Read: *Elephant in a Well* by Marie Hall Ets. Little Elephant falls in a well and
    all of the animals help pull her out. She is not too proud to accept help.
Act out: Use a lightweight rope to pull Little Elephant out of the well. Let one
    child act the role of Little Elephant and sit flat on the floor, holding one
    end of the rope. The others are cat, dog, mouse, etc. Let several children
    play the role of each animal, or add on other animals until everyone is
    on the rope.
Read: *The Chick and the Duckling* by Mirra Ginsburg; illus. by Jose Aruego
    and Ariane Aruego. Translated from the Russian of V. Suteyev. Little chick
    needs help. Duckling gives it.

Read: *The Lion and the Rat* by Jean de la Fontaine; illus. by Brian Wildsmith. Lion thinks he is too proud ever to need the help of a rat.

Make: A "Jim Flying High" picture. With a black magic marker draw a tree trunk on a piece of paper, add branches. Older children can do this. For younger ones, you can provide paper with the trees already drawn on. Instruct the children to rub a glue stick along each branch. Then they paste on tiny paper fish. I pre-cut the fish from yellow, light blue, and chartreuse paper. Just cut these by freehand, about 1 inch long. Ask the children to decide which fish in the tree is Jim Flying Fish. Draw an eye on that fish so that Jim can cut his eye at you and say, "Shew . . . shew . . . shew."

Closing songs.

More books to share:

Galimoto by Karen Lynn Williams; illus. by Catherine Stock. Kondi is *not* too proud to ask for help. He asks everywhere he goes and ends up with materials to make a little wire push toy called a *galimoto*.

Follow-up activities for home or school:

•Act out examples of times a child might need to ask for help. For example: opening a door, opening a jar, etc.

•Demonstrate things you need to ask for help with, such as moving the piano, reaching a high shelf, etc.

•Talk about times when a child might help someone else, for example, a baby who drops a rattle or a dog that wants to be let out the door.

37. Don't Be Shy

Opening songs.

Read: *Youngest One* by Taro Yashima. Bobby slowly lets Momo make friends with him.

Read: *Shy Charles* by Rosemary Wells. Charles, who won't speak to the store lady or take dance class or play football, rescues the injured babysitter in an emergency.

Read: *Play with Me* by Marie Hall Ets. Wild animals are shy of a little girl until she sits quietly.

Act out: Choose one child to be the little girl in *Play with Me*. Give other children the parts of deer, snake, turtle, etc. and have them approach her. If the little girl moves, they must jump and run away. Let the little girl play at making the animals run away a few times, then instruct her to sit very still and let the animals come close so she can pet them. Choose someone else to be the little girl and play the game again.

Read: *The Shy Little Girl* by Phyllis Krasilovsky; illus. by Trina Schart Hyman. The actions of another very shy little girl.

Read: *Throw a Kiss, Harry* by Mary Chalmers. Harry won't throw a kiss until Mother leaves.

Hide a shy bunny: Cut out free-form bushes and trees. Give each child four bushes/trees ranging from 3 to 4 inches in height. Provide one stick-on dot with a face drawn on. This is the shy bunny. An adult must help with

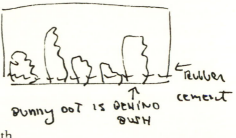

this project by pasting a 1-inch strip of rubber cement across the bottom of an 8½ by 11-inch sheet of paper. The child sticks bushes and trees onto the sticky strip, making a row across the bottom of the paper. The child then hides a bunny face behind one bush and draws on bunny ears. Try to find the hidden bunny on each child's paper. Adults can play with the children, pulling back the tops of first one bush and then another until the bunny is discovered.

Closing songs.

More books to share:

Shy Vi by Wendy Cheyett Lewison; illus. by Stephen John Smith. Attempts to treat Vi's shyness with voice and acting lessons bring dismal results.

Sophie and Lou by Petra Mathers. Shy Sophie gets up her nerve and learns to dance.

What Mary Jo Shared by Janice May Udry; illus. by Eleanor Mill. Mary Jo is too shy to show and tell until she thinks of a special thing to share.

Follow-up activities for home or school:
- •Talk about being shy and being bold.
- •Practice being both shy and bold. Act out situations in which one could respond in either way. For example, offer a cookie, ask a child to play, etc.

38. *I Want to Share with You Today*

Opening songs.

Talk about: Sharing when we have plenty. I use this program the week before
   Thanksgiving.

Read: *Harriet's Halloween Candy* by Nancy Carlson. Harriet refuses to share
   her candy.

Read: *The Good Bird* by Peter Wezel. The good bird brings a worm to share
   with friend fish. The book has no words. Sometimes I let the children
   invent a dialogue for the bird and fish. *Tweet, tweet, tweet* and *glub, glub,
   glub* work well.

Circle songs:
   I want to share with you today,
   With you today,
   With you today.
   I want to share with you today,
   And we'll be friends.

Sing of the different things you will share. "I'll share my blocks with you
   today . . . ."

Music: See the music on page 181.

Read: *On Mother's Lap* by Ann Herbert Scott; illus. by Glo Coalson. It's hard
   to share a mother. Everyone should rock "back and forth" with Michael
   and his mother as the storyteller reads "back and forth, back and forth."

Read: *The Doorbell Rang* by Pat Hutchins. Two children have twelve cookies
   to share until the doorbell rings and company comes . . . and comes . . .
   and comes.

Talk about: Ways to share food. One way to divide: Count out "one for you
   and one for me." Another way to divide: One person cuts the food item
   in half, the second person has first choice of the halves.

Activity: Arrange the group into partners. Give each pair a cup of items to
   share by counting out, "one for you and one for me." Goldfish crackers
   work well. Give each pair two plastic-wrapped pieces of processed cheese
   and a table knife. Let partner number one cut and partner number two
   choose. Then reverse roles and cut the second piece of cheese. Eat the
   crackers and cheese.

Closing songs.

More books to share:

It's Your Turn, Roger by Susanna Gretz. Sharing is especially hard for pigs.

I Do Not Like It When My Friend Comes to Visit by Ivan Sherman. Sharing with a friend is not always easy.

Wilfrid Gordon McDonald Partridge by Mem Fox; illus. by Julie Vivas. A young boy shares with an old woman in the nursing home next door.

Follow-up activities for home or school:

•Find something you would like to share with someone else (food, flowers, toys, etc.). Share this with a friend.

•Sometimes sharing means taking turns. Practice taking turns riding a tricycle, swinging, etc.

39. Small Creatures Meet Big Bullies

Opening songs.

Read: *Swimmy* by Leo Lionni. Small fish cooperate to scare off the big fish.

Read: *The Grouchy Ladybug* by Eric Carle. A small ladybug challenges bigger creatures to fight. A bad idea.

Action chant:

Walking through the jungle,

What did I see?

(walk around the circle)

A big gorilla was roaring at me!

(turn and roar at the person behind you)

Select another intimidating animal and repeat. End with a small animal, such as a singing bird.

Read: *Rosie's Walk* by Pat Hutchins. Rosie *ignores* the fox.

Read: *The Great Big Scary Dog* by Libby Gleeson; illus. by Armin Greder. Jen and friends make a dragon mask to frighten a big scary dog, but he turns out to be friendly.

Make a paper bag dragon: Provide large stick-on dots for eyes, pre-cut a serrated spine for the dragon's back, a long tongue, and teeth.

Play: Scare someone with your dragon puppet. Then assure them that he is really a nice dragon, not a bully.

Closing songs.

More books to share:

> *Loud Mouth George and the Sixth Grade Bully* by Nancy Carlson. Big kid bullies smaller children at school.
>
> *Move Over, Twerp* by Martha Alexander. A bully at school.
>
> *Nine-in-One Grrr Grrr* by Blia Xiong; illus. by Nancy Hom. Adapted by Cathy Spagnoli. Ev bird tricks Tiger.
>
> *Roger Takes Charge!* by Susanna Gretz. Flo bosses Roger around until he's had enough and takes charge.
>
> *Willy the Wimp* by Anthony Brown. A bigger, tougher gorilla bullies Willy.
>
> *Willy the Champ* by Anthony Brown. Willy deals with his bully.

Follow-up activities for home or school:

> •Talk about times you felt intimidated by someone bigger. How could you have dealt with that?

40. Gentle Giants

Opening songs.

Read: *Andy and the Lion* by James Daugherty. A boy befriends a lion and the lion returns the favor.

Read: *The Lion and the Rat* by Jean de la Fontaine; illus. by Brian Wildsmith. A lion shows kindness to a tiny rat.

Sing and act out:

> I am BIG BIG BIG BIG BIG.
> I am STRONG STRONG STRONG STRONG STRONG.
> I am a LION LION LION.
> Hear me ROAR ROAR ROAR ROAR ROAR.
> But I'm GENTLE GENTLE GENTLE,
> To my friend the little boy.

Let children suggest strong animals to act out. Who could that animal be gentle to? (Lion/mouse, boy/cat, horse/dog make good pairs.)

Music: See the music on page 174.

Read: *The Biggest Bear* by Lynd Ward. A boy raises a bear cub. It gets too big.

Read: *The Big Pets* by Lane Smith. A fantasy of small children and large, caring pets. Fine text and striking art.

Make a gentle book: Pre-print booklets for each child. The copy machine makes this easy. Use a folded 8½ by 11-inch page for your booklet. On the cover print, "MY GENTLE BOOK." Inside print, "MY NAME IS _____" and "I CAN BE GENTLE TO _____." Provide several lines to write names of people or creatures the child suggests. The children can decorate the cover. We dipped torn tissue paper scraps in liquid starch and covered the booklet's cover. The dark printing of the title will show through the tissue paper.

Closing songs.

More books to share:

The Great Big Scary Dog by Libby Gleeson; illus. by Armin Greder. Diex and her friends don a New Year dragon head to terrorize the big scary dog on their block, but he turns out to be friendly.

Salt Hands by Jane Chelsea Aragon; illus. by Ted Rand. A deer takes salt from a young girl's hands.

Follow-up activities for home or school:

•Handle something very small very gently (ie., a pet, a delicate toy, a flower). *You* are the gentle giant.

•Talk about friends or animals you know who are very big, but very gentle.

41. Youngest One

Opening songs.

Read: *Youngest One* by Taro Yashima. Shy two-year-old Bobby is teenage Momo's youngest friend.

Talk about: Older friends you have. Do you feel shy around older friends sometimes?

Read: *Happy Birthday, Sam* by Pat Hutchins. Sam is too short to reach things—until his birthday present arrives.

Sing and act out:

What can you do if you're too small?
If you're too small?
If you're too small?

What can you do if you're too small,
To wash your hands in the sink?

Let the children suggest things they are too small to do, such as reaching cookies in a cookie jar. Brainstorm appropriate behavior with the children and parents and then sing of it:

Stand on a stool if you're too small.
You're too small,
You're too small.
Stand on a stool if you're too small,
And wash your hands in the sink.

Discuss safety. Some things may be too high to reach by climbing and require the answer, "Ask someone to help if you're too small."

Music: See the music on page 170.

Read a poem: "Wait, Little Joe" by Lessie Little Jones in *Pass It On: African-American Poetry for Children* selected by Wade Hudson, illus. by Floyd Cooper, p. 10.

Read: *Meatball* by Phyllis Hoffman; illus. by Emily Arnold McCully. A younger best friend at preschool.

Talk about: Do you have a best friend who is smaller than you? How can you help them? Do you have a best friend who is taller than you? How can they help you?

Read: *Oh, Little Jack* by Inga Moore. Little Jack Rabbit is too small for some things, but just right to sit on Grandpa's knee.

Talk about: What things can you do that BIGGER people CAN'T DO?

Activity: Make a "Just the Right Size" picture. Provide a photocopied picture of a room. Provide cut-out pictures of an adult and a child. What can the child do in this room that the adult cannot do? Walk under the table? Hide in a tiny spot? Have the children paste their adult and child onto the picture and discuss why they placed them in those spots.

More books to share:

Billy and Belle by Sarah Garland. Little sister goes to school with brother on pet day and turns all the pets loose!

Hard to Be Six by Arnold Adoff; illus. by Cheryl Hanna. Even six is too young for many things.

Poor Carl by Nancy Carlson. Disadvantages and advantages of a baby brother.

Whose Mouse Are You? by Robert Kraus; illus. by Jose Aruego. Young mouse misses his family.

Follow-up activities for home or school:
- •Talk about people in your family. Who is the youngest? How do the older people help the youngest?
- •Talk about things you can't do yet.
- •Talk about things you couldn't do when you were younger that you CAN do now.

❧ Around Town ❧

42. Policeman to the Rescue

Opening songs.

Read: *Make Way for Ducklings* by Robert McCloskey. Policeman Michael helps
    Mama and her ducklings across a busy Boston street.

Act out *Make Way for Ducklings*: Half of the group are ducks, the other half
    are cars. An adult and child are police. Cars line up and rev their engines.
    Police hold them back while the ducks cross the street chanting, "Quack-
    quack-quack-quack."

Or, you could use this waddling chant:
    Mother duck says, "Quack, quack, quack,
    Follow me to the pond and back."

Read: *The Day the Goose Got Loose* by Reeve Lindbergh; illus. by Steven Kel-
    logg. Policemen bring back the lost goose and take notes on the disaster.

Read: *Shy Charles* by Rosemary Wells. When Charles calls the emergency
    number, policemen, doctors, and firemen all arrive. I told the class he
    dialed 9-1-1.

Read: *Corduroy* by Don Freeman. A night watchman carries the wandering
    teddy bear back to the toy department.

Form a circle and sing:
    If I were a policeman, a policeman, a policeman,
    If I were a policeman, this is what I'd do.
    I'd drive in a police car, police car, police car.
    I'd drive in a police car,
    That is what I'd do.

Let the children suggest things a policeman might do. If they suggest shooting
   guns, I have them turn away from the circle and do target practice.
Music: See the music on page 166.
Activity: I photocopied the picture of the night watchman shining his flash-
   light down the escalator from the book *Corduroy*. I asked the children to
   imagine what he might be checking on and suggested a variety of possibilities: a lost child, an injured person, etc. They colored the picture and
   each child explained what the policeman in his or her picture was doing.
Closing songs.
More books to share:
   Mystery on the Docks by Thacher Hurd. Mouse Ralph captures rat kidnap-
   pers on the docks, saving opera singer Edwardo Bombasto.
   Paddy's New Hat by John S. Goodall. Paddy acts out the life of a policeman.
   A Zoo for Mister Muster by Arnold Lobel. The police try to corral the zoo
   animals who have come to Mr. Muster's apartment.
Follow-up activities for home or school:
   •Invite a police officer to visit. Talk to him or her about the job of a police
   officer.
   •Look for pictures of police in newspapers or magazines and make a
   police photo gallery. Are their uniforms all the same? What different
   kinds of work do they do?

43. To the Grocery Store

Opening songs.
Read: *Tommy at the Grocery* by Bill Grossman; illus. by Victoria Chess. Silli-
   ness with language at the grocery store . . . an ear of corn is confused
   with a person's ear, etc.
Read: *Lollipop* by Wendy Watson. A trip to the store for a lollipop fails.
Read: *Don't Forget the Bacon* by Pat Hutchins. Boy forgets everything he is
   sent for, then remembers again.
Play at remembering: Set up a "storekeeper" on one side of the room. Whis-

per three items to a "shopper" and send them to the store to ask for the items. Prompt when needed. You can send a shopping list along with very small children.

Form a circle and sing:
> My mother gave me a nickel,
> To buy a pickle,
> But I didn't buy a pickle,
> I bought some chewing gum.
> La-da-da-da-da chewing gum.
> La-da-da chewing gum.
> La-da-da-da-da chewing gum.
> La-da-da chewing gum.

Repeat this ditty using in place of the nickel/pickle combination, the rhymes of dime/lime; quarter/water; and dollar/collar.

Music: See the music on page 174.

Read: *General Store* by Nancy Winslow Parker. A child pretends to run a store.

Make a display tray to sell your wares: Fold one long edge of a piece of typing paper over about two inches, to form a tray two inches deep. Staple the sides shut to hold this tray in place. This is your "store." Cut pictures of objects from old magazines and tuck them into this store tray. Help the children decide on a price for each object and label it. Pretend to buy and sell.

Closing songs.

More books to share:

> *Bear Goes Shopping: A Guessing Game Story* by Harriet Ziefert and Arnold Lobel.

> *Going Shopping* by Sarah Garland. A trip to the supermarket. Simple text about a tired mom.

> *Hare and Bear Go Shopping* by Julie E. Frankel; illus. by Ted Smith. Bear eats his way through the grocery store and has to work off his bill.

> *I'll Bet You Thought I Was Lost* by Shirley Parenteau; illus. by Lorna Tomei. A child is temporarily lost in the supermarket.

> *On Market Street* by Arnold Lobel; illus. by Anita Lobel. Imaginative drawings show shopkeepers whose bodies are created from their wares.

> *The Supermarket* by Anne F. Rockwell. Very simple text names objects encountered at the market.

Teddy Bears Go Shopping by Susanna Gretz. Teddy bears at the super-market.

Tom and Annie Go Shopping: A Can You Find? Book by Barry Smith. Tom and Annie visit a bakery, a hardware store, a candy store, a vegetable market, a toy store, a grocery, and a magazine stand. The trick is to find the items they want in the very busy pictures.

Follow-up activities for home or school:

•Take a trip to a grocery store. Bring a list of things to buy. Look for the baked goods and buy a loaf of bread. Look for the produce and buy some carrots. Look for the deli and buy some sliced cheese. Look for the dairy products and buy a carton of milk. Make yourself lunch!

•Make a shoebox store shelf. Stock small boxes of various products such as individual-size raisin boxes or cereal boxes. Add small-sized cans to your miniature grocery store display. Decide how much each item should cost and label each item with a price. Play at buying and selling your food.

44. *Bakers at Work*

Opening songs.

Read: *In the Night Kitchen* by Maurice Sendak. The bakers who bake till the dawn so we can have cake in the morn are surprised when Mickey falls into their batter.

Singing game: Let one child be the cake and stand that child in the center of your circle. All pretend to pour in milk and chant:
Milk in the batter!
Milk in the batter!
We bake cakes and nothing's the matter!

An adult turns the "cake" around as all chant:
Stir it!
Scrape it!

Make it!
Bake it!

The "cake" now stoops down into a pretend pan and all chant:
Bake . . . bake . . . bake . . . bake . . . .

The "cake" slowly rises as we chant. When the "cake" is standing upright, we all shout:

IT'S DONE!

Pretend to put candles on the "cake" and all sing a chorus of "Happy Birthday to You!"

Decorate cookies: Give each child a pre-cut cookie to decorate. Sugar cookies may be bought in refrigerated rolls and simply sliced into rounds. Provide sprinkles and small candies to decorate the cookies. Put in a preheated oven to bake and take them out after reading the next story. Let them cool down during the last story and then eat them.

Read: *The Gingerbread Boy* by Paul Galdone. Traditional folktale of the gingerbread boy who runs away.

Read: *The Doorbell Rang* by Pat Hutchins. More and more friends arrive to share a batch of cookies.

Read: *Chocolate Chip Cookies* by Karen Wagner; illus. by Leah Palmer Preiss. One-word steps to baking cookies: "Stir," "Pour," etc.

Eat your cookies!

Closing songs.

See also: Kitchen! Kitchen!, program 6; Holiday Cake Tales, program 66.

Note: Add one of the holiday books from the list below and this program becomes "Holiday Bakers."

More books to share:

Arthur's Christmas Cookies by Lillian Hoban. Arthur has trouble with the Christmas present he tries to make.

Marcel the Pastry Chef by Marianna Mayer; illus. by Gerald McDermott. Marcel the Hippopotamus is discovered secretly baking pastries at night and is made royal pastry chef.

Mr. Cookie Baker by Monica Wellington. A baker bakes and sells his cookies. Very simple text.

Ruth's Bake Shop by Kate Spohn. Ruth opens a bakery shop featuring an amazing array of pastries. Discuss the many kinds of pastries Ruth makes.

Sofie's Role by Amy Heath; illus. by Sheila Hamanaka. Sofie helps out during the Christmas rush in her parents' bakery.

Follow-up activities for home or school:

- •Visit a bakery. Ask the names of the pastries displayed. Buy one for a treat.
- •Look at pictures of pastries in an illustrated cookbook. Which would you eat if you could choose?
- •Learn the names of several different kinds of cookies. Taste them. Which do you like best?
- •Look at cookie pictures in cookbooks. Select one that looks good to eat. Follow the directions and make the cookies.

❧ A Multicultural Whirl ❧

45. Northern Winter (Inuit/Eskimo)

Opening songs.

Read: *On Mother's Lap* by Ann Herbert Scott; illus. by Glo Coalson. Michael doesn't want to make room on mother's lap for a baby sister. Let the children rock with you as you chant, "back and forth."

Read: *King Island Christmas* by Jean Rogers; illus. by Rie Munoz. Working together, islanders carry an oomiak boat over the island to the calmer lee side so the new priest can disembark for Christmas.

Tell: "A Whale of a Tale" from *Twenty Tellable Tales* by Margaret Read Mac-Donald. A little boy eats so much he explodes. Let the children say the refrain with you, "I'm *still* hungry!"

Act out: Let all of the children be the "hungry little boy." You act out the grandmother's lines and then lead them in wandering about in search of food, gobbling it down, and exclaiming, "I'm *still* hungry!" After you all "explode" at the end of the story, just drift quietly down to the floor and reassemble for the next story.

Read: *Very Last First Time* by Jan Andrews; illus. by Ian Wallace. Eva Padlyat of Ungava Bay goes under the ice at low tide to gather mussels. Gorgeous illustrations and a gripping tale. The unusual concept of the tide going out from beneath the ice may require some explanation during this tale of northern Quebec.

Fill a mussel pan: Free-cut mussels and pink anemones from tag board. Roll the board over a fat marking pen before cutting to give your mussels a slight curl. Add Easter grass for seaweed. Give each child a small aluminum pie tin to use as a mussel pan. Children paste mussels, anemones, and seaweed into their pan.

Closing songs.

More books to share:

Arctic Memories by Normee Ekoomiak. Pictures and brief text describe the Inuit life. Text given also in Inuklitut.

O Canada by Ted Harrison. A glorious illustration of the Canadian national anthem.

Tobias Has a Birthday by Ole Hertz. Trans. from the Danish by Tobi Tobias. A Greenland boy's birthday is celebrated by the whole village.

See also: Tobias Catches Trout; Tobias Goes Ice Fishing; and *Tobias Goes Seal Hunting,* all by Ole Hertz.

Follow-up activities for home or school:

• View *The Owl Who Married a Goose.* 8 min. Sand-over-lightboard animation of Eskimo tale. Owl tries to fly with his goose bride but falls.

• Make a lunch of mussels or codfish.

• See how many can rock on Mother's lap without breaking the rocking chair.

• Let the child pretend to be the mom and rock a lap full of dolls, trucks, puppies, etc.

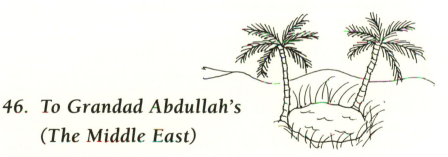

46. *To Grandad Abdullah's (The Middle East)*

Opening songs.

Read: *A Balloon for Grandad* by Nigel Gray; illus. by Jane Ray. Sam's balloon flies over the mountains, ocean, and desert to visit Grandad Abdullah.

Talk about: Grandads. How far would a balloon have to fly to visit YOUR grandad? Over mountains? Oceans? Deserts?

Talk about: Deserts. They are dry . . . hot . . . need wells to provide water.

Read: *Why the Jackal Won't Speak to the Hedgehog: A Tunisian Folktale* by Harold Berson. The jackal and the hedgehog farm together. Jackal gets the tops of the wheat crop and the bottoms of the onion crop. Brief text and delightful illustrations, but the children need to come close to see them well. Showing an onion and a stalk of tall grass before reading would help kids understand the concept of the trick.

Tell: "Biyera Well" from *Look Back and See: Twenty Lively Tales for Gentle Tellers* by Margaret Read MacDonald, pp. 90–94. Duck, Goat, and Donkey farm together. Donkey sneaks out and eats the crop at night. Each swears by the Biyera Well that he did not eat the crop. Donkey swears falsely and falls into the well.

Act out: Form a circle and take turns jumping over the "well" (a piece of blue paper on the floor). Each player tells which animal he/she is acting, then says, "Quack, Quack, if I've eaten it . . . etc." and jumps over the well. Three-year-olds just "Quack" and jump. Five-year-olds will recite the whole dialogue. Some fives will want to be Donkey and fall in.

Read: *Oasis of the Stars* by Olga Economakis; illus. by Blair Lent. Abu wants to settle in one place, but the need for water keeps his family on the move through the desert. Abu digs a well and they settle down. This story will need to be cut for three-year-olds. Five-year-olds can listen to the entire tale.

Make: An oasis picture. Give each child an 8 ½ by 11–inch piece of yellow or buff paper (the desert), an orange strip (a palm tree trunk), three pre-cut green palm leaves, and one pre-cut blue circle (the well). Each child arranges and pastes on these pieces to make an oasis scene. Give each child one red stick-on dot to stick in the sky. This is the balloon coming to see Grandad Abdullah.

Closing songs: Take time to play with the picture. Pretend your finger is the duck and say: "Quack, Quack, if I've eaten it . . . ." Then jump your finger over the well. Sing goodbye to the Oasis and goodbye to Grandad Abdullah.

More books to share:

The Day of Ahmed's Secret by Florence Parry Heide and Judith Heide Gilliland; illus. by Ted Lewin. A water boy in Cairo learns to write his name.

Kassim's Shoes by Harold Berson. Abu Kassim has trouble getting rid of his slippers.

Abu Kassim's Shoes: An Arabian Tale by Nancy Green; illus. by W. T. Mars. Same plot as in *Kassim's Shoes* above.

Nine in a Line by Ann Kirn. When counting his camels, the camel driver fails to count the one he is sitting on.

Follow-up activities for home or school:

•On a map or globe find Tunisia, Egypt, and Saudi Arabia.

•Share a Middle Eastern food treat such as dates from Grandad Abdullah's trees or goat cheese from his little goats.

47. Koala, Kangaroo, and Kookaburra (Australia)

Opening songs.

Show: Australia on a globe.

Read: *One Woolly Wombat* by Trinca, Rod, and Kerry Argent; illus. by Kerry Argent. One to fourteen fanciful Australian animals to count. For example: "Two cuddly koalas sipping gumnut tea." Children like to count the animals in the pictures. Fours and up like to repeat the bouncy rhymes after you.

Sing and act out:
 I wish I were a kangaroo,
 A kangaroo,
 A kangaroo.
 If I were a kangaroo,
 This is what I'd do.

Let the children suggest what a kangaroo might do and sing of this.
 If I were a kangaroo,
 A kangaroo,
 A kangaroo,
 If I were a kangaroo,
 I'd hop all around like this.

Suggest other Australian animals and sing of their actions too. You might sing of a koala, dingo, emu, echidna, and others.

Music: See the music on page 175.

Sing and act:
 Kookaburra sits in the old gum tree.
 Merry, merry king of the bush is he.

Laugh, Kookaburra! Laugh, Kookaburra!
Gay your life must be!

Kookaburra sits in the old gum tree.
Eating all the gumdrops he can see.
Stop, Kookaburra! Stop, Kookaburra!
Leave some there for me!

Put one or two children on a chair or bench. They are the kookaburra. They
flap their wings and laugh as the other children sing to them. In the
second verse, offer the kookaburras each a gumdrop to eat. Let two other
children be the kookaburras and earn their gumdrops too. Play until
everyone has received a gumdrop.

Tell: "Why the Koala Has No Tail" from *Look Back and See: Active Tales for
Gentle Tellers* by Margaret Read MacDonald, pp. 74–80. Koala and Tree
Kangaroo dig for water.

Color a tree kangaroo and koala picture: I photocopied a koala and tree
kangaroo from *Animal Atlas of the World* by E. L. Jordan, p. 27 and p. 31.
Any such illustrations would do. I free-cut around the illustrations, so
that each child had a cut-out of a tree kangaroo and a cut-out of a koala.
They colored them and then were ready to use them in the dramatic play
which follows.

Tell a story: Bring your colored cut-outs back to the circle. Make up a story
about Tree Kangaroo and Koala. What does Tree Kangaroo say or do?
What does Koala say or do? Ask each child to make up a story working
with the adult that accompanied him or her to storytime. Older children
might want to create a group story or share individual story ideas with
the entire group.

Closing songs.

More books to share:

The Bunyip of Berkeley's Creek by Jenny Wagner; illus. by Ron Brooks. A
lonely bunyip seeks his identity.

Possum Magic by Mem Fox; illus. by Julie Vivas. Grandma Possum works
magic and makes Little Hush invisible. They tour Australia looking for a
food to make her visible again.

Where the Forest Meets the Sea by Jeannie Baker. The book takes you into
an aboriginal Australian forest. Gather the children close to look for hidden animals in these dark pictures.

Wombat Stew by Marcia K. Vaughan; illus. by Pamela Lofts. The animals conspire to trick Dingo out of his "gooey, brewy, yummy, chewy, wombat stew."

Follow-up activities for home or school:

•Visit a zoo to see a kangaroo, a koala, and perhaps a tree kangaroo. What other animals from Australia can you find in books or at the zoo?

48. *Indian Festival (India)*

Opening songs.

Read: *The Old Woman and the Red Pumpkin: A Bengali Folk Tale* by Betsy Bang; illus. by Molly Garrett Bang. A fox, a bear, and a jackal threaten the old woman en route to her granddaughter's house, but she returns in a rolling pumpkin.

Read: *The Old Woman and the Rice Thief* by Betsy Bang; illus. by Molly Garrett Bang. When a mouse steals from the old woman's rice pot, Wood-apple, Razor, Scorpion-fish, Alligator, and Cow-pat conspire to oust the pest.

Act out: *The Old Woman and the Rice Thief.* You take the part of the old woman and pretend the children are wood-apples, razors, etc. Move the children who are wood-apples, razors, etc. to hiding places around the room. Now you take the role of the mouse and enter the room (or choose one bold child to be a mouse and accompany you). Let the children jump out and terrorize you as you approach each child's hiding place.

Read: *The Festival* by Peter Bonnici; illus. by Lisa Kopper. Arjuna celebrates a village festival by wearing his first lungi and by dancing with the grown men for the first time.

Paint a sidewalk: Paint festive designs on your sidewalk like those Arjuna's mother made. We used water-soluable tempera paints and each child worked on one square of sidewalk. We drew triangles, circles, or squares in concentric patterns using red, blue, and yellow paints. Older children caught the idea of drawing a circle within a circle within a circle. Younger ones just had fun making colored lines. The actual doorstep drawings in India are made by sprinkling colored powders.

Closing songs.

More books to share:

The First Rains by Peter Bonnici; illus. by Lisa Kopper. Arjuna waits for the rainy season to arrive.

Leela and the Watermelon by Marilyn Hirsh and Maya Narayan; illus. by Marilyn Hirsh. Leela thinks a pregnant woman has a watermelon growing in her tummy.

49. Shoes and Songs (South Africa and Zimbabwe)

Opening songs.

Read: *Not So Fast, Songololo* by Niki Daly. Songololo's grandmother takes him shopping and he gets a bright new pair of shoes!

Play: A Zimbabwean shoe-passing game. Sit in a circle on the floor and each remove one shoe. Pound this shoe on the floor in time with the song's rhythm as you sing the first part of the song, "Mmbera" (see below). During the chorus of the song you each pass a shoe to the right on each beat of the song. Sing very slowly at first until everyone catches on. Your own shoe will travel around the circle and you keep passing on the shoe which has just been passed over to you from your left. Keep the game going until everyone has his or her own shoe back. Confusion is to be expected.

Shoe-pounding verse:
    Mmbe-e-ra
    Mmbe-e-ra
    Mmbe-e-ra
    Mmbera ya stimela.

Shoe-passing chorus:
    NA na
    (*pass shoe*)
    na NA na
    (*pass shoe*)
    NA na
    (*pass shoe*)
    na NA na
    (*pass shoe*)

Music: See the music on page 176.

Read: *Jafta's Father* by Hugh Lewin; illus. by Lisa Kopper. Jafta's father comes home from the city and plays with his child.

Read: *At the Crossroads* by Rachel Isadora. South African boys wait for their fathers to come home from the mines. They greet them singing, with homemade instruments.

Make an instrument: Cover a lidded juice or nut can with construction paper and decorate. Put seeds or rocks inside to make a shaker. Or decorate a large plastic pail with magic markers. Turn it upside down and play on it with hands or sticks.

Play and sing: Make up your own tune and sing and play "Our fathers are coming home today!"

Closing songs.

More books to share:

All the Magic in the World by Wendy Hartman; illus. by Niki Daly. A South African odd-job man spins magic from the string, shells, and pop-tops in his special tin.

Come Home Soon, Baba by Janie Hampton; illus. by Jenny Bent. A Zimbabwean family make bricks for a new home and count the days until father, who is away working, can return.

Over the Green Hills by Rachel Isadora. A rural South African child travels to visit his grandmother.

Straw Sense by Rona Rupert; illus. by Mike Dooling. An older man's scarecrows bring a smile and a voice to a young boy.

Where Are You Going, Manyoni? by Catherine Stock. A Zimbabwean girl crosses the veld on her way to school.

Follow-up activities for home or school:

•Find South Africa on a map or globe. Trace with your finger the route you would take to fly there from your home. What countries or oceans would you fly over?

50. Reaching the Sky: A Tanabata Storytime (Japan)

The Japanese Tanabata celebration is held on the Seventh Day of the Seventh Moon. On this day, according to legend, the Heavenly Maid and her lover the Cowherd are allowed to meet crossing the Milky Way. The two were banished to the heavens and set on opposite sides of the Milky Way because she neglected her weaving duties after marrying a mortal cowherd. One day of the year they are allowed to meet. It always rains on this night—tears of their joy at meeting and sorrow at parting again. All magpies fly to heaven on this night to form a bridge for the lovers to cross. Children in Japan sometimes write poems to the lovers and hang them decoratively on branches on this day.

Opening songs.

Read: *The Badger and the Magic Fan* by Tony Johnston; illus. by Tomie de Paola. Badger makes the nose of the princess grow long with a magic fan, but ends up having his own nose grow to the heavens.

We stopped the story after the first page and played at fanning our noses on the right side to make them grow longer, and on the left side to make them grow smaller. We used our right hands to fan our noses, and with our left hands we showed how long or short they were growing.

Read: *Taro and the Bamboo Shoot: A Japanese Tale* by Masako Matsuno. Taro is stuck on a magically growing bamboo shoot which carries him to the sky.

Read: *The Legend of the Milky Way* by Jeanne M. Lee. A Chinese version of the legend of the Cowherd and the Heavenly Weaver Maid. The pair were turned into stars but are allowed to meet once a year on the Seventh Day of the Seventh Moon.

Read a poem: Use selected poems from *In a Spring Garden* by Richard Lewis; illus. by Ezra Jack Keats. Haiku.

Make a poem paper: Let each child choose three words to put on a poem paper. Show samples such as "Bird. Sky. Fly," or "Apple. Red. Tree." Have

adults write each child's three-word poems
on the paper. The children decorate the
poem paper. Hang them from a tree branch
and admire the poems as they flutter in the
breeze. I provided 8 ½ × 2 ½-inch strips of
brightly colored paper with a hole punched
in one end for the ribbon that ties
the paper to the tree branch. The children
walked around under the tree to see each other's poems as the parents
read them out. Older children, of course, could write more lengthy
poems.

More books to share:

Cricket Songs: Japanese Haiku by Harry Behn; illus. from Sesshu. A fine
collection of evocative haiku. Read them aloud and just let the children
think about them. Black-and-white reproductions of paintings by Sesshu.
Haiku: Vision in Poetry and Photography by Ann Atwood. Illustrated with
photographs by Atwood.

Follow-up activities for home or school:

•In Japan the poem papers are tossed into a stream on the day after
Tanabata and carried off. You might do this too.

🎋 *From Paper to Book to Library* 🎋

51. What Is Paper?

Opening songs.

Read: *The Paper Airplane* by Fulvio Testa. Flying a paper airplane.

Talk about: How is paper used in this story?

Show: Paper of all kinds.

Read: *What a Good Lunch!* by Shigeo Watanabe; illus. by Yasuo Ohtomo. How does baby bear use paper in this story?

Talk about and demonstrate with paper samples: What can you do with paper? Write on it; cut it; paste it; hold water in it (paper cup); absorb with it (paper towel); tie things up with it (paper ribbon); fold things out of it (paper airplane, oragami); wrap things in it; make noise with it (experiment with crumpling paper, flapping paper in air, slapping papers together . . . to make noises). Older children can think of even more.

Form a circle and sing:
> What can you do with a piece of paper?
> What can you do with a piece of paper?
> What can you do with a piece of paper?
> Show me what you can do.

Give each child a sheet of typing paper. Hold the paper high in the air and drop it. Sing "Let it float to the ground. Let it float to the ground. Let it float to the ground. That's what you can do." Other possibilities: "Fold it into a paper airplane." "Wad it up and throw it in the air." "Tear it up into little pieces." "Throw it into the wastepaper basket."

Music: See the music on page 170.

Read: *Paper, Paper, Everywhere* by Gail Gibbons. How paper is used.

84

Make a Valentine picture or other holiday card: Have available snippets of all
sorts of paper, cellophane, crepe paper, curling ribbon, paper doilies, and
a few pre-cut heart shapes. Pass out paper for cards, scissors, and paste.
Let children decorate their own cards.

Closing songs.

More books to share:

Curious George Rides a Bike by H. A. Rey. George has a newspaper route.

Paper John by David Small. Fantasy of a paper village.

For more background on paper see:

"Paper" Through the Ages by Shaaron Cosner; illus. by Priscilla Kiedrowski. A history of paper and earlier materials to write on. An I-Can-Read
format.

Writing It Down by Vicki Cobb; illus. by Marilyn Hafner. History of paper
and writing implements.

Follow-up activities for home or school:

•Use paper to fold paper airplanes. Fold airplanes from tissue paper, construction paper, wax paper, etc. Which fly best?

•Fold paper fans. Use them to move the air around.

•Fold paper cones and fill them with popcorn for a snack.

52. *What Is a Book?*

Opening songs.

Talk about: How a book is made and the materials from which it is made.
Show a board book, a plastic book, and a cloth book made for babies.

Read: *I Like Books* by Anthony Brown. A monkey child reads comics, song
books, fat books, thin books.

Read a board book: *My Clothes* by Sue Porter. In this wordless book a baby
gets dressed. Let the children tell you what is happening. *Any* board book
may be used here.

Read a book with unusual split pages: *Kangaroo* by Sylvie Selig. This has half-
size pages between every two regular-size pages. Let the children recount
the story as you turn the pages. Little kangaroo is stolen by a large bird,
rescued, and returned home by a little girl and her family. A different
book with split pages could be substituted here.

Show other kinds of books: A huge atlas; a miniature doll house book with print so tiny you must use a magnifying glass; a scroll . . . I used a copy of the Bayeux Tapestry in a fold-out book which we expanded and held up with help from parents until it encircled the children, who walked around inside and "read" the pictures.

Read a book poem: "What If . . . " by Isabel Joshlin Glaser in *Good Books, Good Times!* by Lee Bennett Hopkins; illus. by Harvey Stevenson, p. 21.

Read a singing book: *Old MacDonald Had a Farm;* illus. by Pam Adams. Let everyone sing with you. Assign parts and repeat the entire song. Have each animal stand and make its sound at the appropriate time.

Read a pop-up book: *Peekaboo!* by Matthew Price and Jean Claveria. This pop-up book has very effective movement, and it's about a *reading* family!

Play peekaboo: After playing the game a few times, you keep *your* eyes covered and let the *children* initiate the peekaboo.

Read another pop-up book: *Dinner Time* by Jan Pienkowski; text by Anne Carter; paper engineering by Marcin Stajewski and James Roger Diaz. Shark eats Crocodile, who eats Gorilla, etc. Talk about paper engineering and show how the various effects are achieved.

Make a book: Provide a stack of old book jackets or magazines. Ask one child to select an illustration, cut it out, and paste it on a sheet of paper. Ask the children to suggest a story about this picture and write their story by the picture. Let them select another illustration and paste this on a second sheet of paper, adding the group's created story for this picture. Staple the two stories together. Read this book that the group has created. Send everyone to the craft tables to make their own books. Adults help write out the stories for the children.

Closing songs: Sing goodbye to the books. Since this craft takes a long time for some children, we just sing goodbye as we work rather than returning to our story circle for a formal goodbye as we usually do.

More books to share:

Dora's Book by Michelle Edwards. Dora writes. Tom types and prints. Dora folds and collates. Together they build the books.

Petunia by Roger Duvoisin. Petunia the goose wants to read her book but hasn't learned to read yet. Video also available.

Too Many Books! by Caroline Feller Bauer; illus. by Diane Paterson. Can you have too many books?

Follow-up activities for home or school:

•Make a library shelf in your room to hold your books.

•Bring your favorite book to share with someone. Tell why you like that book.

53. What Is a Library?

Opening songs.

Read: *Quiet: There's a Canary in the Library* by Don Freeman. Cory imagines a library full of reading zoo animals.

Read: *Story Hour—Starring Megan* by Julie Brillhart. Megan's mom is the librarian, and when baby brother cries during storytime Megan saves the day by reading to the children. These are small illustrations so gather your audience close for this one.

Sing and play:
    Let's go to the library,
    The library,
    The library.
    Let's go to the library,
    And see what we can do.

Let the children suggest activities they can do at the library and sing of these.
    Look at books at the library,
    The library,
    The library.
    Look at books at the library.
    That's what we can do.

Our choices were: "Listen to stories," "drop books in the bookdrop," "color with crayons." You may choose also to sing about how you get to the library, with accompanying actions. "Drive your car to the library," "take a walk to the library," "push baby's stroller to the library." We sang first about how we got to the library, then sang of the things we did there.

Music: See the music on page 166.

Read a poem: "Read to Me!" in *The Three Bears Rhyme Book* by Jane Yolen; illus. by Jane Dyer.

Read: *Andy and the Lion* by James Daugherty. Andy checks a book about lions out of the library and strange adventures follow.

Make a library diorama: Pre-cut strips of stiff paper, 4 × 12 inches. Fold the ends of this paper in toward the center 3 inches from either side. This is your diorama and should stand alone when you sit it on a table top. In the center panel of this diorama,  trace around a 3½ × 5-inch card in the center panel to form a "bulletin board." Draw horizontal lines on the side panels of your diorama to represent bookshelves. Cut tiny rectangles of brightly colored paper and fold each in the center to make "book jackets." Paste these on the bulletin board. Draw the spines of books onto the bookshelves. Stand the library diorama up on a table top and admire it.

Closing songs.

More books to share:

Check It Out: The Book About Libraries by Gail Gibbons. All about libraries in simple drawings and brief text.

Clara and the Bookwagon by Nancy Smiler Levinson; illus. by Carolyn Croll. A turn-of-the-century farm girl yearns for books. An I-Can-Read format.

How My Library Grew, by Dinah by Martha G. Alexander. A new library is built.

Mike's House by Julia L. Sauer; illus. by Don Freeman. Robert calls the library "Mike's House" because of *Mike Mulligan and His Steam Shovel*, but the policeman who rescues him when he gets lost has trouble finding "Mike's House."

Something Queer at the Library by Elizabeth Levy; illus. by Mordicai Gerstein. Gwen and Gill catch the culprit who has been cutting pictures from the library's dog books . . . at the dog show.

❧ Spring ❧

54. Cra-a-ack!

Opening songs.

Talk about: Dyeing eggs at Easter and hunting for them.

Read: *The Golden Egg Book* by Margaret Wise Brown; illus. by Leonard Weisgard. A duck in "a small dark world" hatches to meet a bunny in a "big
bright world."

Talk about: How it might feel to be inside an egg—cramped, dark, damp,
etc. When you hatched, would things seem bright? Confusing?

Read: *Where's My Mommy?* by Colin Hawkins & Jacqui Hawkins. A baby
duck hatches and approaches a dog, a cat, and other animals, looking for
its mother. You might also want to read the Spanish version of this book,
Donde Esta Mi Mamá? You can read the line first in Spanish and then
repeat it in English. I encouraged the children to repeat the duckling's,
"Hola Mamá!" each time.

Read: *The Chick and the Duckling* by Mirra Ginsburg, translated from the Russian of V. Suteyev; illus. by Jose Aruego & Ariane Aruego. A baby duckling and a chick hatch. The chick copies the duckling's moves until the
duck goes for a swim.

Read: *Good Morning, Chick* by Mirra Ginsburg, adapted from a story by Korney Chukovsky; illus. by Byron Barton. Another newborn chick tries to
get the hang of things. Let the children help peck, cluck, crow, as you
tell the story.

Sing a chicken song:
> I wish I were a chicken, a chicken, a chicken.
> If I were a chicken,
> I'd walk through the barnyard like this.

Form a circle and sing this song, walk around clucking and showing off your feathers at the end. Let the children suggest other things a chicken will do and sing of them. Peck at grain; ruffle your feathers; drink your water; etc. End with "I'd lay an egg like this!" Talk about how long you must sit on your egg and sing "I'd sit on my egg like this." Lastly, pretend to BE the egg and hatch! "I'd hatch from my egg like THIS!" Curl up on the ground as an egg and then all leap up on the last word.

Music: See the music on page 166.

Read: *Horton Hatches the Egg* by Dr. Seuss. Horton the elephant takes over the egg-sitting task of Mayzie bird. This book is too long for toddlers, but works well with four-year-olds and five-year-olds.

Color: Draw with crayons on hard-boiled eggs. Then dip them in egg coloring. Let them dry in egg cartons as you sing closing songs.

Closing songs.

More books to share:
> *The Egg Book* by Jack Kent. Hatching egg silliness.
> *The Happy Egg* by Ruth Krauss; illus. by Crockett Johnson. A chick hatches.

Follow-up activities for home or school:
> •Peel a hard-boiled egg. Examine its insides, then eat it.
> •Color eggs at home and have fun hiding and hunting them.
> •Visit a children's zoo or a real farm to see eggs in an incubator or hens in a hen house.
> •For more chick ideas, see "Feathered Babies" in *Booksharing: 101 Programs to Share with Preschoolers* by Margaret Read MacDonald, pp. 71–78.

55. *Trick an April Fool*

Opening songs.

Talk about: Playing tricks on April Fool's Day (April 1).

Read: *Whistle for Willie* by Ezra Jack Keats. Peter hides under a carton and tricks his dog Willie.

Read: *George and Martha One Fine Day* by James Marshall. George tries to scare Martha, but she turns the tables on him.

Have a tricking parade: The leader holds up a flag. Parade in a circle to any marching music. When the leader lowers the flag, everyone must stop. If the leader turns around and parades in the other direction, everyone must follow. Give each child a chance to be leader for a time. The object is for the leader to try to trick the others into a wrong move.

Read: *Which Horse Is William?* by Karla Kuskin. William tries to trick his mother by turning into various animals, but she spots him every time.

Read: *Swimmy* by Leo Lionni. Swimmy teaches the little red fish to swim in formation as one GREAT fish to trick the big fish.

Make a hiding picture: Pre-cut seaweed shapes from paper doilies. (See the forms Lionni used for his seaweed in *Swimmy*). Smear a strip of wet rubber cement across the bottom of each child's paper. The children lay the seaweed forms onto their paper, gluing them fast to the rubber cement strip. Thus they are attached only at the bottom. Give each child three small pre-cut fish shapes to hide behind the seaweed. They may want to draw eyes on their fish. Let the children try to trick their parents and friends with these hidden fish. The parent or friend tries to guess where the fish are hiding.

Closing songs.

More books to share:

Arthur's April Fool's Day by Marc Brown. Arthur worries over the magic tricks he will perform for the school assembly.

The April Rabbits by David Cleveland; illus. by Nurit Karlin. On the first day of April, Robert meets one rabbit. On the second day, he meets two rabbits, etc. The rabbits play tricks on Robert.

Tom by Tomie de Paola. Tommy uses chicken feet from Grandpa's grocery store to scare the girls at school.

Tulips by Jay O'Callahan; illus. by Debrah Santini. A young boy plays innumerable tricks on his Parisian grandmama and her staff.

Follow-up activities for home or school:

•Plan a simple April Fool's Day trick to play on an adult with a sense of humor.

•Read stories about tricksters from folk literature such as *Raven: A Trickster Tale from the Pacific Northwest* by Gerald McDermott and *Zomo the Rabbit* by Gerald McDermott.

56. *Groundhog Day*

Opening songs.

Talk about: Groundhog Day and talk about hibernating animals.

Read: *Chipmunk Song* by Joanne Ryder; illus. by Lynne Cherry. A chipmunk
emerges from its winter nest, plays, stores nuts, curls up to sleep again.
A small boy imitates the animal's movements.

Sing and act out:

Groundhog's sleeping underneath the ground.
February second he wakes and looks around.
Climbs up from his hole so sleepily.
That's my SHADOW! It's back to bed for ME!

(or) No more SHADOW! It's SPRINGTIME now for me!

Children squat on the floor "underneath the ground" as they sing the first
lines. Poke their head up on the second line, and stand up on the third
line. On the fourth line, they either return to the floor ("back to bed") or
leap up in joy ("Springtime now").

Music: See the music on page 176.

Read: *A Garden for a Groundhog* by Lorna Balian. Farmer O'Leary and wife
wait out the long winter, watch Groundhog emerge from his hole and
return, plant a garden—only to have Groundhog appropriate the whole
garden.

View: *Mole and the Green Star.* 8 min. Video or 16 mm film. Mole cleans his
hole and emerges for springtime, finds a green star, and tries to put it
back in the sky.

Make a groundhog hole: Poke a hole in the bottom of a styrofoam cup. Tape
a groundhog picture to one end of a straw and insert the other end of
the straw through the hole inside the cup. Push the straw up and down
to make the groundhog go in and out of his "hole." Color the cup and
groundhog picture before assembling. For a groundhog picture, I used a

photocopy from *Come Visit a Prairie Dog Town* by
Eugenia Alston; illus. by St. Tamar, p. 8. I reduced it
once to a smaller size. A drawing of an actual
groundhog would be better if you can find one.

Closing songs: Sing "Groundhog's Song" again, acting it
out with your paper-cup groundhog. Play with your
groundhog cups by poking the groundhog up, letting him ask "Is it spring yet?" and answering, "No."
Have him jump back into his hole, calling "Back to
bed!"

More books to share:

Has Winter Come? by Wendy Watson. Groundhog
children prepare for winter.

Wake Up, Groundhog by Carol Cohen. Groundhog re-
fuses to wake up though his friends bring watches, clocks, and town hall
bells. Spring finally does the trick.

Follow-up activities for home or school:

•Walk through a field or forest looking for entrances to underground
homes, large or small. Speculate about what animal or insect might live
in these.

•Check out books about hibernating animals. Look at pictures of their
dens and talk about their lives.

57. *Ducklings Dawdle*

Opening songs.

Read: *Make Way for Ducklings* by Robert McCloskey. Mrs. Mallard searches
for the right spot to raise her ducklings. Policeman Mike holds up traffic
to help them waddle through town.

Act out *Make Way for Ducklings*: Assign adults or more mature children to be
police and stop the traffic. Some of the children take the part of cars,
others are the ducks. Mark streets on the floor with masking tape. Lead
the ducks through intersections while police hold up the cars. Circle
around and repeat. You may want a leader for the cars as well. Let them
honk and swerve at will.

Read: *Good Morning, Chick* by Mirra Ginsburg; adapted from a story by Kar-
ney Chukovsky; illus. by Byron Barton. "A chick . . . small and yellow

and fluffy . . . like this" has adventures. Every line ends in, "like this."
Listeners will repeat it with you.

Read: *Three Ducks Went Wandering* by Ron Roy; illus. by Paul Galdone. Three
ducklings busily escape one disaster after another.

View: *The Ugly Duckling*. 15 min. Video or 16 mm film. Weston Woods version based on the Hans Christian Andersen classic. Or view Disney classic film, *The Ugly Duckling*. 8 min.

Make a chick-mobile: Cut bird shapes in three sizes: 1
inch long, 2 inches long, and 3 inches long. Let the
children decorate the birds and paste on a curl of
ribbon as tail feathers. Help them tape the birds to
a length of yarn, with the smallest bird on top.
Hang it up as a mobile.

More books to share:

Across the Stream by Mirra Ginsburg; illus. by
Nancy Tafuri. Simple tale, simple illustrations of
real animals.

Angus and the Ducks by Marjorie Flack. Ducks
frighten a wee Scottish terrier.

A Duckling Is Born by Hans Heinrich Isenbart; trans. by Catherine Edwards Sadler; photos by Othmar Baumli. Photos document a duckling's
birth.

Have You Seen My Duckling? by Nancy Tafuri. A mother duck searches for
a missing duckling.

Little Chick's Story by Mary DeBall Kwitz; illus. by Cyndy Szekeres.
Mother Hen lays five eggs, but keeps one for herself . . . Little Chick!

Follow-up activities for home or school:

•Visit a pond to watch ducks swim, feed, fly. Or visit a farm to watch
baby chicks.

58. Beatrix Potter Day

Opening songs.

Read: *The Tale of Peter Rabbit* by Beatrix Potter. Peter is caught in Mr. Mac-
Gregor's garden.

Read: *The Tale of Benjamin Bunny* by Beatrix Potter. Peter's cousin Benjamin
gets into trouble.

Form a circle and sing:
> Peter Rabbit, Hop! Hop! Hop!
> Wiggles his nose when he stops, stops, stops!
> Peter Rabbit, Hop! Hop! Hop!
> Wiggles his ears with a flip, flip, flop!
> Peter Rabbit, Hop! Hop! Hop!
> Wiggles his tail with a bip, bip, bop!
> Peter Rabbit, Hop! Hop! Hop!
> Nibbling carrots all the way!

Move around in a circle with three big hops on the words "Hop! Hop! Hop!" Stand still during the other lines, making nose-wiggling motions, flopping your hands like ears, and wiggling your tail.

Note: If this program is used at Easter, the last line should be "Bringing us baskets for Easter Day!"

Music: See the music on page 177.

Sing and dance:
> Pretty Peter Pink Ears!
> Pretty Peter Pink Ears!
> Pretty Peter Pink Ears!
> Pretty Peter Pink Ears!

> Run, run, run, run, hop, hop!
> Run, run, run, run, hop, hop!
> Run, run, run, run, hop, hop!
> Run, run, run, run, JUMP, JUMP!

Children stand still and flop their ears on the first lines. They run in a circle on the "run, run, run, run" line and add two hops on the "hop, hop!" The song ends with two big jumps on "JUMP, JUMP!"

Music: Song by Martha Nishitani. See the music on page 178.

Read: *The Tale of Mr. Jeremy Fisher* by Beatrix Potter. Frog Jeremy Fisher catches a fish so large it pulls him right off his lily pad.

View: A selection from the movie *Tales of Beatrix Potter.* 86 min. This is available as video or 16 mm film. Cue up the scene in which Jeremy Fisher dances. Show the film clip. Rewind the video to the beginning of this scene. Run it again and this time everyone dance *with* Jeremy Fisher. Just watch the screen and do everything Jeremy Fisher does. This takes a lot of energy but is great fun! You will have to demonstrate the dancing to lead the children, of course.

Have a rabbit food judging contest: Arrange a plate for each child with one lettuce leaf, one sprig of parsley, and one carrot with greenery still attached. Taste each in turn. Taste lettuce first, then parsley, then carrot. Vote on the favorite rabbit food. Eat your rabbit lunch. Be sure to give the children carrots with their leafy tops still attached. The children find eating these delightful as the ends swish around while they nibble.

Closing songs.

More books to share:

The Story of a Fierce Bad Rabbit by Beatrix Potter. Another naughty rabbit. *The Tale of Mrs. Tiggy-Winkle* by Beatrix Potter. About the hedgehog washerwoman of Peter's neighborhood.

The Tale of the Flopsy Bunnies by Beatrix Potter. Peter's sisters.

Follow-up activities for home or school:

•Read several of Beatrix Potter's books. Be sure to use them in the tiny editions in which they were first printed. They are perfect for little hands to hold.

•View the entire film *Tales of Beatrix Potter*. This film shows the Royal London Ballet in performance, dancing a selection of Beatrix Potter's stories. The costuming is convincing and the dancing extravagant. Share the Beatrix Potter books with your children before viewing the movie, so they know the storylines. The movie includes: *A Tale of Two Bad Mice, The Tale of Mr. Jeremy Fisher, The Tale of Pigling Bland, The Tale of Squirrel Nutkin,* and *The Tale of Jemima Puddleduck.* Peter, Mrs. Tiggywinkle, and other characters move in and out during the ballet, stringing the stories together.

❧ Fall ❧

59. The Enormous Vegetable Harvest

Opening songs.

Read: *The Little Mouse, the Red Ripe Strawberry, and the Big Hungry Bear* by Don and Audrey Wood. One strawberry is a meal for a mouse.

Read: *The Carrot Seed* by Ruth Krauss; illus. by Crockett Johnson. It takes a lot of work to grow a carrot.

Read: *The Great Big Enormous Turnip* by Alexei Tolstoy; illus. by Helen Oxenbury. This turnip is too big to pull, so grandma, grandpa, boy, and cat all help.

Act out: *The Great Big Enormous Turnip.*

Read: *The Pea Patch Jig* by Thacher Hurd. A mouse family in their vegetable garden home.

Read: *Mousekin's Golden House* by Edna Miller. A pumpkin makes a fine house for a mouse.

Make a mousekin's golden house: Cut pumpkin shapes out of orange paper. Cut holes in these for the eyes, nose, and mouth of a jack-o-lantern. The children paste the pumpkins on sheets of white paper. Provide stick-on dots that have been cut in half to represent little mice. The children stick these in and around the pumpkin (in its eye and mouth holes, on top of its head, etc.). They can draw an eye, whiskers, and tail on each mouse.

Closing songs.

More books to share:

The Giant Vegetable Garden by Nadine Bernard Westcott. A villager attempts to win a prize at the county fair. He grows enormous vegetables.

Growing Vegetable Soup by Lois Ehlert. Big bright vegetables are named.

The Rosy Fat Magenta Radish by Janet Wolf. Nora plants her first radish with the help of Jim the gardener.

Follow-up activities for home or school:
- •Visit the grocery store or a vegetable market. Name all of the vegetables you see. Buy several of them and make a salad.
- •Arrange a vegetable display on a table. Name all of the vegetables. Feel their textures and smell them. Later, wash them and snack on them.
- •Start your own vegetable garden. Go to the grocery store or a nursery and select seeds to begin your own miniature garden. Make sure the crops get enough light and water each day. Watch them grow and enjoy eating the harvest!

60. A Fruitful Harvest

Opening songs.

Talk about food: Discuss the concept of having an abundance of food. Have a basket of fruit ready to hand out when class ends.

Read: *Apple Pigs* by Ruth Orbach. Plenty of apples to share with "man and bird and woolley beast."

Read: *Mama's Secret* by Maria Polushkin; illus. by Felicia Bond. A blueberry harvest of plenty.

Read: *Oranges* by Zach Rogow; illus. by Mary Szilagyi. Traces an orange from seed to tree to fruit to picker to packer to store.

Sing and act out:
> Reach up high and pick an apple,
> Reach up high and pick an apple,
> Reach up high and pick an apple.
> Put it in my basket.

> Take my basket home to share it,
> Take my basket home to share it,
> Take my basket home to share it.
> Take it home and share it.

Music: See the music on page 170.

Read: *Country Bear's Good Neighbor* by Larry Dane Brimner; illus. by Ruth Tietjen Councel. Little girl shares her apples and supper with country bear.

Read: *Eat Up, Gemma* by Sarah Hayes; illus. by Jan Ormerod. Gemma tries to eat a hatful of fruit!

Activity: Set a white piece of paper and crayons (red, yellow, orange, purple, and green) at each child's place. Arrange a bowl of fruit at each table for children to use as an inspiration for their drawings. Ask the children to do as you do, then pick up the green crayon. Starting at the bottom of the page, draw across the sheet back and forth and back and forth to make the plate. Look at the fruit. Ask the children, "What color is the apple?." When the response comes, pick up the red crayon and draw in a circular motion saying, "around and around and around . . . ." Repeat with a yellow banana, "up and down," or purple grapes, "teeny weeny around and around," and an orange "around and around" again. Watch the children to make sure they are following you on these strokes as they create their own fruit pictures.

Closing songs.

More books to share:

Frannie's Fruits by Leslie Kimmelman; illus. by Petra Mathers. A young girl helps run the family fruit stand on Highway 57.

Jamberry by Bruce Degen. Bouncing berry rhyme.

Mr. Rabbit and the Lovely Present by Charlotte Zolotow; illus. by Maurice Sendak. A little girl selects fruits for her mother's present.

The Seasons of Arnold's Apple Tree by Gail Gibbons. A year in the life of a tree.

Follow-up activities for home or school:

•Arrange a display of fruits. Handle them, feel their textures, smell them. Compare their colors. Cut one into pieces and share it for a snack.

•Visit the supermarket or a fruit stand. Name the many fruits there. Select several to buy. Make a fruit salad.

61. Scarecrows

Opening songs.

Talk about scarecrows: Show photos from *The Scarecrow Book* by James Giblin and Dale Ferguson.

Read: *Ma nDa la* by Arnold Adoff. A family harvests corn.

Talk about: Why do we need scarecrows?

Chant: Pretend you are a scarecrow with a blackbird on each shoulder and do the following fingerplay.

> Two little blackbirds sitting on a hill.
> (*one finger extended, perched on each shoulder*)
> One named Jack and the other named Jill.
> (*wiggle right finger, then wiggle left finger*)
> Fly away Jack.
> (*hide right finger behind back*)
> Fly away Jill.
> (*hide left finger behind back*)
> Come back Jack.
> (*bring right finger back to shoulder*)
> Come back Jill.
> (*bring left finger back to shoulder*)

Read: *The Wedding Procession of the Rag Doll and the Broom Handle and Who Was in It* by Carl Sandburg; illus. by Harriet Pincus. A straw broom marries a rag doll.

Action song: "The Scarecrow Song"
> Granny is putting her scarecrow out,
> Her scarecrow out,
> Her scarecrow out.

Granny is putting her scarecrow out,
To scare away the crows.

The crows are pecking the corn all up,
The corn all up,
The corn all up.
The crows are pecking the corn all up.
Peck, peck, peck!

The scarecrow is waving its floppy arms,
Its floppy arms,
Its floppy arms.
The scarecrow is waving its floppy arms,
Flop, flop, flop!

Think of other actions for the scarecrow and crows and sing of them.
Music: See the music on page 178.
Read: *My Mother Is the Most Beautiful Woman in the World* by Becky Reyher;
    illus. by Ruth Gannett. A wheat harvest.
Make a scarecrow of raffia:

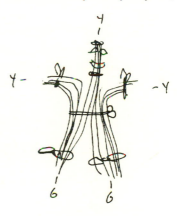

    You will need twelve strands of
raffia. Tie them in the middle with
string or more raffia to form the
scarecrow's waist. Divide the lower
strands, six to each leg. Tie the
ankles. Fold four of the upper
strands out for each arm and tie
the wrists. Leave four strands
sticking straight up for the head.
Tie it at neck and top of head.
Paste on eyes and mouth of colored
paper or felt.

Use your scarecrow as a puppet and chant:
    I am the scarecrow.
    Watch me scare crows.
    Shhh, Shhh, Shhh, Shhh!
    Go away crows!

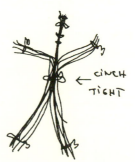

Closing songs.
More books to share:

Barn Dance! by Bill Martin, Jr.; illus. by Ted Rand. Scarecrow fiddles, and the animals dance.

Joji and the Amanojaku by Betty Jean Lifton; illus. by Eiichi Mitsui. A Japanese scarecrow frightens goblins. See also: Joji and the Dragon by Betty Jean Lifton; illus. by Eiichi Mitsui.

The Scarebird by Sid Fleischman; illus. by Peter Sis. A farmer learns friendship from a young man who helps him and his scarecrow.

Pebbles, a Pack Rat by Edna Miller. Pebbles hides in a scarecrow and ends up scaring the children.

Straw Sense by Rona Rupert; illus. by Mike Dooling. South African setting. An older man's scarecrows bring a smile and voice to a young boy who has lost his ability to speak.

The Strawman Who Smiled by Mistake by Paul Tripp; illus. by Wendy Watson. A grouchy farmer learns to smile from his scarecrow.

Witch Hazel by Alice Schertle; illus. by Margot Tomes. A lady scarecrow comes alive in a boy's dreams.

Follow-up activities for home or school:

•Take a drive in the fall and look for scarecrows.

•Make your own scarecrow. Stuff old clothing with newspaper. Add straw at arms, feet, and neck. Stuff an old pillow case for a head and add a hat.

62. Across the Bright Blue Sea: A Columbus Day Sail

Opening songs.

Read: In 1492 by Jean Marzollo; illus. by Steve Bjorkman. The journey of Columbus in simple couplets. Good for even very young listeners.

Talk about: Sailing a long way over the sea.

Read: Little Fox Goes to the End of the World by Ann Tompert; illus. by John Wallner. Little Fox's pretend trip to the forest where bears, tigers, monkeys, and crocodiles frighten, ends with a sail to the end of the world.

Act out Little Fox Goes to the End of the World: Let some children hide under tables and pretend to be bears, tigers, and crocodiles. Others perch on top of tables as monkeys or one-eyed cats. The leader and one or two children who want to play the role of Little Fox walk around the room as you "sail" from one group to another. Each group should roar to terrify you, but you send them back into their lairs with your honey, drum, etc. Sail home safely in the end.

Read: *Whiffle Squeek* by Caron Lee Cohen; illus. by Ted Rand. Whiffle Squeek sails away to encounter the monster Gazook Gaboot. Sing this to the tune of "Aiken Drum," or make up your own tune.

Music: See the music on page 179.

Let the children say "Whiffle Squeek" with you at the end of each line and "Gazook Gaboot." Let them slurp as Gazook eats things up.

Read: *Baby's Boat* by Jeanne Titherington. A baby sails away in a lullaby. You may want to invent a song and sing the text. It seems to call for a lullaby treatment.

Make a paper sail: Pass out small triangles cut from light-weight typing paper. Fold one corner over to form a base for your boat. The tallest point of your triangle becomes the sail. Decorate these with crayons or markers. Stand them up on your table top, lean down so you can direct your wind into their sails, and blow. Make two and have a sailboat race with them.

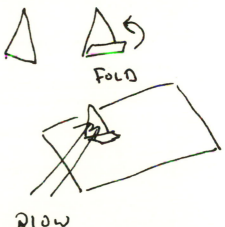

More books to share:

All Pigs on Deck: Christopher Columbus's Second Marvelous Voyage by Laura Fischetto; illus. by Letizia Galli. A humorous tale of the pigs Columbus brought along.

Follow the Dream: The Story of Christopher Columbus by Peter Sis. Detailed illustrations for older viewers. Brief text.

I Saw a Ship A-Sailing by Janina Domanska. Mice sailors.

❧ Winter Celebrations ❧

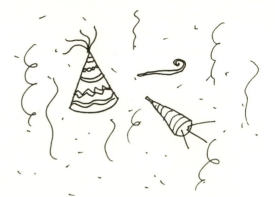

63. Parties!

Opening songs.

Read: *The Birthday* by Hans Fischer. The animals plan a wondrous party for old Lisette, the old woman whose home they share.

Read: *The Cat on the Dovrefell* by Tomie de Paola. Trolls invade on Christmas Eve, but use this story at any time of year.

Act out: *The Cat on the Dovrefell.*

Read: *May I Bring a Friend?* by Beatrice Schenk De Regniers. The king and queen give a party every day!

Read: *Bear Party* by William Pène Du Bois. The bears dress up and throw a party.

Make a party hat: Provide head circlets of brightly colored construction paper approximately 2 ½ inches wide. Kids paste on snippets of gold or silver paper.

Closing: Admire your party hats.

Closing songs.

For a Christmas theme, add some of these titles:

Merry Christmas Ernest and Celestine by Gabrielle Vincent. Celestine convinces Ernest to throw a party.

The Christmas Party by Adrienne Adams. Bunny and his friends plan a huge Christmas party.

More books to share:

Carl's Masquerade by Alexandra Day. Dog Carl takes baby to a masquerade party.

Little Bear's Pancake Party by Janice; illus. by Mariana. Little Bear throws a party.

The Surprise Party by Pat Hutchins. The animals learn it is hard to keep a surprise party secret.

Follow-up activities for home or school:

•Plan a party for wild teddy bears and bring your own bears. Make hats for the bears, provide music and dance with them. Tell them a story, feed them a treat . . . then share it yourself.

64. Winter Birds

Opening songs.

Read: *Hamilton Duck* by Arthur Getz. Hamilton discovers a frozen pond. Winter has come.

Read: *Petunia's Christmas* by Roger Duvoisin. Petunia rescues the gander Charles from becoming Christmas dinner, and weds him, too!

Read: *A Year of Birds* by Ashley Wolff. Birds that visit each month are named.

Action song:

Bluebird, Bluebird, fly through my window,
Bluebird, Bluebird, fly through my window,
Bluebird, Bluebird, fly through my window,
Early in the morning.

Make a circle holding hands. Let one child fly in and out the windows made by your raised arms. Or form a small line of children all holding hands and lead them back and forth through the windows. This second approach works only if you have plenty of adults to make the windows you fly through.

Music: See music on page 168.

Read: *Din Dan Don, It's Christmas* by Janina Domanska. The birds come in procession to see the infant Jesus. Let the children sing with you on the "Din Dan Don, It's Christmas" refrain.

Make a wee bird decoration: Free-cut little wrens from gold or silver paper. Fold a 3 × 4-inch square in half and cut, using fold as the bird's back. Cut a slit as shown:

Now cut a wing from a 1 × 3-inch strip of paper. Insert the wing through

the slot in the wren's back. Add stick-on dots for eyes. Bird can perch on a branch, or can be hung by a thread.

Closing songs.

To eliminate the Christmas emphasis, substitute any of these titles for *Petunia's Christmas* and *Din Dan Don, It's Christmas*:

Tico and the Golden Wings by Leo Lionni. Golden wings make Tico special.

Florina and the Wild Birds by Selina Chönz. Florina feeds the birds of her Austrian mountains in winter.

Winterbird by Alfred Olschewski. Birds join forces to excite a cat and a dog.

Follow-up activities for home or school:

•Make a bird feeder and hang it on a bush near your home.

•Take a winter walk to look for birds.

•Start a list of the birds you see each month.

65. Holiday Stars

Opening songs.

Read: *The Tomten and the Fox* by Astrid Lindgren; illus. by Harald Wiberg. On a starry winter night the little Swedish elf, the Tomten, guards the farm.

Read: *Good Night* by Elizabeth Coatsworth; illus. by Jose Aruego. A little star watches through the window as a child goes to bed.

Film/Video: *Mole and the Green Star*. 8 min. Mole tries to return a fallen star to the sky.

Action song:

Catch a star,
Falling from the sky.
Reach it back,
Way up high!

Reach up to catch the star, hold it for a moment, then stretch to put it back.

Music: See the music on page 180.

Read: *Dikou and the Baby Star* by Elzbieta. Trans. of *Dikou et le Bébé Etoile*. Little Dikou tries to care for a fallen baby star.

Make a silver splinter star: Pre-cut lots of long triangular slivers of silver paper to serve as points for your star. I cut mine about 3 inches long and ½-inch wide at the base, tapering out to a point. Tell children to place one drop of glue at the base of each piece. Then stick all the pieces together with their points sticking out. There is no *wrong* way to do this. They need not be symmetrical to be attractive. Attach a piece of ribbon with tape in order to hang the ornament!

Closing songs.

To emphasize a Christmas theme, add some of these titles:

The Story of the Three Wise Kings by Tomie de Paola. The Three Kings follow the star.

The Silver Christmas Tree by Pat Hutchins. Squirrel's Christmas tree star vanishes in the daylight. His friends are all hiding mysterious packages. Does one of them contain his star?

More books to share:

A Christmas Story by Mary Chalmers. A little girl seeks a star for her tree.

Nine Days to Christmas: A Story of Mexico by Marie Hall Ets and Aurora Labastida. A Christmas star piñata becomes a real star when it is broken.

Follow-up activities for home or school:

•Look at stars in several picture books, noting the ways in which illustrators depict stars. See in particular *Din Dan Don, It's Christmas* by Janina Domanska. A different star on every page!

66. Holiday Cake Tales

Opening songs.

Read: *The Cake That Mack Ate* by Rose Robart; illus. by Maryann Kovalski. "This is the corn that fed the hen that laid the egg that went in the cake that Mack ate." Mack turns out to be a dog.

Read: *Benny Bakes a Cake* by Eve Rice. Benny helps make a cake, but dog Ralph eats it.

Read: *The Birthday* by Hans Fischer. Dog Bello bakes a cake and prepares a party for his mistress, Old Lisette.

Act out making a cake: Put sugar, flour, milk and eggs into a bowl, stir, pour into a pan, lick the bowl, bake, take out of the oven, cut, and taste!

Sing and play:
> If I'd known you were coming,
> I'd have baked a cake,
> Baked a cake,
> Baked a cake.
> If I'd known you were coming,
> I'd have baked a cake.
> How d'you do?
> How d'you do?
> How d'you do?

Act this song out: First knock on an imaginary door. Then pretend to open it and act surprised because company has come! Now sing the song. Walk around shaking hands with everyone on the "How d'you do" part and encourage the children and adults to shake hands with each other.

Ask the children to suggest other good things to offer a guest and sing: "If I'd known you were coming, I'd have baked chocolate chip cookies," etc. Sing and act out this song with various goodies offered.

Music: For tune, listen to *Happy Birthday* by Sharon, Lois, and Bram.

Read: *The Surprise* by George Shannon; illus. by Jose Aruego and Ariane Dewey. Squirrel's attempts to bake a cake fail, so he sends a better gift.

Read: *Happy Christmas, Gemma* by Sarah Hayes; illus. by Jan Ormerod. Baby Gemma gets into everything, including the Christmas cake. An enjoyable story at any time of the year.

Paste up a cake: Provide glue sticks, a white paper cake shape, and colored strips of paper to form the icing. Free-cut the cake shapes by simply rounding off the two top corners of a rectangle. Select several colored papers exactly the same size as the paper from which you cut your cake. Pre-cut narrow strips from these colored papers and provide each child with several colored strips. These are the icing for the cake. The children paste the icing strips onto their cake. They can also add small red circles (or tiny stick-on dots) to the cake's top for cherries.

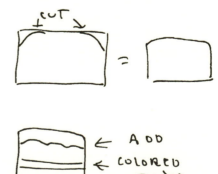

Note: This program can be used for Christmas, Valentine's Day, Thanksgiving, Easter, Fourth of July, etc., by changing the colors of the icing.

See also: Bakers at Work, program 44.

More books to share:

A Cake for Barney by Joyce Dunbar. Barney doesn't want to share his cake.

Country Bear's Good Neighbor by Larry Dane Brimner; illus. by Ruth Tietjan Councel. Country Bear borrows all the ingredients for a good cake.

The Duchess Bakes a Cake by Virginia Kahl. The duchess bakes a high-rising cake.

Ruth's Bake Shop by Kate Spohn. Ruth bakes cakes, cookies, croissants, you name it.

Follow-up activities for home or school:

•Bake a cake. Under adult supervision help measure, mix, and pour in ingredients. Eat it when it is done.

•Decorate cookies. To do this very simply, cut rounds from prepackaged cookie dough rolls. You can buy these in tubes at the supermarket. Provide icing in tubes and/or sprinkles to decorate.

67. *Company's Coming*

Opening songs.

Read: *The Patchwork Lady* by Mary K. Whittington; illus. by Jane Dyer. The patchwork lady gets ready for company and a birthday party.

Read: *Merry Christmas Ernest and Celestine* by Gabrielle Vincent. Ernest and Celestine prepare for a party.

Talk about: Getting ready for company. What do we have to do? Act out each thing. Sweep the floors, dust the furniture, decorate the house, bake goodies, get dressed up, greet the guests at the door.

Form a circle and sing: "If I'd known you were coming, I'd have baked a cake." See Holiday Cake Tales, program 66, for words and directions.

Read: *Chita's Christmas Tree* by Elizabeth Fitzgerald Howard; illus. by Floyd Cooper. Chita's family comes for Christmas dinner in this warm story of a turn-of-the-century African-American family.

Make a welcome mat: Print "WELCOME" on an 11 × 17-inch sheet of paper and make photocopies, one for each child. Or prepare a sample and ask the adults in your group to print them before the children start their decorative work. Provide lots of crayons, markers, and glitter to decorate the "welcome mat."

Closing songs: Take time to sing "Goodbye to the company" as part of your closing song sequence.

To use this program at other seasons, substitute the following titles for the two Christmas books in this program:

For fall:

Over the River and Through the Woods by Lydia Francis Child; illus. by Brinton Turkle. Grandma's house is ready for company.

The Big Sukkah by Penninah Schram; illus. by Jacqueline Kahane. Berl's house is too small for company, but he builds an enormous sukkah and invites the whole family.

For summer:

The Relatives Came by Cynthia Rylant; illus. by Stephen Gammell. Relatives come to visit and *stay* awhile.

For a birthday celebration:

"Birthday Soup" in *Little Bear* by Else Holmelund Minarik; illus. by Maurice Sendak. Little Bear makes his own birthday feast.

For Christmas:

Christmas in Noisy Village by Astrid Lindgren. A Swedish Christmas.

68. *Light a Candle*

Opening songs.

Read: *One Luminaria for Antonio* by Flora Hood; illus. by Ann Kirn. Antonio has no candle and paper bag to make a luminaria. When he returns from midnight mass, a surprise awaits him.

Read: *King Island Christmas* by Jean Rogers; illus. by Rie Munoz. There will be no candlelit Christmas mass unless the priest can get to shore through stormy seas.

Act out a candle riddle:

Little Nancy Etticotte,
In a white petticoat,
And a red nose.
The longer she stands,
The shorter she grows.

Stand straight as the candle, then melt slowly to the ground as you burn down.

Play a candle game:
> Jack be nimble,
> Jack be quick.
> Jack jump over
> The candlestick.

Line up and take turns being Jack and jumping over the candlestick. Bring a real candlestick for the children to jump over . . . a short one is best. After "Jack" jumps, let everyone jump again using his or her own name. "Anne be nimble, Anne be quick."

Read: *An Early American Christmas* by Tomie de Paola. A German immigrant family makes candles, decorates the house, and introduces the Christmas celebration to an early New England village.

Read: *Bring a Torch, Jeanette Isabella!* A Provençal carol attributed to Nicholas Saboly, 17th century; illus. by Adrienne Adams. A candlelight procession. Sing it, but pause long enough to examine the pictures as you go.

Make a candle holder: Prepare a 3-inch cardboard square and a 6-inch square piece of aluminum foil for each child. Pre-cut four "petals" from aluminum foil for each child. Cut each petal from a piece of foil 3 inches long and 1½ inches wide. Taper one end to form a petal. Wrap the foil square around the cardboard square. This forms a base for your candle. Paste or tape the flat ends of the petals to the bottom of the foil candle holder, one to each side of the square. Turn the candle holder right side up and glue a votive candle in its center. Roll the foil petals up to encircle the candle. Curl the petals' tips over your finger to shape them.

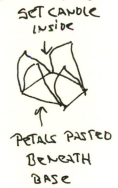

Closing songs.

More books to share:

> *I Love Hanukkah* by Marilyn Hirsh. Explanation of Hanukkah traditions, which include the lighting of one candle each night.

> *Treasures of Chanukah* by Greg Hildebrandt. This book has several sections that discuss various aspects of Chanukah. The section entitled "The Festival of Lights" by Bernice Slater reads aloud well and has lovely, glowing illustrations.

Four Candles for Simon by Gerda Marie Scheidle; illus. by Marcus P. Fister. Simon shares his candles with a robber, a wolf, a beggar, and the Christ Child.

Candle Love Feast by Julia M. Street; illus. by Anna Marie Magagna. Celebration of the Moravian "Candle Love Feast" held on Christmas Eve.

Follow-up activities for home or school:

•Make a display of candles of different shapes and sizes.

•Have a candlelit snack time. Place several large candles on the table. Turn off the lights and dine by candlelight.

69. *Youngest One at Christmas*

Opening songs.

Read: *Happy Christmas, Gemma* by Sarah Hayes; illus. by Jan Ormerod. Baby Gemma destructs Christmas.

Read: *Morris's Disappearing Bag* by Rosemary Wells. Youngest one, Morris, can't play with his older siblings' presents until *he* discovers a bag that can make things disappear!

Read: *Max's Christmas* by Rosemary Wells. Max's bossy big sister is amazed when Max meets Santa.

Action song:

Up on the housetop reindeers pause.

(*paw at the ground*)

Out jumps good old Santa Claus!

(*jump up with arms spread*)

Down through the chimney with lots of toys,

(*arms up, slide down the chimney to the floor*)

All for the little ones' Christmas joys.

(*pass out toys*)

HO HO HO . . . who wouldn't go?

(*pat tummy*)

HO HO HO . . . who wouldn't go?

Up on the housetop, click, click, click!

(*snap fingers*)

Down through the chimney with good Saint Nick.

(*arms up, slide down to the floor*)

Music: See the music on page 180.

Read: *Rotten Ralph's Rotten Christmas* by Jack Gantos; illus. by Nicole Rubel. Ralph is jealous when a younger cat comes to stay.

Read: *Noël for Jeanne-Marie* by Françoise. Jeanne-Marie helps little Patapon have a happy Nöel.

Make a Christmas book ornament for your tree: Fold a small piece of silver or gold paper in half to form a booklet. Punch a hole in the upper left corner and tie a ribbon through the hole in order to hang this as an ornament. Assemble these before the children arrive. Children decorate them by pasting snippets of Christmas ribbon and foil paper on the booklet cover. A message or drawing can be written inside if you like.

Closing songs.

See also: Youngest One, program 41.

More books to share:

Bah, Humbug by Lorna Balian. Big brother says there is no Santa but little sister finds out otherwise.

Merry Christmas, Ernest and Celestine by Gabrielle Vincent. Young Celestine plans a party.

Something for Christmas by Palmer Brown. Little mouse wants to give mother a present.

Follow-up activities for home or school:

•Talk about plans for December celebrations. Be sure your children know what to expect during the confusing rush of the holidays.

70. Christmas Tree!

Opening songs.

Read: *Mog's Christmas* by Judith Kerr. Mog the cat is terrified by what appears to be a walking tree, when the Christmas tree is being brought in the door.

Read: *Christmas at Long Pond* by Willliam T. George; illus. by Lindsay Barrett George. A trip to Long Pond to cut a Christmas tree.

Activity: Examine sprigs from several evergreens. Pass them around. Smell them. Notice the needle arrangement on the twig and the size, shape, and color of the needles.

Activity: Go on a mini field trip. Walk around outside and notice evergreens. Look at their shape and size, feel their needles, examine their bark. Discuss their suitability as Christmas trees.

Read: *Christmas Tree Farm* by David Budbill; illus. by Donald Carrick. Tells of a tree being planted, tended, harvested, and trucked to the city. For smaller children, just show pictures and tell about each step briefly.

Read: *Pigs at Christmas* by Arlene Dubanavich. The pigs go buy a Christmas tree . . . the last one on the lot. Very small pictures in this book, so it is difficult to use with large groups.

Decorate a Christmas tree: Before the children arrive, free-cut Christmas tree shapes from poster board. Do not try to make these symmetrical. I cut mine about 7 inches tall and 5 inches wide at the base. You will need two tree pieces for each child. Cut halfway DOWN the center of one tree piece, starting at the top. Cut halfway UP the center of the second tree piece, starting at the bottom. Fasten these two pieces together and adjust them so that the tree will stand upright on a table top. Stand these around the tables before the children arrive. Provide many stick-on dots. Let the children decorate the trees by applying the stick-on dots as tree ornaments. These are simple to prepare, look great, and kids love them. I used one sheet of light green poster board and one of dark green for each tree, giving an interesting look.

Closing songs.
More books to share:
> *Night Tree* by Eve Bunting; illus. by Ted Rand. A trip to the woods to decorate a special tree for the birds and animals.
>
> *Stopping by Woods on a Snowy Evening* by Robert Frost; illus. by Susan Jeffers. The woods in winter.
>
> *The Tree That Came to Stay* by Anna Quindlen; illus. by Nancy Carpenter. The tree is thrown out, but mother fills a basket with pine needles to remember its scent.

Follow-up activities for home or school:
> •Decorate a small tree. Make all of the decorations yourself using colored papers, scissors, and paste. Foil stars or bright snippets of ribbon add sparkle.

71. *Christmas Sharing*

Opening songs.
Talk about: Sharing and gift-giving.
Read: *The Doorbell Rang* by Pat Hutchins. Cookies are shared . . . and shared . . . and shared.
Read: *Angelina's Christmas* by Katherine Holabird; illus. by Helen Craig. Angelina plans a Christmas surprise for lonely old Mr. Bear.
Read: *Christmas Present from a Friend* by Yuriko Kimura; illus. by Masako Matsumura. Rabbit shares her carrot with Donkey, who shares with Sheep, who shares with . . . . As I read, I ask the children to help me

pretend to knock on each animal's door and call, "Donkey! Donkey! Anybody home?" or "Rabbit! Rabbit! Anybody home?"

Act out *Christmas Present from a Friend:* Form a circle. Assign animal parts, adding more animals if necessary so everyone can have a part. Rabbit carries a carrot to Donkey's home and knocks. Donkey has his back turned, so Rabbit knocks on his back, calling, "Donkey, Donkey! Anybody home?" Rabbit leaves the carrot on the floor behind Donkey and goes back to his own house. Donkey turns around, picks up the carrot, and takes it to Sheep's house. The play repeats itself as each child carries the carrot on to another character.

Sing while shaking hands with your neighbors:
Shake my hand and you'll be my friend,
You'll be my friend,
You'll be my friend.
Shake my hand and you'll be my friend.
We'll all be friends.

Sing of sharing and let kids suggest things to share, such as "Share my cookies and you'll be my friend."

Music: See the music on page 181.

Share a carrot: Count the number of children in the group and cut a carrot so that each person gets a piece. Share and eat.

Read: *Paddy's Christmas* by Helen A. Monsel. Paddy finds the best part of Christmas is giving to others.

Make two tree ornaments: Each child can make one to keep and one to share. Paste stars or stick-on dots on green pre-cut triangles to decorate a Christmas tree. Punch a hole in the tree tip and insert a ribbon to hang it.

Closing songs.

More books to share:
Merry Christmas Mom and Dad by Mercer Mayer. Little Monster tries to help.
Something for Christmas by Palmer Brown. Little mouse wants to give a present to mother.

Follow-up activities for home or school:
•Make a gift for a friend.
•Arrange a plate of holiday cookies and candies to share

❧ What Can You Do With . . . ? ❧

72. What Can You Do with a Balloon?

Opening songs.

Talk about: What you can do with a balloon? Fly it, chase it, sit on it.

Read about flying away with a balloon: *I'm Flying* by Alan Wade; illus. by Petra Mathers. Attaching weather balloons to his lawn chair, our hero flies to a tropical island. Humorous and satisfying. This concept is a bit over the heads of three-year-olds and younger, but still fun.

Read about chasing a balloon: *Louella and the Yellow Balloon* by Molly Cone. Louella the Pig's balloon escapes at the circus and she pursues it.

Play with a balloon by making a circle and singing:

Pass the balloon,
Pass the balloon,
Pass the balloon,
All around the room.

Toss the balloon from person to person as you sing this. Sing other rounds of the song using "Tap the balloon" or "Blow the balloon." End by tapping the balloon high in the air and letting it fall to the floor singing "Watch the balloon . . . Falling to the ground."

Music: See the music on page 182.

Make a jet balloon: Blow up several balloons, but do not tie them. Let the children hold them and on the count of three, all release the balloons at once. Repeat.

Read: *A Balloon for Grandad* by Nigel Gray; illus. by Jane Ray. A small boy's balloon flies over mountains, seas, and deserts to reach his Grandad Abdullah's home.

Read: *Miss Eva and the Red Balloon* by Karen M. Glennon; illus. by Hans Poppel. A magical balloon changes Miss Eva's life. On the last page she passes it on to the traffic policeman. Ask the children what might happen to the traffic policeman next. Or what would happen to them if *they* had the magical balloon?

Make a balloon creature: Put pre-cut eyes, feet, and noses on the tables. Free-cut these in any shape you like. Children tape them to the balloon.

Closing songs.

More books to share:

> *The Highest Balloon on the Common* by Carol Carrick; illus. by Donald Carrick. Paul is lost on the town common during a fall festival, but his balloon reveals his location to his father.
>
> *Wilbur's Space Machine* by Lorna Balian. Violet and Wilbur escape the crowded town by fastening balloons to their homestead and flying it away.

Follow-up activities for home or school:

> •See the video *The Red Balloon,* written and directed by Albert Lamorisse. 34 min. A boy's balloon flies off over the rooftops of Paris to an adventure of its own.
>
> •Inflate three different kinds of balloons. Observe them for several days. Which deflate fastest?
>
> •Inflate balloons made of three different types of material. Try to pop them by putting pressure on them. Pile books on top of the balloons. How many books can each balloon support before it pops?
>
> •Give each child a balloon. Feel it. Smell it. Try to pop it.
>
> •Think of a way to make someone feel magical with a balloon.

73. What Can You Do with an Umbrella?

Opening songs.

Talk about: Things you can do with an umbrella.

Read: *Umbrella* by Taro Yashima. Momo uses her new umbrella for the first time.

Talk more about: What can you do with an umbrella?

> •Keep the sun off.

•Keep the wind out of your eyes.

•Poke things with it.

•Use it as a cane.

•Point with it.

•Use it as decoration.

•Twirl it.

•Use it as a boat.

•Carry things in it.

•Fly away with it like Mary Poppins.

Read: *The Umbrella Day* by Nancy Evans Cooney; illus. by Melissa Bay Mathis. Missy pretends her umbrella is a toadstool, a circus tent, a boat.

Play an umbrella marching game: March to music as the leader carries an umbrella high overhead. When the leader lowers the umbrella, all STOP. Take turns being leader.

Read: *Roger's Umbrella* by Honest Dan'l Pinkwater; illus. by James Marshall. Roger has an uncooperative umbrella. Three strange ladies teach him how to talk to it so it will behave.

Play with an umbrella: Ask the class to say Roger's magic words to make the umbrella fly off. Let it carry you around the room. Call to the class to say the magic words to make it fold up again.

Film: *Mole and the Umbrella*. 9 min. Ask the class to watch and see what Mole will do with his umbrella. Encourage them to call out things they see him doing during the movie.

Talk about: What did Mole do with his umbrella? Float in it, fly with it, roll it, mend it, use it as a stand to sell things, shelter under it, get caught in it, open it.

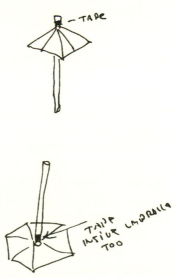

Make a paper umbrella: Pre-fold squares of paper. Do this by folding the square first lengthwise, then sideways, and into a triangle, matching corner to corner. The folds become the ribs of the umbrella. Poke a very tiny hole in the exact center of the square. Let the children decorate the paper umbrella with crayons. Have adults help insert a straw through the hole as the umbrella handle. Wrap a piece of colored adhesive tape around the straw end protruding above the umbrella and on the underside wrap tape around the straw just below where the straw pokes through the umbrella. This should keep the umbrella from slipping off its straw handle.

Walk a tightrope: Place a strip of masking tape across the floor and "walk the tightrope." Use your paper umbrellas to help balance. To explain about tightrope walking show the picture of mother rabbit walking the tightrope from *Runaway Bunny* by Margaret Wise Brown; illus. by Clement Hurd.

Closing songs.

More books to share:

> *The Enchanted Umbrella* by Odette Meyers; illus. by Margot Zemach. A flying umbrella and a boy who learns kindness. A very brief history of umbrellas is appended.
>
> *Little Bear Marches in the St. Patrick's Day Parade* by Janice; illus. by Mariana. Little Bear raises his umbrella and it rains. He lowers it and the rain stops.
>
> *My Red Umbrella* by Robert Bright. An umbrella shelters many.

Follow-up activities for home or school:

- •Walk in the rain with your own umbrella.
- •Listen to the rain on your roof, on your umbrella, on the sidewalk.
- •Walk in the sun with your umbrella. Hold it high. Hold it low. Tilt it to the left, the right, front, back. Does its shade always cover your body in the same way?
- •Put a teddy bear on the ground. Arrange the umbrella so that only his feet are in the sun. Can you arrange the umbrella so that he is almost totally in the sun, yet still sitting under the umbrella?

74. What Can You Do with a Broom?

Opening songs.

Talk about: Things you can do with a broom.

Read: *If You Give a Mouse a Cookie* by Laura Joffe Numeroff; illus. by Felicia Bond. A mouse sweeps the house in a chain of events following his request for a cookie.

Talk about: What else can you do with a broom? Suggest reaching with it to knock things down.

Read: *Wing-a-ding* by Lyn Littlefield Hoopes; illus. by Stephen Gammell. A Wing-a-ding (cardboard box toy) sticks in a tree and kids try throwing things at it, poking it with a broom, etc. to knock it down. They finally sing it down. Let the children sing the song with you several times, adding this singing to the text. Show the title page and explain that the box is a "wing-a-ding" before you start the book. Explain that the objects are stuck in the tree as you read.

Sing a broom song:
> Sweep, sweep, sweep so high.
> Sweep, sweep, sweep the sky!
>
> Sweep, sweep, sweep so low,
> Sweep, sweep, down below.

Music: See the music on page 182.

Read a book about marrying a broom: *The Wedding Procession of the Rag Doll and the Broom Handle and Who Was in It* by Carl Sandburg; illus. by Harriet Pincus. Lead the children in pretending to lick spoons, bang pots and pans, wipe their dirty finger on bibs as you read.

Read a book about flying on a broom: *Hester* by Byron Barton. Hester goes trick-or-treating and meets up with a real witch, who takes her for a ride.

Play "Pass the Witch's Broomstick": The game and music are found on the record *Halloween* (Den-Lan Music, 1964). The game consists of passing a broom around the circle until the music stops. The one who ends up with the broom rides it around the circle while everyone claps. If the *Halloween* recording is not available, you could play this game to another piece of music. And if witches are taboo in your storytime, you could pretend the broom is a hobby horse to ride.

Paint a picture with a broom: First the children make free-form crayon marks on their paper. Next they spackle them with a whisk broom. I set up three spackling stations, each with a whisk broom and a plate heavily coated with thick tempera paint. As they completed their drawings, the children brought their papers to the spackling table. Under adult supervision, they dipped the tips of their whisk brooms in the paint plate and then dabbed their picture. Demonstrate the dabbing technique beforehand so the children don't try to use the whisk broom as a brush. Use short up-and-down movements, just touching the tips of the broom to the paper to make many specks of paint. I set out purple and blue crayons and magenta paint for an interesting effect.

Closing songs.

More books to share:
> *Housekeeper of the Wind* by Christine Wideman; illus. by Lisa Disimini. The wind's housekeeper sweeps and sweeps.

The Leaky Umbrella by Demi. Silly Wako mistakes a broom for an umbrella and gets wet. Japanese setting. Tiny black-and-white line drawings.
Wobble Pop: Noisy Words by John Burningham. A toddler cleans house. One word per page.
"The Teeny Weeny Bop" in *Look Back and See: Twenty Lively Tales for Gentle Tellers* by Margaret Read MacDonald. A tale to tell. Sweeping the house, the Teeny Weeny Bop finds a silver coin and starts a chain of events.

Follow-up activities for home or school:

•Take a broom and sweep your sidewalk clean.

•Take a tour of your broom closet to see what brooms and mops are there. What are they used for? How are they different? How are they the same?

75. What Can You Do with a Box?

Opening songs.

Read: *Baby in a Box* by Frank Asch. Baby, fox, and blocks in box.

Read: *Boxes! Boxes!* by Leonard Everett Fisher. Many uses for boxes are shown.

Activity: Show boxes of many sizes and shapes. Pass out the boxes. Let each child decide what pretend object should be put inside the box. An adult writes the name of the object on a slip of paper and puts it in the box. Pile the boxes up and let each child pick a box from the pile. Open the boxes one at a time, read out the contents, and marvel over the pretend prizes in the boxes.

Read: *The Surprise* by George Shannon; illus. by Jose Aruego and Ariane Dewey. A box in a box in a. . . .

Read: *Sitting in My Box* by Dee Lillegard; illus. by Jon Agee. A child and his animals in a box.

Play with boxes: Have enough large boxes for each child to sit in one (or just pretend to climb into a box). Ask each child to invite an imaginary animal into the box. Serve it a picnic lunch. Tell it goodbye.

Decorate a box: Shoeboxes or any small box will do. Provide paste and colored paper snippets or other decorations to glue onto the box.

Closing songs.

More books to share:

Boxman by Irina Hale. Bob wears a box over his head all day as "Boxman."
The Christmas Box by Eve Morrison; illus. by David Small. Only one long, long box under the tree.

The Gift by John Prater. Two children climb into a cardboard box and pretend to sail away for adventures. Good imagination starter for sitting-in-a-box play.

I Need a Lunch Box by Jeannette Caines; illus. by Pat Cummings. A child dreams of using lunch boxes, but big sister is going to school, not him.

Follow-up activities for home or school:

•Stack boxes.

•Arrange boxes by size, shape.

•Squash boxes.

•Drum on boxes.

•Wear boxes.

•Hide under boxes.

•Stand on boxes.

❧ Just Me! ❧

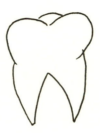

76. A Tooth! A Tooth!

Opening songs.

Talk about: Losing teeth.

Read: *One Morning in Maine* by Robert McCloskey. Sal loses her tooth while
digging for clams and worries she might not get her wish without it. This
is long, but the episodes hold attention well.

Poem: "This Tooth" by Lee Bennett Hopkins, in *A Cup of Starshine: Poems and
Pictures for Young Children* by Jill Bennett; illus. by Graham Percy, p. 19.

Read: *The Bear's Toothache* by David McPhail. A bear with a toothache appears
under a child's window at night. The child helps pull the aching tooth.

View: *Doctor De Soto* by William Steig. 10 min. Film or video. Mouse dentist
treats a fox at great peril.

Read: *Arthur's Tooth* by Marc Brown. A seven-year-old is the only one in his
class who hasn't lost a tooth yet.

Make a tooth picture: Pass out bread slices. Bite into, but not through, the
bread, biting a design around the edge. Compare your artwork. Eat your
artwork!

Closing songs.

More books to share:

Airmail to the Moon by Tom Birdseye; illus. by Stephen Gammell. Mac
loses her lost tooth before the tooth fairy can exchange it for money, and
what a fuss she makes!

My Dentist by Harlow Rockwell. A look at objects encountered in a dental
visit.

Follow-up activities for home or school:
- •Use a mirror to look at your own teeth.
- •Count them. How many do you have?

77. Bathtime

Opening songs.

Read: *To Bathe a Boa* by C. Imbior Kudrna. A boa is hard to catch and harder to bathe.

Read: *Harry the Dirty Dog* by Gene Zion; illus. by Margaret Bloy Graham. Harry hides his scrub brush and runs away.

Form a circle and sing:
> Scrub a dub dub,
> Scrub a dub dub,
> Scrub a dub dub dub,
> Scrub a dub dub.

Pretend to pour hot water into a washtub and wash your clothes as you sing this. Pretend to take a bath and sing it again.

Pretend to sink under the bubbles and sing:
> Blub a blub blub,
> Blub a blub blub,
> Blub a blub blub blub,
> Blub a blub blub!

Extend your arms over your head and sink to the floor as if sinking under the bubbles.

Music: See the music on page 183.

Sing and act out:
> This is the way we wash our clothes,
> Wash our clothes,
> Wash our clothes.
> This is the way we wash our clothes,
> So early in the morning.

Sing the song again and pretend to be the washing machine. Sing "This is the way we dry our clothes" and pretend to be the dryer. Sing of folding the clothes. Sing of putting them away.

Music: See the music on page 183.

> Older children will enjoy singing and playing the story of *Harry the Dirty Dog* to this tune. "This is the way I hide my scrub brush." "This is the way I play in the train yard," etc. End very softly with, "This is the way I take my nap."

Read: *Three Little Kittens;* illus. by Masha. After reading the poem once, read it again, and this time let the children make motions to accompany the text. They can meow, wash mittens, eat pie, etc.

Read: *There's a Hippo in My Bath!* Adapted from a story by Kyoko Matsuoka; illus. by Akiko Kayashi. A young Japanese boy imagines huge animals sharing his bath.

Read a poem: "After a Bath" by Aileen Fisher in *Days Are Where We Live and Other Poems* compiled by Jill Bennet; illus. by Maureen Roffey.

Make a picture of bubbles and baths: Draw white bubbles on dark blue construction paper with a bar of soap. Closing songs.

More books to share:

> *The Beast in the Bathtub* by Kathleen Stevens; illus. by Ray Bowler. Imaginary company in the tub.
>
> *I Can Take a Bath* by Shigeo Watanabe; illus. by Yasuo Ohtomo. Baby Bear scrubs in tub with Daddy. Very brief text.
>
> *King Bidgood's in the Bathtub* by Audrey Wood; illus. by Don Wood. Silliness in an overcrowded royal tub.
>
> *Let's Give Kitty a Bath* by Steven Lindbloom; illus. by True Kelley. A wordless picture book.
>
> A film to view: *Let's Give Kitty a Bath.* 12 min. Video or 16 mm film. Live action film retells the picture book by Lindbloom and Kelley.

Follow-up activities for home or school:

> •Pour water into three large plastic tubs. Add three different kinds of bubble bath or dishwashing liquid and stir. Which makes the most bubbles? Smell them. Which scent do you prefer?
>
> •From discarded plastic containers make a toy boat to play with in the bathtub. You will need two containers, one larger than the other. Invert the small container, place it upside down inside the larger container to form the boat's cabin. Put glue on the rim of the smaller, inverted container to hold it in place. Decorate the boat with waterproof markers.

78. Bedtime

Opening songs.

Read: *Winifred's New Bed* by Lynn and Richard Howell. Winifred gets a big new bed, but each night she adds another stuffed animal until she falls out.

Sing a fingerplay:
>There were ten in the bed,
>(*hold up ten fingers*)
>And the little one said,
>"Roll over! Roll over!"
>(*roll hands forward on each "roll over"*)
>So they all rolled over, and one fell out.
>(*Drop one finger, leaving nine*)

Repeat the song until only one finger remains.
>There was one in the bed,
>And the little one said,
>"Aaaaaahhhhhh . . . ."

The song ends with a satisfied sigh.

Music: See the music on page 184.

Sing and act out: Put a blanket on the floor with pillows at one end to make a bed. Make it big enough to hold several children at a time. Line them up side by side in the bed and sing "There were five in the bed . . . ." All roll over and the one on the end falls off the blanket. Repeat until all but one have fallen out. Repeat the game until all have had a turn.

Read: *The Bed Just So* by Jeanne R. Hardendorff; illus. by Lisl Weil. A wee elf called a "hudgin" complains nightly about the beds a tailor makes for it: "Too soft and too tickly"; "Too high and too hard"; etc. A bed that is a walnut shell is "just so." The pictures in this book are tiny. For large groups you might tell the story without the pictures. Or enlarge the pictures of the beds on a copy machine and tell the story showing the beds mentioned. You can make a simple flannel board by putting loops of masking tape on the backs of photocopied pictures and sticking them to a large sheet of poster board as you tell. Show a real walnut shell at the end.

Read: *The Napping House* by Audrey Wood; illus. by Don Wood. Cumulative tale of granny, child, dog, cat, mouse, napping—until flea starts a chain reaction that awakens all.

View: *The Napping House*. 5 min. Video or film. Follow the reading of the book with this delightful film.

Make a bed full of toys: Photocopy the big bed on page 5 of *Winifred's New Bed*. To create an empty bed for your picture, you will have to cut out Winifred's head, paste blank paper over the space, and redraw the sheet pattern. Now, using this as a master, make a copy of the empty bed for each child. Cut out the bed and cut a slit along the top of the top sheet. (You are going to slide the cut-out toys into bed here.) Paste the cut out bed onto a larger sheet of paper. Leave an unpasted strip about 1½ inches deep under your top sheet slit. You will tuck the cut-out toys into this slit. Photocopy the toys from *Winifred's New Bed* and make a master with toy pictures. Make a copy of these toy pictures for each child. Pre-cut them for younger children, let older children or those with parents cut them out themselves. The children color the toys and insert them under the bed sheet.

Closing songs.

More books to share:

The Bed Book by Sylvia Plath; illus. by Emily McCully. A sailing bed poem.
Goodnight Moon by Margaret Wise Brown; illus. by Clement Hurd. A bunny in bed says goodnight to every thing in the room.
The Princess and the Pea by Hans Christian Andersen; illus. by Paul Galdone. A royal bed is piled high with mattresses and a hidden pea to detect a true princess.

Follow-up activities for home or school:

•Bring your favorite bedtime book to class. Let everyone pretend to tuck into bed and listen to the bedtime story.
•Make a bedtime book basket. Gather your favorite bedtime picture books and put them in a box or basket beside your bed.

❧ Concepts ❧

79. Plain and Fancy

Opening songs.

Talk about: Plain vs. fancy. I wore a plain T-shirt, then pulled out a fancy one to wear over it; showed a plain scarf and a fancy one; a plain necklace and a fancy one; kept these items in a plain bowl and a fancy bowl, etc.

Read: *Hey, Al* by Arthur Yorinks; illus. by Richard Egielski. Al lives in a plain apartment. He flies off to a fancy new environment.

Play: "This little pig went to market." Younger groups can remove their shoes and adults can play it with them. With older kids, we used the fingers of our left hand to play the game. I showed a simple illustration for this poem from *Mother Goose* by Tomie de Paola, p. 41.

This little pig went to market.
(*wiggle big toe or thumb*)
This little pig stayed home.
(*wiggle second toe/finger*)
This little pig had roast beef.
(*wiggle third toe/finger*)
This little pig had none.
(*wiggle fourth toe/finger*)
And this little pig went WEE, WEE, WEE, WEE, WEE,
All the way HOME.
(*wiggle little toe/finger rapidly*)

Read: *This Little Pig* by Leonard B. Lubin. Fancy illustrations for the rhyme.

Read: *Frida the Wondercat* by Betsy Everitt. A plain cat becomes fancy when she wears a magic collar.

Play: Form a circle and sit down and purr as plain cats. Strike a gong to signal that all have now turned into fancy cats. The fancy cats pretend to dance, drive buses, make bean soup, and do other things that Frida could do. When the gong is struck again, all drop to the ground, turned into plain cats. Repeat. I end by sticking a "fancy cat" sticker on each child one by one, turning them into permanent fancy cats. Any sticker will do, just call it a "fancy cat" sticker.

Read: *The Patchwork Lady* by Mary K. Whittington; illus. by Jane Dyer. The Patchwork Lady wears fancy clothes, eats fancy food, lives in a fancy house, throws a fancy party, and receives a fancy gift.

Make: A fancy (or plain) card for someone. Show your cards to the group. I used this program at Valentine's Day, but any season would work.

More books to share:

A Bargain for Frances by Russell Hoban; illus. by Lillian Hoban. Frances wants a fancy tea set, but settles for a plain one.

Just Plain Fancy by Patricia Polacco. An Amish girl, raised to prize the plain, is horrified when her hen hatches a *fancy* chick.

Follow-up activities for home or school:

•Find several fancy items in your room. Find several plain ones. Make a display of fancy objects.

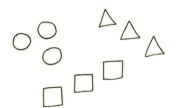

80. *Three*

Opening songs.

Show: Shamrock or clover. Discuss its three leaves.

Talk about: The number three. Show a triangle. It has three sides and three corners. Hold up three fingers and count them.

Read: *Three Little Kittens*, illus. by Masha. Stress the number three. Let the kittens meow THREE times rather than four times when you read the book. Let the children meow or purr with you and hold up three fingers as you meow one, two, three times.

Tell: "The Three Bears." Let the children help as you pretend to mix up the porridge, pour it out, taste it. For an easy-to-tell version of this story, see *A Parent's Guide to Storytelling* by Margaret Read MacDonald.

Read: "Porridge" and "Three Bears Walking" from *The Three Bears Rhyme Book* by Jane Yolen; illus. by Jane Dyer. Go on a bears' walk in the woods. Form a circle. Read "Three Bears Walking" again. Act the rhyme out as you read. Repeat each refrain twice ("Three bears walking down the lane, down the lane, down the lane . . . Three bears walking down the lane, down the lane, down the lane.") This allows the children to chime in with you the second time you speak the lines. Stop walking in a circle and ask each other the bears' questions: "Do you think it's going to rain? Do you think it's going to rain?" Then begin circling again: "Three bears walking . . . ," etc.

Play a squirrel game: Form groups of three. Two people hold both hands to form a "tree." One person is inside the circle of their arms as a squirrel. Call out, "One . . . two . . . three! Squirrels run to another tree!" Squirrels run out of their tree and run into another tree. To calm them down between the runs call out, "Squirrels, STOP! Eat your peanuts!" They mime eating nuts. Then repeat the running chant. End with, "One . . . two . . . three . . . Squirrels run to your home tree!" Squirrels now change places with one of the tree persons, and you repeat the play.

Read: *3 × 3: Three by Three* by James Kruss; illus. by Eva Johanna Rubin. Three cats chase three mice. Three dogs scare three cats.

Read: *Wynken, Blynken and Nod* by Eugene Field; illus. by Barbara Cooney. Tell the kids that Wynken, Blynken, and Nod are two eyes and a head. Point to eyes and head as you say, "Wynken, Blynken and Nod." As you read, have them point to first one eye, then the other, then the head.

Make: A picture of threes. I used this at St. Patrick's Day and sprinkled paper shamrocks in the center of each table. Each child chose three shamrocks to paste on a paper. You could use three triangles, three clovers, etc.

Closing songs.

More books to share:

Three Kittens by Mirra Ginsburg; illus. by Giulio Maestro. Trans. from the Russian of V. Suteyev. Three kittens get into flour, soot, etc., and keep changing color.

Three Yellow Dogs by Caron Lee Cohen; illus. by Peter Sis. Introduces the concepts "dogs," "yellow," and "three" in very brief text.

Follow-up activities for home or school:

•Sort items into piles of three. M & M candies, paper clips, or pennies would do.

•Provide three items at snack time. Try three carrot sticks, three crackers, or three raisins.

81. Small and Tall

Opening songs.

Read: *Ton and Pon: Big and Little* by Kazuo Iwamura. Is it better to be big or little? Each has its advantages.

Poem: "Drinking Fountain" by Marchette Chute in *A Cup of Starshine: Poems and Pictures for Young Children* by Jill Bennett; illus. by Graham Percy, p. 15.

Read: *Elephant Buttons* by Noriko Ueno. An elephant unbuttons his skin and out steps a horse, who unbuttons his skin and out steps a lion, and so on.

Act out: *Elephant Buttons.*

First recite and act out this poem.
>An elephant goes like this and that.
>He's terribly big and he's terribly fat.
>He has no fingers, he has no toes,
>But OH my goodness, what a nose!

Next act out all of the animal changes in *Elephant Buttons.* I hold the book in one hand and turn the pages to show the next animal change as we act them out. End as an elephant with a repeat of the elephant poem.

Read: *The Biggest Bear* by Lynd Ward. Sometimes big is *too* big. A boy brings home a pet bear . . . which grows!

Sing and act out:
>I'm not small.
>I'm so tall.
>I can walk with an elephant on my back.

Let the children suggest other things to carry on their backs, or other things to do when tall. Sing of these.

Music: See *I'm Not Small*. Songs by Patty Zeitlin and Marcia Berman. This audiocasette and booklet contain the words and music. If this is not available you could substitute the song "I Am Big" from this book. See the music on page 174.

Read: *Blue Sea* by Robert Kalan; illus. by Donald Crews. Little fish, big fish, bigger fish, biggest.

Make a Mr. Small/Mr. Tall doll: Accordian-fold a strip of paper 1 inch wide by 4 inches long. Make four folds about 1 inch deep each. This is the doll's body. Give each child one pre-pleated strip and an inch-diameter stick-on dot to serve as the doll's head. The child pastes the stick-on dot on one end of the body and draws on a face. The body can be decorated with crayons. Fold the doll up to make Mr. Small. Extend it to make Mr. Tall.

Closing songs: Sing "I'm Not Small" using your paper Mr. Small/Mr. Tall dolls. Play with them asking, "Where is Mr. Tall?" Stretch the doll out. "Where is Mr. Small?" Fold the doll up.

More books to share:

George Shrinks by William Joyce. What if you grew smaller and smaller?

Happy Birthday, Sam by Pat Hutchins. Sam is too small to reach things.

Follow-up activities for home or school:

•Make a display of small and tall objects, such as books, pencils, jars, etc.

•Make a mark on the wall to show how high you can reach.

•Who is tallest in your family? Ask your family to stand in a row. Who is smallest?

•Make a growth chart. Stand against the edge of a door and have someone mark your height there. Add the date. Remember to come back in three months to do it again. This way you can measure your own growth.

82. Inside, Outside, Upside Down!

Opening songs.

Read: *Where Is My Friend?* by Betsy and Giulio Maestro. Harriet goes up, down, in, out, etc., in search of her friend.

Read: *Rosie's Walk* by Pat Hutchins. Rosie walks *around* the pond, *over* the haystack, etc.

Read: *Mushroom in the Rain* by Mirra Ginsburg; adapted from the Russian of V. Suteyev; illus. by Jose Aruego and Ariane Dewey. Five animals sheltered under a mushroom.

Act out: *Mushroom in the Rain.* Let adults or some of the kids be the mushroom.

Sing and play:

Bluebird, bluebird, fly through my window.
Bluebird, bluebird, fly through my window.
Bluebird, bluebird, fly through my window.
Early in the morning.

Let each child decide if he/she wants to be a bluebird, rabbit, frog, etc. Adjust your words accordingly.

Music: See the music on page 168.

Read: *Three Kittens* by Mirra Ginsburg; translated from the Russian of V. Suteyev; illus. by Giulio Maestro. Three kittens go *in* a flour bin, come *out* again.

Read: *Inside, Outside, Upside Down* by Stan and Jan Berenstain. Read it through once. Then repeat, letting the children chant each phrase after you.

Make: A Brother Bear and a box. Photocopy Brother Bear from the book *Inside, Outside, Upside Down.* You can make a master sheet by photocopying the bear several times, cutting the bear pictures out and pasting up one page of bears. Give each child one bear picture. The child can color the bear and then paste it onto a folded piece of cardboard so the bear will stand up. The child can also decorate a paper cup or small box with magic markers. This is the "box" for Brother Bear to hide in.

Play: Put Brother Bear in his box, under his box, beside his box, etc. Let each child tell where they want the group to put Brother Bear. All follow his/her directions.

Closing songs.

More books to share:

Everything Has a Place by Patricia Lillie; illus. by Nancy Tafuri. A bird *in* a nest, a baby *on* a lap . . . a place for everything.

You Think It's Fun to Be a Clown! by David Adler; illus. by Ray Cruz. A clown falls *down*, is shot *up*, and is stuffed *inside* a cannon.

Follow-up activities for home or school:

•Play with a large cardboard box. Get inside it, outside it, under it, on top of it.

83. *Green*

Opening songs.

Read: *Colors* by John S. Reiss. After reading, go back to the "green" page and talk about more green things.

Read a poem: "What Is Green?" from *Hailstones and Halibut Bones* by Mary O'Neil; illus. by John Walner.

Read: *What Do You See?* by Janina Domanska. Think about green environments.

Read a poem: "Green Stems" from *Nibble Nibble* by Margaret Wise Brown.

Read: *Under the Greenwillow* by Elizabeth Coatsworth; illus. by Janina Domanska.

Read: *A House of Leaves* by Kiyoshi Soya; illus. by Akiko Hayashi. A green leafy hiding place.

Read a poem: "The Butterbean Tent" by Elizabeth Maddox Roberts in *Golden Journey: Poems for Young People* by Louise Bogan and William Jay Smith, p. 52.

Activity: Go outside and look into the green worlds of grass, bushes, treetops, etc. Give each child a paper cup. Bring back bits of green grass, leaves, moss, etc. Make a miniature green environment that a bug or very tiny person might enjoy.

Closing songs.

More books to share:

> *Inch by Inch* by Leo Lionni. A green inchworm vanishes in a grassy jungle.
> *Little Blue and Little Yellow* by Leo Lionni. Blue and Yellow hug and turn green!
> *Greens* by Arnold Adoff; illus. by Betsy Lewin. Color in rhyme.

Follow-up activities for home or school:

> •Touch every green thing you can find in the room.
> •Go outside. Name all the green things you see.
> •Eat a green snack: lettuce, peas, Jello, etc.

84. The Quiet Storytime

Opening songs.

Read: *Quiet* by Peter Parnall; illus. by Byrd Baylor. A young boy lies so quietly that chickadees and a chipmunk climb onto his tummy to eat seeds.

Read: *Play with Me* by Marie Hall Ets. A little girl moves too quickly and frightens animals away. Later she sits still and they all approach.

Act out: *Play with Me.* Form a circle. One child is the little girl or boy in the circle center. We decide which animal we will be and then all creep closer to "it." We are chipmunks, frogs, snakes, etc. The child who is "it" waits until we get close, then waves arms at us and we scamper away. Repeat with a different "it." Give each child a chance to be "it" and frighten us all off.

Read: *A House of Leaves* by Kiyoshi Soya; illus. by Akiko Hayashi. Another little girl sits quietly. This time, insects approach.

Read: *The Listening Walk* by Paul Showers; illus. by Aliki. A boy hears all sorts of things on his listening walk.

Take a quiet walk: Collect sounds as you go. Do not make a sound yourself. Move slowly and stop often. Point out small sounds the group may miss. Make a list of the sounds you hear. Go back to the story room and talk about the sounds you heard on your walk. Suggest more listening at home.

Play "Guess the sound": Form a circle. Ask everyone to close their eyes. You make a sound. The group guesses what it is. Try clapping hands, banging on a pot, crinkling paper, etc.

Closing songs.

More books to share:

> *Helen and the Great Quiet* by Rick Fitzgerald; illus. by Marilyn MacGregor.

Helen thinks the world is too quiet until her aunt and uncle teach her to listen.

The Quiet Noisy Book by Margaret Wise Brown; illus. by Leonard Weisgard. Muffin the dog listens.

Follow-up activities for home or school:

•Set up a "noise trap" path. Scatter dry leaves, aluminum tins, crinkled newspaper, peanut shells. See how quietly you can walk this path.

ᕁ *What If You Were a Goose?* ᕁ

85. Bears in Their Dens

Opening songs.

Read: *Blueberries for Sal* by Robert McCloskey. Little Sal and Little Bear get
    their mothers mixed while picking blueberries.

Talk about: Hibernating bears.

Form a circle and sing:
    Old Brown Bear
    Sleeping in his den.
    Little Chipmunk tickles him,
    And runs back home again.

Let one child be "Old Brown Bear" another be "Chipmunk," or several can
    be bears at once and everyone else can be chipmunks.

Music: See the music on page 184.

Read: *Bear* by John Schoenherr. A bear wakes to find his mother gone and so
    begins a life on his own. Striking illustrations of an Alaskan bear in the
    wilderness.

Play: "Let's Go on a Bear Hunt!" For text see: *A Parent's Guide to Storytelling*
    by Margaret Read MacDonald.

Read: *The Biggest Bear* by Lynd Ward. Johnny's baby bear grows up.

Make: A bear in a den. Photocopy a picture of a sleeping bear. Make a master
    with several copies of your chosen picture on it and run off enough
    bears for the class. Each child colors a bear, pastes it on a piece of black
    construction paper. The adult helper staples a piece of brown or green

construction paper to this paper at the top, letting it cover the bear to form a "cave." Lift this brown/green flap and peek at the bear in his den.

Closing songs: Sing the "Old Brown Bear" song again. As you sing, lift the cave cover and peek at the sleeping brown bear, tickle him, and close the cover quickly.

More books to share:

Backyard Bear by Jim Murphy; illus. by Jeffrey Greene. A bear, driven from its territory, enters the suburbs.

Bears Are Sleeping by Yulya; illus. by Nonny Hogrogian. A Russian lullaby about hibernating animals.

Cully Cully and the Bear by Wilson Gage; illus. by James Stevenson. Cully Cully and the bear chase each other around the tree.

Nobody Listens to Andrew by Elizabeth Guilfoile; illus. by Mary Stevenson. A bear in Andrew's room!

Shadow Bear by Joan Hiatt Harlow; illus. by Jim Arnosky. A polar bear cub and an Eskimo boy frighten each other.

Two Little Bears by Ylla. Black-and-white photos of bear cubs tell a single tale.

Follow-up activities for home or school:

•Check out some books on bears from the library to learn more about them.

•Tell or read, "Grandfather Bear is Hungry" from *Look Back and See: Twenty Lively Tales for Gentle Tellers* by Margaret Read MacDonald. Act out the story.

•Make a pretend bear cave using a blanket draped over a chair or box. Pretend to be a bear crawling into the cave, going to sleep, waking up, smelling the spring air, going out to look for food, etc.

86. Bats, Bats, Bats

Opening songs.

Read: *Bat Time* by Ruth Horowitz; illus. by Susan Avishai. Leila can't wait for night to fall so she and her father can watch the bats fly.

Talk about: It's fun to pretend that bats are scary, but bats are really relatively harmless little creatures.

Read: *Stellaluna* by Janell Cannon. A baby fruit bat is raised by a family of birds. She learns to love two families.

Read: *Creatures of the Night* by Judith Rinard. Read only page 20. Show the bat pictures slowly so everyone can look carefully. Notice the bat's fur and face.

Talk about: Is a bat a bird or an animal?

Read: *A Bat Is Born* by Randall Jarrell; illus. by John Schoenherr. A night in the life of a baby bat and its mother. Scientific fact presented through poetry.

Act out: A night in the life of a bat. Begin by hanging in your cave, wings folded. Fly about . . . scoop up insects . . . etc.

Read for older groups: *Hattie the Backstage Bat* by Don Freeman. Hattie lives backstage in an empty theater and makes a startling performance on opening night.

Read for younger groups: Poem from *From King Boggen's Hall to Nothing at All* by Blair Lent.

Bat, Bat, come under my hat,
And I'll give you a slice of bacon.
And when I bake, I'll give you a cake,
If I am not mistaken.

Make: A bat. Give children pre-cut bats.
This is a paper folding craft, very simple.

1. Fold the bat in half.
2. Fold down each wing. Show the children how to get the edges even, then press down their folds. Let them do it themselves with guidance.
3. An adult must help the child tape a black thread to the top of the bat's back right in the middle, so that the bat hangs properly balanced when the child holds the thread.

Play with bats: Dangle them on their threads and chant,
One little bat flying through the air,
Eee! Eee! Eee! Who can I scare?

Shake your bat and pretend to scare someone.
Closing songs.

If this is a Halloween program, add:

> *Haunted House* by Jan Pienkowski. A huge pop-up bat is on the last page.
>
> *A Woggle of Witches* by Adrienne Adams. Witches ride, return home to make bat stew.

More books to share:

> *Rufus* by Tomi Ungerer. Rufus the bat wants to see the bright colors of day.
>
> *Shadows of the Night: The Hidden World of the Little Brown Bat* by Barbara Bash. Bat facts.

Follow-up activities for home or school:

> •Read aloud *The Bat Poet* by Randall Jarrell; illus. by Maurice Sendak. This is a short novel about a poetic bat.
>
> •View: *Bats*. Produced and directed by Paulle Clark. 8 min. Video.

87. *Spiders*

Opening songs.

Read: *Be Nice to Spiders* by Margaret Bloy Graham. Helen, the spider, visits each zoo animal in turn, ridding them of flies!

Read: *The Lady and the Spider* by Faith McNulty; illus. by Bob Marstall. A spider sets up house in a head of lettuce. The lady gardener spares her. From a spider's eye view.

Read: *What Do You See?* by Janina Domanska. The world as seen from a frog's eye, a fly's eye, a bat's eye, a fern's eye, and a lark's eye point of view.

Read: *There Was an Old Lady Who Swallowed a Fly* illus. by Pam Adams. Sing it as you go. The peek-through pages show each animal inside the other. Drawings in the round are confusing to young children though, so you must take time to point out the dog, cow, etc.

Sing and act out "The Eensy Weensy Spider":

> The Eensy Weensy Spider,
>
> Went up the waterspout.
>
> Down came the rain and washed the spider out.
>
> Out came the sun and dried up all the rain,
>
> So the Eensy Weensy Spider went up the spout again.

Music: See the music on page 184.

Make climbing motions with your fingers as the spider climbs. Swoosh your hands down as the water washes him out. Raise arms in a circle as the sun emerges.

Sing and act out "Little Arabella Miller":
> Little Arabella Miller
> Found a baby caterpillar.
> (*bend over and pretend to pick up caterpillar*)
> First she put it on her brother.
> (*pretend to put it on neighbor to your right*)
> Then she put it on her mother.
> (*pretend to put it on neighbor to your left*)
> They said, "Arabella Miller!
> Take away that caterpillar!"
> (*wave hands to fend off Arabella*)

Music: See the music on page 185.

Draw a spider web: For each child put four chalk points on a piece of black paper. The children draw chalk lines between the four points, connecting the dots. Then have them draw lines within the "web," connecting the dots across the middle of the circle. Lastly have them add spiral lines within the web. Review the spider web building page in *Be Nice to Spiders* before beginning to work.

Closing songs.

More books to share:
> *I Know an Old Woman Who Swallowed a Fly* illus. by Nadine Bernard Westcott. Another version of the song.
> *My Daddy Longlegs* by Judy Hawes; illus. by Walter Lorraine. A beginning science book about daddy longlegs, another arachnid.
> *The Spiders' Dance* by Joanne Ryder; illus. by Robert J. Blake. A poetic look at spiders.
> *Spiders in the Fruit Cellar* by Barbara M. Josse; illus. by Kay Chorao. A young child is afraid to go down to the fruit cellar because of the spiders.
> *Wolfie* by Janet Chenery; illus. by Marc Simont. A wolf spider in a jar.

Follow-up activities for home or school:
> •Locate a spider on a web to observe. Stop by to watch it working at several different times. Discuss what you see.
> •Take a walk to look for spider webs. Are they all alike? Talk about the ways in which they differ.
> •Get a guide to spiders from your library and learn the names of some of the spiders you see.

88. The Timid Deer

Opening songs.

Read: *Deer at the Brook* by Jim Arnosky. Deer come to drink at a sparkling brook.

Read: *Salt Hands* by Jane Chelsea Aragon; illus. by Ted Rand. A deer takes salt from a young girl's hands. Read slowly; this is magical.

Read: *Play with Me* by Marie Hall Ets. A young girl sits very still and animals come to sit near her.

Act out "Salt Hands": Let one child be the little girl/boy who holds out the salt. A second child takes the role of a deer and approaches slowly. If the child with the "salt" moves, the deer backs off. A wrapped candy can serve as the "salt." Take turns until everyone has had a chance to be a deer and snatch a "salt" from a partner's hands.

View: *Bell on a Deer*. 16 min. 16 mm film. A charming film made in Shanghai. Chinese watercolor backgrounds of mountains and delightful Chinese music. A wounded deer is cared for by a girl. It leaves her when its parents return.

Make a Chinese mountain picture: Tear heavy construction paper into pieces. Lay a set of these pieces on the table top for each child and tape a white sheet of paper over them. Using the side of a green crayon, make a rubbing. The result should simulate mossy rocks, mountains and bushes. Provide several different shades of green and yellow crayons for varying effects. Talk about where your deer might hide in this picture. Might it leap from peak to peak on your "mountains"?

Closing songs.

More books to share:

Dash and Dart by Mary and Conrad Buff. Lengthy text, story of deer in the forest.

Deer in the Snow by Miriam Schlein; illus. by Leonard P. Kessler. Children help three deer through a hard winter.

Fawn in the Woods by Irmengarde Eberle; photos by Lilo Hess. Photographs of a fawn's life.

Oats and Wild Apples by Frank Asch. Deer meets cow.

Parsley by Ludwig Bemelmans. Parsley the deer peacefully watches the hunters.

Follow-up activities for home or school:

•Visit an area where wildlife is abundant (birds, squirrels, insects, etc.). Sit very still for a while and see if any animals approach.

89. Crafty Chameleons

Opening songs.

Read: *A Color of His Own* by Leo Lionni. Chameleon wants a color of his own but settles for a friend to change colors *with* him.

Read: *Lizard in the Sun* by Joanne Ryder. Imagine yourself a lizard for a day.

Act out *Lizard in the Sun*: Using your arms as legs, drag your tail (feet) and move around the room. Stay very still and catch flies. Lap up water from a leaf. Stick your head in the air and puff out your neck to show your pride. Do push-ups using your tail for balance.

Read: *Crafty Chameleon* by Mwenye Hadithi; illus. by Adrienne Kennaway. Chameleon tricks Leopard and Crocodile into a tug-of-war.

Act out *Crafty Chameleon*: Use several leopards and crocodiles. Provide a rope to serve as the vine.

Make a chameleon picture: Photocopy the picture of a lizard on a wall from *Lizard in the Sun*. Provide green, yellow, orange, and brown crayons. Color the lizard any color you like, then color a background of the same color (green leaves, brown twigs, etc).

Closing songs.

More books to share:

How to Hide a Gray Tree Frog and Other Amphibians by Ruth Heller. Amphibians shown against their camouflage backgrounds.

Izzard by Lonzo Anderson; illus. by Adrienne Adams. A pet lizard adopts Jamie.

The Mixed-up Chameleon by Eric Carle. A bored chameleon tries other colors.

Follow-up activities for home or school:

•Look for other animals or insects who use camouflage to hide.

•Play at hiding small colored objects (blocks, tiddly winks, buttons, etc.). Are they harder to find when placed on objects of the same color?

90. Happy Hippos

Opening songs.

Read: *How Hippo!* by Marcia Brown. Hippo learns his "How's," especially, "How, Help!"

Read: *Hot Hippo* by Mwenye Hadithi; illus. by Adrienne Kennaway. Hippo promises not to eat the little fishes if he can live in the cool streams.

Film: *Hot Hippo.* 6 min. Video or 16 mm film.

Read: *There Is a Hippo in My Bath* adapted from a story by Kyoko Matsuoka; illus. by Akiko Hayashi. A rubber duck, a turtle, two penguins, a seal, a hippo, and a whale all in one bath!

Read: *George and Martha One Fine Day* by James Marshall. George scares the pants off Martha, but Martha gets her revenge.

Make a hippo puppet: Start with a closed brown paper bag. Cut out a rectangle of brown paper just slightly larger than the folded-over bottom of the bag. Round the corners. Paste this onto the folded-over bottom of the bag. Add two stick-on dots for eyes. Paste on two small squares of brown paper for ears. Round their corners. Paste on two small squares of white paper for teeth (one if you are making a George). If you like, add a bow which can be used as a tie for George or hairbow for Martha.

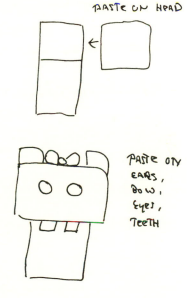

More books to share:

The Boy Who Was Followed Home by Margaret Mahy; illus. by Steven Kellogg. What if hippos followed you everywhere? A witch tries to help Robert.

The Happy Hippopotami by Bill Martin, Jr.; illus. by Betsy Everett. Rhyming hippos at the beach.

Ten Little Hippos: A Counting Book by Babette McCarthy. Ten hippos on stage. They fall off, one at a time. All return for a curtain call.

The Hippopotamus Song by Michael Flanders and Donald Swann; illus. by Nadine Bernard Westcott.

The Secret Hiding Place by Rainey Bennett. Little hippo leaves life with the big herd.

Follow-up activities for home or school:
  •Learn about hippos. Why do they like water? How well can they swim? How long can they hold their breath?

91. Cow, Bull, Ox

Opening songs.

Read: *A Brown Cow* by Bijou Le Tord. A little brown cow lives in my backyard. Simple, gentle.

Read: *The Cow Who Fell in the Canal* by Phyllis Krasilovsky; illus. by Peter Spier. Hendrika falls into the canal and floats to the cheese market. Detailed illustrations of the countryside along a canal in The Netherlands.

Read: *How the Ox Star Fell from Heaven* retold and illus. by Lily Toy Hong. Sent to Earth with a message, the heavenly Ox Star blunders and is banished to work for humans henceforth. A Chinese myth with striking illustrations.

Form a circle and sing or chant:
  Hey, diddle diddle, the cat and the fiddle,
  The cow jumped over the moon.
  The little dog laughed to see such sport,
  And the dish ran away with the spoon.

Assign partners before you begin this song. Everyone pretends to fiddle along with the cat. Let children take turns being the cow and jumping over the moon. They can jump in pairs. You can place a moon cut from yellow or silver paper on the floor to jump over if you like. All laugh with the little dog. Repeat until everyone has had a turn at jumping. All lock arms with their partner and swing around on "the dish ran away with the spoon." I count "1-2-3-STOP!" as we swing our partners. This restrains overeager swingers.

Music: See the music on page 186.

Read: *The Story of Ferdinand* by Munro Leaf, illus. by Robert Lawson. Ferdinand likes to sit just quietly and smell the flowers. Then he is taken away to the bullfights in Madrid!

Make a cow/bull/ox puppet: Pre-cut brown circles for the cow's head. Precut horns. To make the horns I used gold paper and simply cut a small rectangle just big enough to fit the top of the "cow head." Then I scooped out a semi-circle in the top of the rectangle, and rounded the bottom corners to turn the rectangle into crescent-shaped horns. The children paste the horns on their cow head, add stick-on dots for eyes, and paste the head onto a tongue depressor.

Closing songs: Carry on some snorting, butting play with your cow puppets. Let the puppets sing goodbye to each of the books you have read.

More books to share:

A Calf Is Born by Joanna Cole; photos by Jerome Wexler. Photographs of a calf's birth.

Daisy by Brian Wildsmith. A cow dreams of seeing the world.

Flip and the Cows by Wesley Dennis. A foolish colt meets the cows.

Santa Cows by Cooper Edens; illus. by Daniel Lane. Santa Cows bring gifts.

Black and White by David Macaulay. Four tales interwoven, some featuring cows.

Follow-up activities for home or school:

•Visit a farm or a fair to see cows up close.

•Have a "Thank You, Cow" party and sample the things we eat made of milk: butter, cheese, cottage cheese, milk, buttermilk, yogurt, ice cream.

92. *Watching Foxes*

Opening songs.

Read: *Watching Foxes* by Jim Arnosky. Foxes play till mother returns.

Read: *What's in Fox's Sack?* An old English tale retold and illustrated by Paul Galdone. When fox's bee is eaten he takes the rooster who ate it. Through a series of such exchanges he ends up with a little boy in his bag.

Act out *What's in Fox's Sack?*: Bring a shawl to serve as your "sack." Wrap it around the child, pig, etc. as they are put into the sack. I ask for volunteers for fox, bee, pig, boy, dog. I place an adult with each group of bees, pigs, etc. Fox approaches each group and asks if he may leave his sack. The adult accepts the sack and promises not to open it. The "roosters" then fly out and eat the "bee," etc. Several children can play the part of the fox at once if they wish. I teach my foxes to chant *trot . . . trot . . . trot, trot, trot* as they move about the room.

Form a circle and play: "Fox goes traveling." All circle, chanting, "*Trot . . . trot . . . trot, trot, trot.*" The circle stops. We all open imaginary bags, and the children become bees and buzz around inside the circle. Children rejoin the circle and we circle again. We open the bags again and they fly out as roosters. Repeat with pig, boys and girls, dog. The dogs come out barking and the tale is over. We all pretend to eat a bit of gingerbread, then go back and sit down.

Read a poem: "The Red Fox" in *Earth Verse and Water Rhymes* by J. Patrick Lewis; illus. by Robert Sabuda, p. 11.

Read: *The Tomten and the Fox* by Astrid Lindgren. From a poem by Harald Wiberg. Tomten feeds a hungry fox who tries to steal hens.

Read and sing: *The Fox Went Out on a Chilly Night* by Peter Spier. I usually show only the double-page color spreads if the group is large. I talk a bit about the fact that foxes like to eat chicken before I begin. The music is on the last page of the book.

Make a fox and full moon picture: On sheets of dark blue paper, children paste one large yellow stick-on dot or a pre-cut yellow moon. Then they paste on one small brown stick-on dot as the fox's head. Provide a green crayon and a brown crayon for each child. Children draw on the fox's ears, body and tail with the brown crayon. With the green crayon they draw tall grass for the fox to hide in.

Closing songs: Begin with a reprise of the first verse of "Fox Went Out on a Chilly Night."

More books to share:

> *Father Fox's Pennyrhymes* by Clyde Watson; illus. by Wendy Watson. Fanciful rhymes recited by Father Fox to his young.
>
> *Fox's Dream* by Keizaburo Tejima. A fox travels in a winter forest.

Follow-up activities for home or school:

> •Play "Fox and Geese." This is most enjoyably played in winter when snow lies on the ground, but if there is no snow you can simply draw the game lines on the ground. To make your playing area, tramp out a large circle in the snow, perhaps 20 feet across. Tramp out spokes passing through the center of the circle. The "fox" stands in the circle center. The "geese" walk around the circumference, using only the paths you have made. The fox must venture out to catch a goose. If a goose can reach the circle center without being tagged by the fox, that goose is home free. Geese caught are brought to the center and held there. A caught goose can be freed by being tagged out by another goose. No one may step out of the snow trail and cut across where no trail has been made.

93. Whale Song

Opening songs.

Read: *The Life Cycle of the Whale* by Paula Z. Hogan; illus. by Karen Halt. Large illustrations and clear information about the life cycle of the humpback whale.

Read: *Winter Whale* by Joanne Ryder; illus. by Michael Rothman. Pretend you are a whale under the sea. Children may act this out with whooshing sounds and gentle diving motions as they listen.

Form a circle and sing:
I'm a whale.
I'm a whale.
See what I can do.
I can dive.
I can dive.
If you're a whale, you can too.

Ask the children to suggest things a whale can do—swim, spout, breach, slap their flippers—and sing of those.

Music: See the music on page 186.

Read: *I Wonder If I'll See a Whale* by Frances Ward Weller; illus. by Ted Lewin. On a whale-watching expedition, a girl sees a humpback up close. Great illustrations carry the somewhat wordy text for even young listeners.

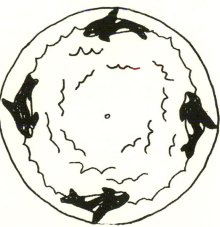

Make a whale wheel: Fold a sheet of 8½ × 11-inch paper in half and cut a slit 3 inches deep. Photocopy the whale wheel shown here enlarged to 225% (about 5¼" across) and cut out one wheel for each child. Kids color the whale wheel, adults fasten it to the paper with a brad. Slip the wheel up through the slot in the page.

Fasten it about 1 inch *below* the slot in the paper in the exact center. Children can draw on waves, seagulls, boats, etc.

SLIP WHEEL IN SLOT

← FASTEN WITH BRAD

Closing songs.

More books to share:

The Grouchy Ladybug by Eric Carle. A grouchy ladybug challenges ever larger creatures to fight, until it meets a WHALE, who gives it such a SLAP.

John Tabor's Ride by Blair Lent. A whaling ballad.

Sing a Whale Song by Tom Chapin and John Forster; illus. by Jerry Smath. Picture book version of Tom Chapin's ecological song.

Whale in the Sky by Anne Siberell. Whale chases salmon, but Thunderbird carries Whale away.

The Whale's Song by Dyan Sheldon; illus. by Gary Blythe. A grandmother recalls a visit from the whales. Lily hears them call her name.

Follow-up activities for home or school:

•Check out books from the library and learn more about whales. Find pictures in magazines or photocopy pictures from books and make a gallery of whale pictures. Learn the names of the different whales.

•Listen to a recording of whale song.

•View: *Burt Dow, Deep-Water Man.* Based on the book by Robert McCloskey. If the film is not available, read the book. It will need some cutting for younger listeners, as it is a bit lengthy.

94. The Goose Got Loose

Opening songs.

Read: *Catching the Wind* by Joanne Ryder; illus. by Michael Rothman. A girl imagines she is a Canada goose for a day.

Act out: Tell the children, "Pretend you are a Canada goose. Stretch out your neck. Flap your big wings. Fly away. Fly over trees. Fly over houses." Let the children suggest what you are flying over. Then suggest: "Let's all land in that pond. Land with a SPLASH. Float around in the pond. Paddle with your big feet and swim around. Take a long drink of water. Stretch your neck high and let the water run down your throat." Next, climb up on the shore, waddle around, eat some grass, fly back home, and all sit down.

Read a poem: "Wild Geese" by Sandra Liatsos in *Side by Side: Poems to Read Together* by Lee Bennett Hopkins; illus. by Hilary Knight, p. 22.

Read: *Lost in the Fog* by Irving Bacheller; illus. by Loretta Krupinski. A boy's rowboat is towed home by geese! Cut the text slightly for very young listeners. The illustrations carry well, but the text is a bit long.

Read: *Angus and the Ducks* by Marjorie Flack. Two ducks terrorize curious Angus, a Scottish terrier.

Sing and play:
> Flap your wings!
> You're a goose.
> Flap your wings!
> You're a goose.
> Flap your wings!
> You're a goose.
> You're a goose, my darling!

Ask the children what else geese do, and sing of those actions—"waddle around," "swim in the pond," etc. Your actions will be similar to those of your creative play after reading *Catching the Wind*. End by settling down on the shore with your head under your wing and going to sleep.

Music: See the music on page 171. Adapt the words to fit the tune of "Old Brass Wagon."

Read: *The Day the Goose Got Loose* by Reeve Lindbergh; illus. by Steven Kellogg. Bouncy chant about wild animal antics on "the day the goose got loose." Read this with a lilt and let the children join on the refrain, "The day the goose got LOOSE."

For older listeners add: *Ducks* by Daniel Pinkwater. A giant duck gives Scott a heavenly chariot, then drags Scott to heaven and takes the chariot back.

Make a snow goose: Pre-cut goose bodies and wings. Using a sheet of white typing paper, free-cut a goose body with a long neck. Fold a piece of white typing paper in half and free-cut two  identical goose wings. Children assemble the geese by folding the end of each wing over as a tab and gluing it to the bird body. Children draw on feathers and eyes. If you hold the goose by its tummy and wave it up and down, the wings should flap.

Closing songs. Sing a refrain or two of "Flap your wings, you're a goose" while flapping your paper birds around the room.

More books to share:

Iktomi and the Ducks: A Plains Indian Story by Paul Goble. Iktomi tricks the ducks by making them dance with their eyes closed and then whacking them over the head. Kindergarten and older children appreciate Iktomi's errant ways. This can be used with preschoolers if they have already been introduced to Iktomi's character through Goble's other books.

Springtime for Jeanne-Marie by Françoise. Jeanne-Marie's pet duck Madelon swims away.

Follow-up activities for home or school:

•Visit a lake or pond to watch ducks and geese. Make a list of things the children observe about them. How do they eat? How do they land in the water? How do they take off?

•Visit a farm where geese or ducks are raised. How does the farmer care for them? Why does he raise them?

•Create a collage using goose down or feathers.

•Examine goose down and goose feathers. How does the goose keep warm?

•Stuff a small pillow with goose down or feathers. Craft shops carry a variety of feathers, but it might be cheaper to watch for a sale and buy a feather pillow to cut up for your feather supply.

♪ Music ♪

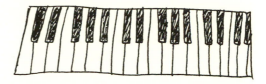

These music storytimes are planned to incorporate extended rhythm instrument play and musical activities centered on a book-related theme. Each program features one book and extends that book through dance, creative drama, musical instrument play, and a craft activity. I use the instruments to teach dynamics and rhythm and to accompany ourselves as we sing, march, and dance.

In order to use the rhythm instruments effectively, you need to take a great deal of time in your initial session. Discuss the instruments as you pass them out and ask the children not to begin playing them until they are given the signal. This seems restrictive, but if you do not do this the room soon turns into chaos. The children sit in a circle with their instrument on the floor in front of them. As director, you instruct them to pick up their instruments when you give the command, "Pick up your instruments." Then give the command, "Get ready, get set, play your instruments!" Count the beat for them as they play:

"One, Two, Three, Four!" Practice just playing a four/four beat at first. Call, "Rest!" and tell them that means to stop playing.

To practice dynamics, I let them bang away on their instruments in a total cacaphony, playing without rhythm. I tell them to play louder if I raise my arms high, softer if I lower them. They must stop all together when I place my instrument on the floor and call out, "Rest!" Even very young children can learn to follow these commands with a little practice.

You can now lead them in playing to the beat as you sing or you can march and play to a recording. I like Hap Palmer's *Modern Tunes for Rhythms and Instruments.* It has very simple rhythms—so simple we can even perform in two-part rhythm after a few weeks of practice!

A good song to sing for rhythm instrument play is "Play Your Instruments and Make a Pretty Sound" from the Ella Jenkins album of that name. We sing this over and over, letting each instrument take a solo chorus at the song's end, until everyone has had a turn to be part of a solo chorus.

My "rhythm instrument play" section of the storytime might consist of these activities:

1. Pass out instruments.
2. Practice dynamics.
3. Practice a rhythm.
4. Sing a song while clapping in rhythm.
5. Sing the same song while playing our instruments.
6. March or dance to a recording while playing our instruments.
7. Put our instruments away and sit back down.

Your rhythm instrument activities need not be elaborate. For this young age group, keep it simple and keep it controlled.

95. Frida the Wondercat

Opening songs.

Rhythm instrument play.

Read: *Frida the Wondercat* by Betsy Everitt. When Frida the cat wears her magic collar she can drive a bus, cook, and even play the piano!

Put on a Wondercat concert: Show a blue paper collar. Pretend it is like Frida's. I use crepe paper with silver stars to make mine. Put it on one child at a time. Announce a concert by Frida the Wondercat! The child then runs to the piano, plays a quick tune (in other words, strikes several random keys), runs back, and sits down amid applause. I do not go with the child to the piano, but stay with the group. I select bold children for the first few players, and the rest follow their lead. Any note the child hit was greeted with approval. When wearing the Wondercat collar, *anyone* is empowered to perform!

Make a Wondercat collar: We pasted stars on strips of blue crepe paper and taped them into a circular collar to wear.

Closing songs.

96. *Rattle, Rattle, Rattlesnake*

Opening songs.

Rhythm instrument play.

Read: *Baby Rattlesnake* by Te Ata; adapted by Lynn Moroney; illus. by Veg Reisberg. Baby Rattlesnake wants a rattle SO bad, but is just too young to use it properly.

Act out: *Baby Rattlesnake*. Let the children acting the part of the Rattlesnake hide maracas behind their backs, then leap out to scare the passing animals. I use one rabbit, a turtle, and the chief's daughter, though other animals could be added. The rest of the children play the role of the baby rattlesnake and all leap out at once to terrorize the passing animal.

Make a Baby Rattlesnake: Put a few grains of popcorn in a long envelope. Shake all the grains to one end of the envelope and then fold over about one inch of envelope with the rattling grains trapped in the fold. Staple this to hold the fold in place. Give one to each

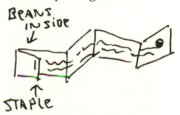

child. (The part of the envelope with the grains in it is the snake's tail.) The children affix a stick-on dot to the other end of the envelope as an eye. They draw lines along the length of the envelope to decorate the rattlesnake.

Act out *Baby Rattlesnake* again: The teacher acts the parts of rabbit, turtle, and girl. This time, let all of the children scare YOU with their rattlesnakes.

Closing songs.

97. *Whiffle Squeek!*

Opening songs.

Rhythm instrument play.

Read: *Whiffle Squeek!* by Caron Lee Cohen; illus. by Ted Rand. Whiffle Squeek wears a hat of octopus arms, boots of jellyfish squish, etc.

Play with *Whiffle Squeek!*: Give each adult-child group a copy of one stanza of the poem. I usually photocopy the stanzas describing Whiffle Squeek's attire and Gazook Gaboot's tongue, fire, etc. Ask each adult-child group to read the poem aloud and decide which rhythm instrument would best make a sound effect to illustrate the "jellyfish squish," "sea-green weed," etc. Let each child select his/her instrument and practice with the adult. If you do not have adults included in the storytime, read each stanza aloud to the group. Then let a child volunteer for that stanza and go select an instrument. Perform the poem with the children playing their sound effect instruments as their stanzas are spoken. In adult-child groups, the adult should read aloud the child's stanza while the child performs. I usually perform this through the descriptions of Whiffle and Gaboot and stop before Gaboot begins his eating routine.

Paste up a Whiffle Squeek: Photocopy Whiffle Squeek from the title page. Paste on green cellophane. Easter grass is excellent for "sea-green weed" and "octopus arms"; pink or white cellophane for "jellyfish squish"; tiny cut-out silver fish for "misfit fish," etc.

Closing songs.

98. Dancing Puppets

Opening songs.

Rhythm instrument play.

Read: *Coppelia: The Story of the Ballet* by Krystyna Turska. The illustrations in this story from the ballet are fine for preschoolers, but you will need to retell the story in simpler language. This story of a lifesize doll has pre-school appeal.

Pretend: To be marionettes! Show a marionette first, if possible. Lift its legs one at a time and make its hands wave to illustrate how the strings lift the limbs. Now pretend YOU are a marionette. Lift one leg. Lift the other. Lift one arm. Lift the other. Bend from the waist, etc.

Sing and dance:
> See them dance, dance, dance.
> See the little marionettes!

See them dance, dance, dance.
One small turn and then they stop.

Sing it also in French if you like:
    Ainsi font, font, font,
    Les petites marionettes!
    Ainsi font, font, font.
    Trois petits tours et puis s'en vont.

Ask the children what else a marionette could do, and sing: "See them jump,
    jump, jump"; "See them kick, kick, kick"; "See them wave, wave, wave";
    "See them bend, bend, bend."
Music: See the music on page 187.
Make a simple marionette: Cut paper into
    pieces measuring 3 × 2 inches. Split
    the paper three quarters of the way up
    the middle to make two legs. Fasten a
    piece of yarn about 10 inches long to
    the bottom of the right leg with a large
    stick-on dot.

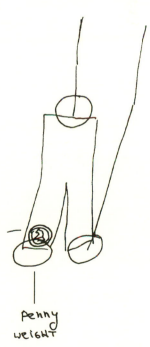

Fasten a piece of yarn the same length to
    the top for head using a large stick-on
    dot. This dot also forms the head. Add
    a third stick-on dot to the left leg for
    symmetry, but no yarn. Fasten a penny
    behind the left leg with tape to weight
    it down. Your puppet can kick his
    right leg, bow, and jump. It takes
    about five minutes to make, and pre-
    schoolers can do it with little help.
Closing songs: Sing the marionette song
    again and make your paper marionette
    dance, kick, jump, and bow.

penny
weight

99. The House That Jack Built

Opening songs.

Rhythm instrument play.

View: *The House That Jack Built*. 15 min. Video. Billy Seago signs the tales. Lively telling, with a voice-over by Ted Hinkey. Discuss a few of Billy's signs before viewing: house, corn, rat, cat, dog, cow with crumpled horn, maiden all forlorn, man all tattered and torn, priest all shaven and shorn, cock that crowed in the morn. Play rhythm sticks during the telling, clacking them each time Billy uses his hammer to "knock knock."

Act out "The House That Jack Built": Keep a rhythmic beat going as you recite. Make the signs as you go along. Different children might act out the corn, rat, and so on.

Read: *A Very Special House* by Ruth Krauss; illus. by Maurice Sendak. Emphasize the beat of the story. All join in on the "Oooie, Oooie," "Snore, snore, snore," etc.

Make rhythm sticks: Give each child two foot-long pieces of wooden dowel to use as rhythm sticks. The children can decorate them with crayons. Use them to play "knock, knock, knock" as you recite, "This Is the House That Jack Built."

Note: If you need the text, see: "This Is the House That Jack Built" in *Mother Goose: The Classic Volland Edition* by Eulalie Osgood Grover; illus. by Frederick Richardson, pp. 60–61.

Closing songs.

100. Skip to My Lou

Opening songs.

Rhythm instrument play.

Read: *Skip to My Lou* by Nadine Bernard Westcott. An illustrated version of this folk song.

Sing and dance: "Skip to My Lou."

Music: See the music on page 187.

Sing the story: Read *Skip to My Lou* again, this time *singing* and letting the children join in on the refrain.

Make a dancing hoop: Bend florist's wire into a circle and fasten ends together. Cover the ends with tape to hold them fast. Give one hoop to each child. The children tape on streamers of crepe paper or ribbon. Hold your hoops and wave them as you dance. (You can also make the hoops from coffee can lids by cutting out the plastic in the middle, leaving a ring.)

Closing songs. Dance, waving your hoops.

Note: My favorite recording for dancing to "Skip to My Lou" is by Mike and Peggy Seeger, *American Folk Songs for Children*. Play your dancing music as the children enter the room and during the craft work, as well as during your dancing period.

101. The Jumblies

Opening songs.

Rhythm instrument play.

Talk about floating: Float objects in a pan of water and watch them bob. Try to float objects that will not float. Include a sieve (which sinks).

Sing:
> All the ducks are floating in the water.
> Floating in the water,
> Floating in the water.
> All the ducks are floating in the water,
> Heigh-ho, rowly rowly day!

Sing about other things that float. Pretend you are the ducks, boats, ferry boats, whales, etc. Let the children suggest floating objects.

Music: See the music on page 165.

Read: *The Jumblies* by Edward Lear; illus. by Ted Rand. Encourage the children to join in the refrain, "Their heads are green and their hands are blue, and they went to sea in a sieve."

Activity: Make a "Jumblie goes to sea" picture. Make two copies of the title page of *The Jumblies*. Cut out the Jumblies and paste up a master, then reproduce enough Jumblies for each child to have one. Cut them out roughly. Give each child a Jumblie, a piece of paper, a green crayon, and a blue crayon. Cut from magazines or book jackets a number of objects on which the Jumblie might "go to sea." Chairs, cars, cribs, cereal boxes, cups—anything you can find will do, the sillier the better. Let each child select the picture of the object upon which his or her Jumblie will go to sea. Each child draws a line of blue water across his page. Paste the silly object onto the page so that it is floating on the blue water line. Paste the Jumblie onto the object. Color his head and hands.

Admire your Jumblies: Hold each child's picture up and chant together, "Far and few, far and few, are the lands where the Jumblies live / Their heads are green, their hands are blue / And they went to sea on a . . . CEREAL BOX!" Refer to whatever the child has used in the picture. Encourage the group to chant the refrain with you each time you hold up a picture.

Closing songs. Take time to sing, "Goodbye to the Jumblies!"

Appendix: Musical Notation for Songs

Opening Song
Jenny, Jenny, Are You Here?

Child answers

Jen- ny Jen- ny are you here? Yes yes I am here.

Hello Song
Hello Everybody

Hel - lo ev - ery - bo - dy yes in - deed.

Yes in - deed. Yes in - deed. Hel - lo ev - ery - bo - dy

yes in - deed. Yes in - deed my dar - ling.

Hello Song
Hello, Hello, We Are Glad to Meet You

Hel - lo hel - lo we are glad to meet you.

Hel - lo hel - lo hel - lo ev - ery one.

Goodbye Song
Goodbye to the (Airplanes) (substitute storytime topic)

Goodbye Song
Our Storytime Is Over

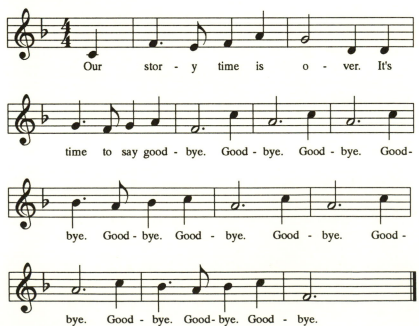

Program 1
I See the Moon   Ditty by M. MacDonald

Programs 2 and 101
At the Bottom of the Pond   Folk Song

166

Program 3
Walking in the Woods   Chant by M. MacDonald

Programs 5, 8, 22, 27, 30, 42, 53, 54
I Wish I Were a Baby   Folk Song

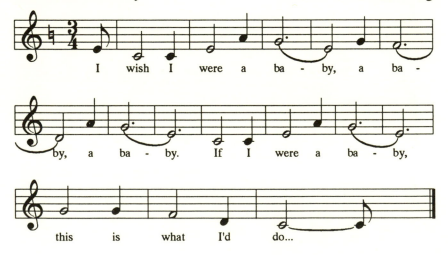

Program 6
Kitchen! Kitchen!   Ditty by M. MacDonald

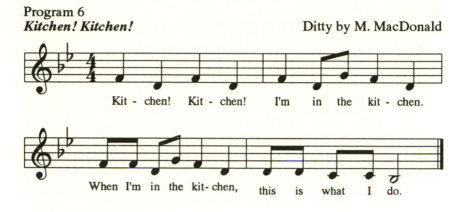

Kit - chen! Kit - chen! I'm in the kit - chen.

When I'm in the kit- chen, this is what I do.

Program 7
The Fat Cat Song   Ditty by M. MacDonald

I will eat eat eat eat eat. Till I'm

fat fat fat fat fat. I will eat eat eat eat

eat. I'm a fat fat fat fat CAT!

Programs 10, 16, 64, 82
Bluebird, Bluebird, Fly Through My Window

Blue-bird, blue-bird, fly through my win-dow.
Blue-bird, blue-bird, fly through my win-dow. Blue-bird, blue-bird,
fly through my win-dow, ear-ly in the mor - ning.

Program 15
Trot Trot   Ditty by M. MacDonld

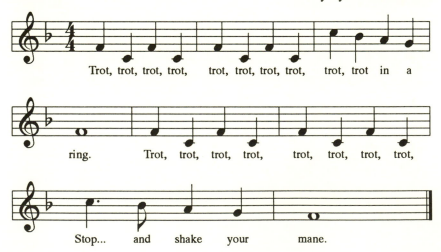

Trot, trot, trot, trot, trot, trot, trot, trot, trot, trot in a
ring. Trot, trot, trot, trot, trot, trot, trot, trot,
Stop... and shake your mane.

Program 18
I'll Dress Up   Ditty by M. MacDonald

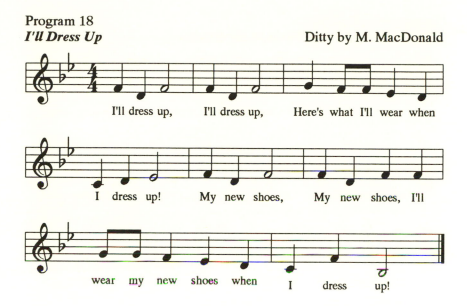

I'll dress up, I'll dress up, Here's what I'll wear when

I dress up! My new shoes, My new shoes, I'll

wear my new shoes when I dress up!

Program 23
Los Maderos de San Juan   Folk Song

As - e- rin, as - e-ran, los ma-de-ros de San Juan.

As - e- rin, as - e-ran, los ma-de-ros de San Juan.

Programs 24, 41, 51, 60
The Recycling Song (What Shall We Do with the Drunken Sailor?)

What shall we do with a piece of pa - per?

What shall we do with a piece of pa - per?

What shall we do with a piece of pa - per?

How can we re - cy - cle?

Program 25
When I Go to Grandma's House

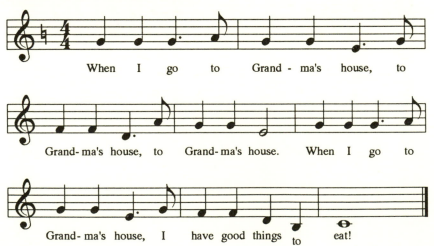

When I go to Grand - ma's house, to

Grand- ma's house, to Grand- ma's house. When I go to

Grand- ma's house, I have good things to eat!

Program 29
Circle Time Song: The Old Brass Wagon

Cir - cle to the left, the old brass wa - gon.

Cir-cle to the left, the old brass wa-gon. Cir-cle to the left, the

old brass wa-gon. You're the one, my dar - ling.

Program 32
Did You Ever Go A-Fishin'?   Folk Song

Did you ev- er go a-fish-in' on a hot sum-mer day?

Sit - tin' on a log, and the log rolls a - way.

Al - li - ga - tor bites you by the seat of the pants, and

all the lit - tle fish-ies do the hoo - chy koo - chy dance.

Program 33
Rock-a-Bye Baby   Folk Song

Rock - a - bye ba - by, in the tree top.

When the wind blows, the cra - dle will rock.

When the bough breaks, the cra - dle will fall, and

down will come ba - by cra - dle and all.

Program 34
Whoops Song   Adapted by M. MacDonald

When I was play - ing yes - ter - day, when

I was play - ing yes - ter - day, when I was play - ing

yes - ter - day, some - thing hap - pened to me! I

(continued)

fell off my be - d   yes - ter - day, I   fell off my be - d

yes - ter - day, I   fell off my be - d   yes - ter - day,

that's   what   hap - pened   to   me!

Program 35
Look What I Can Do!   Ditty by M. MacDonald

Look what I can   do.   Look what I can   do.

I can do most   an - y-thing!   Look what I can   do!

Program 40
I Am BIG BIG BIG   Ditty by M. MacDonald

I am BIG BIG BIG BIG BIG. I am
STRONG STRONG STRONG STRONG STRONG. I'm a
LI-ON LI-ON LION. Hear me ROAR ROAR ROAR ROAR
ROAR. But I'm GEN-TLE GEN-TLE GEN-TLE with my
friend the lit-tle boy.

Program 43
The Chewing Gum Song   Folk Song

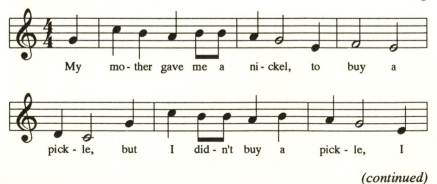

My mo-ther gave me a ni-ckel, to buy a
pick-le, but I did-n't buy a pick-le, I

(continued)

bought some chew - ing gum. La da da da da

chew-ing gum, la da da chew-ing gum. La da da

chew-ing gum. La da da chew - ing gum.

Program 47

The Kookaburra Song

Folk Song

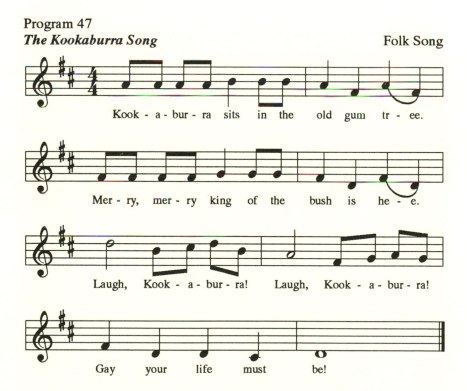

Kook - a - bur - ra sits in the old gum tr - ee.

Mer - ry, mer - ry king of the bush is he - e.

Laugh, Kook - a - bur - ra! Laugh, Kook - a - bur - ra!

Gay your life must be!

Program 49
Mmbera

Mm - ber - a.   Mm - ber - a.   Mm - ber -

a   Mm - ber - a   ya   sti - me - la.

Pass shoe on first beat of each measure.

NA   na   na   NA   na   NA   na   na   NA   na.

NA   na   na   NA   na   NA   na   na   NA   na.

Program 56
The Groundhog Song   M. MacDonald

Ground - hog's   sleep - ing   un - der - neath   the   ground.

Feb - ru - a - ry   sec - ond,   he   wakes   and   looks   a - round.

Climbs   up   from   his   hole   so   sleep - i - ly.

(continued)

"That's my SHA - DOW! It's back to bed for me!"

Program 58
Peter Rabbit, Hop! Hop! Hop!

Jennifer MacDonald

Pe - ter Rab - bit Hop! Hop! Hop!

Wig-gles his nose when he stops, stops, stops! Pe - ter Rab - bit

Hop! Hop! Hop! Wig-gles his ears with a flip, flip, flop!

Pe - ter Rab - bit Hop! Hop! Hop! Wig-gles his tail with a

bip, bip, bop! Pe - ter Rab - bit Hop! Hop! Hop!

Nib - bl - ing car - rots all the way!

Program 58
Pretty Peter Pink Ears

Martha Nishitani

Pret - ty Pe - ter   Pink Ears!   Pret - ty Pe - ter

Pink Ears!   Pret - ty Pe - ter   Pink Ears!   Pret - ty Pe - ter

Pink Ears!   Run, run, run, run,   hop,   hop!

Run, run, run, run,   hop,   hop!   Run, run, run, run,

hop,   hop!   Run, run, run, run,   JUMP,   JUMP!

Program 61
The Scarecrow Song

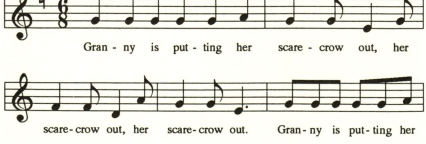

Gran - ny is put - ting her   scare - crow out, her

scare - crow out, her   scare - crow out.   Gran - ny is put - ting her

(continued)

scare - crow out, to scare a - way the crows.

Program 62
Aiken Drum   Scottish Folk Song

The - re was a man lived in the moon, lived

in the moon, lived in the moon, The - re was a man lived

Chorus

in the moon, and his name was Ai - ken Drum. And he

played up-on a la - dle, a la - dle, a la - dle, and he

played up-on a la - dle, and his name was Ai-ken Drum.

Program 65
A Falling Star Stretch

M. MacDonald

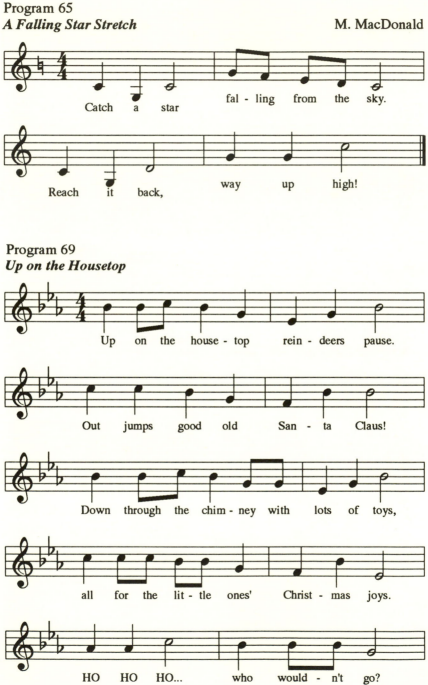

Catch a star fal - ling from the sky.

Reach it back, way up high!

Program 69
Up on the Housetop

Up on the house - top rein - deers pause.

Out jumps good old San - ta Claus!

Down through the chim - ney with lots of toys,

all for the lit - tle ones' Christ - mas joys.

HO HO HO... who would - n't go?

(continued)

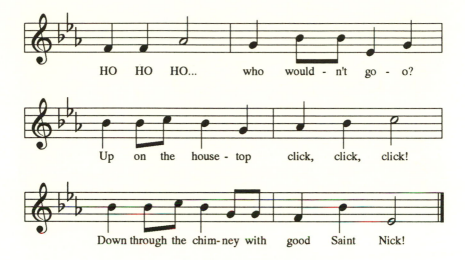

HO HO HO... who would-n't go - o?

Up on the house-top click, click, click!

Down through the chim-ney with good Saint Nick!

Programs 38, 71
Shake My Hand and You'll Be My Friend

Shake my hand and you'll be my friend, you'll

be my friend, you'll be my friend. Shake my hand and you'll

be my friend. We'll all be friends.

Program 72
Pass the Balloon

Action Song by M. MacDonald

Pass the bal - loon, pass the bal - loon,

pass the bal - loon, all a - round the room.

Program 74
The Sweeping Stretch

M. MacDonald

Sweep, sweep, sweep so high. Sweep, sweep, sweep the sky! -

———— Sweep, sweep, sweep so low.

Sweep, sweep down be - low.————

Program 77
Scrub-a-dub-dub
Ditty by M. MacDonald

Scrub - a - dub - dub, scrub - a - dub - dub,

scrub - a - dub - dub - dub, scrub - a - dub - dub.

Program 77
This Is the Way We Wash Our Clothes
Folk Song

This is the way we wash our clothes,

wash our clothes, wash our clothes.

This is the way we wash our clothes, so

ear - ly in - the morn - ing.

Program 78
Ten in the Bed   Folk Song

There were ten in the bed, and the lit-tle one said, "Roll o-ver! Roll o-ver!" So they all rolled o-ver and one fell out...

Program 85
Old Brown Bear   M. MacDonald

Old Brown Bear, sleep-ing in his den. Lit-tle chip-munk tick-les him and runs back home a-gain.

Program 87
The Eensy Weensy Spider   Folk Song

The Een-sy Ween-sy Spi-der went up the wa-ter

(continued)

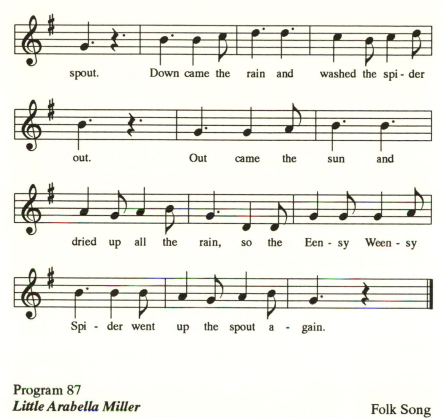

spout. Down came the rain and washed the spi - der

out. Out came the sun and

dried up all the rain, so the Een - sy Ween - sy

Spi - der went up the spout a - gain.

Program 87
Little Arabella Miller

Folk Song

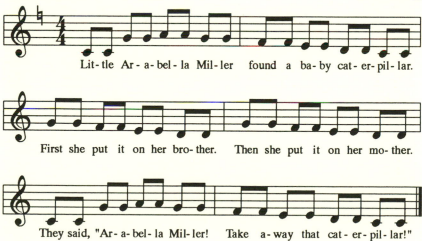

Lit-tle Ar - a-bel-la Mil-ler found a ba-by cat-er-pil-lar.

First she put it on her bro-ther. Then she put it on her mo-ther.

They said, "Ar-a-bel-la Mil-ler! Take a-way that cat-er-pil-lar!"

Program 91
Hey, Diddle Diddle
Folk Song

Hey, did-dle did-dle, the cat and the fid-dle, the cow jumped o-ver the moon. The lit-tle dog laughed to see such sport, and the dish ran a-way with the spoon.

Program 93
I'm a Whale
M. MacDonald

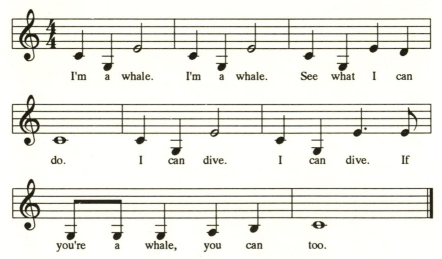

I'm a whale. I'm a whale. See what I can do. I can dive. I can dive. If you're a whale, you can too.

Program 98
Marionettes

Folk Song

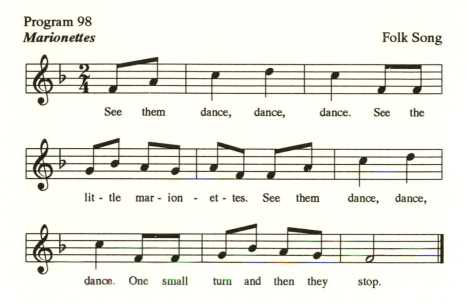

See them dance, dance, dance. See the
lit - tle mar - ion - et - tes. See them dance, dance,
dance. One small turn and then they stop.

Program 100
Skip to My Lou

Folk Song

Lou, Lou, skip to my Lou. Lou, Lou, skip to my Lou.
Lou, Lou. skip to my Lou. Skip to my Lou, my dar - ling.

Bibliography

* The item is used in the suggested program
# The item is an additional source for the program

Books and Recordings

Abercrombie, Barbara. *Charlie Anderson*; illus. by Mark Graham. New York: Margaret K. McElderry, 1990. *31 Families, Families, and More Families.

Ackerman, Karen. *Song and Dance Man*; illus. by Stephen Gammell. New York: Knopf, 1988. *18 Dress Up; #28 Grandpa and Me.

Adams, Adrienne. *The Christmas Party*. New York: Scribner's, 1978. #63 Parties.

Adams, Adrienne. *A Woggle of Witches.* New York: Scribner's, 1971. #86 Bats, Bats, Bats.

Adams, Pam. *Old MacDonald Had a Farm*; illus. by Pam Adams. Wiltshire, England: Child's Play, 1975. *52 What Is a Book?

Adams, Pam. *There Was an Old Lady Who Swallowed a Fly*. Purton, Wiltshire, England: Child's Play, 1973. *#87 Spiders.

Adler, David. *You Think It's Fun to Be a Clown!*; illus. by Ray Cruz. Garden City, N.Y.: Doubleday, 1980. *9 Upside Down Day. *#82 Inside, Outside, Upside Down.

Adoff, Arnold. *Greens;* illus. by Betsy Lewin. New York: Lothrop, Lee and Shepard, 1988. #83 Green.

Adoff, Arnold. *Hard to Be Six*; illus. by Cheryle Hanna. New York: Lothrop, Lee & Shepard, 1991. #41 Youngest One.

Adoff, Arnold. *Ma nda la*. New York: Harper & Row, 1971. *61 Scarecrows.

Alexander, Martha. *How My Library Grew by Dinah*. New York: H.W. Wilson, 1982. #52 What Is a Library?

Alexander, Martha. *Move Over, Twerp*. New York: Dial, 1981. #39 Small Creatures Meet Big Bullies.

Alexander, Martha. *Nobody Asked Me If I Wanted a Baby Sister*. New York: Dial, 1971. #8 Bad Babies.

Aliki. *Hush Little Baby*. Englewood Cliffs, N.J.: Prentice-Hall, 1968. *#33 Lullaby.

Alston, Eugenia. *Come Visit a Prairie Dog Town*; illus. by St. Tamar. New York: Harcourt Brace Jovanovich, 1976. #56 Groundhog Day.

American Folk Songs for Children by Mike and Peggy Seeger. Cambridge, Mass.: Rounder Records, 1987. Rou–8001/02/03. *#100 Skip to My Lou.

Andersen, Hans Christian. *The Princess and the Pea*; illus. by Paul Galdone. New York: Clarion, 1978. #78 Bedtime.

Anderson, Lonzo. *Izzard*; illus. by Adrienne Adams. New York: Scribner's, 1973. #89 Crafty Chameleon.

Andrews, Jan. *Very Last First Time*; illus. by Ian Wallace. Vancouver: Douglas & McInytre, 1985. *45 Northern Winter.

Aragon, Jane Chelsea. *Salt Hands*; illus. by Ted Rand. New York: Dutton, 1989. *1 A Walk in the Moonlight; #40 Gentle Giants; *#88 Timid Deer.

Argent, Trinca, Rod, and Kerry. *One Woolly Wombat*; illus. by Kerry Argent. Brooklyn, N.Y.: Kane/Miller, 1985. *47 Koala, Kangaroo, and Kookaburra.

Arnosky, Jim. *Come Out Muskrats*. New York: Lothrop, Lee & Shepard, 1989. *2 At the Bottom of the Pond.

Arnosky, Jim. *Deer at the Brook*. New York: Lothrop, Lee & Shepard, 1986. *88 The Timid Deer.

Arnosky, Jim. *Raccoons and Ripe Corn*. New York: Lothrop, Lee & Shepard, 1987. *1 A Walk in the Moonlight.

Arnosky, Jim. *Watching Foxes*. New York: Lothrop, Lee & Shepard, 1985. *92 Watching Foxes.

Asch, Frank. *Baby in a Box*. New York: Holiday House, 1989. *75 What Can You Do with a Box?

Asch, Frank. *Just Like Daddy*. New York: Simon Schuster, 1981. *32 Gone Fishing.

Asch, Frank. *Oats and Wild Apples*. New York: Holiday House, 1988. #88 The Timid Deer.

Ata, Te. *Baby Rattlesnake*. Retold by Lynn Moroney; illus. by Veg Reisberg. San Francisco: Children's Book Press, 1989. #96 Rattle, Rattle, Rattlesnake.

Atwood, Ann. *Haiku—Vision in Poetry and Photography*. New York: Scribner's, 1977. #50 Reaching the Sky.

Aylesworth, Jim. *Country Crossing*; illus. by Ted Rand. New York: Atheneum, 1991. * 14 Out the Train Window.

Bacheller, Irving. *Lost in the Fog*; illus. by Loretta Krupinski. Boston: Little, Brown, 1990. *#94 The Goose Got Loose.

Baker, Alan. *Benjamin's Book*. New York: Lothrop, Lee & Shepard, 1982. *#22 If I Were a Painter.

Baker, Alan. *Benjamin's Portrait*. New York: Lothrop, Lee & Shepard, 1986. *#22 If I Were a Painter.

Baker, Jeannie. *Where the Forest Meets the Sea*. New York: Greenwillow, 1987. *#4 Into the Rain Forest. #47 Koala, Kangaroo, and Kookaburra.

Baker, Keith. *Who Is the Beast?* San Diego: Harcourt Brace Jovanovich, 1990. *#4 Into the Rain Forest.

Balian, Lorna. *Bah Humbug.* Nashville: Abingdon, 1982. #69 Youngest One at Christmas.

Balian, Lorna. *A Garden for a Groundhog.* Nashville: Abingdon, 1985. *56 Groundhog Day.

Balian, Lorna. *Wilbur's Space Machine.* New York: Holiday House, 1990. #72 What Can You Do with a Balloon?

Bang, Betsy. *The Old Woman and the Red Pumpkin: A Bengali Folk Tale*; illus. by Molly Garrett Bang. New York: Macmillan, 1975. *48 Indian Festival.

Bang, Betsy. *The Old Woman and the Rice Thief*; illus. by Molly Garrett Bang. New York: Macmillan, 1978. *48 Indian Festival.

Bang, Betsy. *Tuntuni the Tailor Bird*; illus. by Molly Garrett Bang. New York: Greenwillow, 1978. #10 Parrot Parties.

Bang, Molly. *Delphine.* New York: Morrow, 1988. *13 Safe Biker!

Bang, Molly Garrett. *Tye May and the Magic Brush.* New York: Greenwillow, 1981. #22 If I Were a Painter.

Barraca, Debra and Sal. *Maxi the Hero*; illus. by Mark Buehner. New York: Dial, 1991. #11 Toothgnasher Superflash.

Barton, Byron. *Hester.* New York: Greenwillow, 1975. *74 What Can You Do with a Broom?

Barton, Byron. *I Want to Be an Astronaut.* New York: Crowell, 1988. *21 Space Place.

Bash, Barbara. *Shadows of the Night: The Hidden World of the Little Brown Bat.* San Francisco: Sierra Club, 1992. #86 Bats, Bats, Bats.

Bate, Lucy. *How Georgina Drove the Car Very Carefully from Boston to New York*; illus. by Tamar Taylor. New York: Crown, 1989. #12 On the Road.

Bauer, Caroline Feller. *Midnight Snowman*; illus. by Catherine Stock. New York: Atheneum, 1987. *3 Winter Wonderland.

Bauer, Caroline Feller. *Too Many Books!*; illus. by Diane Paterson. New York: Viking Kestrel, 1984. #52 What Is a Book?

Bayley, Nicola. *Parrot Cat.* New York: Knopf, 1984. *16 Where Is the Green Parrot?

Behn, Harry. *Cricket Songs: Japanese Haiku*; illus. from Sesshu. New York: Harcourt, Brace and World, 1964. #50 Reaching the Sky.

Bemelmans, Ludwig. *Parsley.* New York: Harper, 1955. #88 Timid Deer.

Bennett, Jill. *A Cup of Starshine: Poems and Pictures for Young Children*; illus. by Graham Percy. San Diego: Harcourt Brace Jovanovich, 1991. *76 A Tooth! A Tooth!; *81 Small and Tall.

Bennett, Jill. *Days Are Where We Live and Other Poems*; illus. by Maureen Roffey. New York: Lothrop, Lee & Shepard, 1981. *77 Bathtime.

Bennett, Rainey. *The Secret Hiding Place.* Cleveland: World, 1960. #90 Happy Hippos.

Berenstain, Stan and Jan. *Bears in the Night.* New York: Random House, 1971. *17 Dance-a-Path.

Berenstain, Stan and Jan. *The Berenstain Bears and Mama's New Job.* New York: Random House, 1984. #29 Quilts to Remember.

Berenstain, Stan and Jan. *The Bike Lesson.* New York: Random House, 1964. *13 Safe Biker!

Berenstain, Stan and Jan. *Inside Outside, Upside Down.* New York: Random House, 1968. *9 Upside Down Day. *82 Inside, Outside, Upside Down.

Berson, Harold. *Kassim's Shoes.* New York: Crown, 1977. *46 To Grandad Abdullah's.

Berson, Harold. *Why the Jackal Won't Speak to the Hedgehog: A Tunisian Folktale.* New York: Seabury, 1969. *46 To Grandad Abdullah's.

Birdseye, Tom. *Airmail to the Moon;* illus. by Stephen Gammell. New York: Holiday House, 1988. #76 A Tooth!, A Tooth!

Blake, Quentin. *Cockatoos.* Boston: Little, Brown, 1992. *10 Parrot Parties.

Blos, Joan W. *The Grandpa Days;* illus. by Emily Arnold McCully. New York: Simon & Schuster, 1989. #23 Good Wood.

Bodsworth, Nan. *A Nice Walk in the Jungle.* New York: Puffin, 1989. *4 Into the Rain Forest.

Bogan, Louise and William Jay Smith, eds. *Golden Journey: Poems for Young Readers.* Chicago: Reilly & Lee, 1965. *83 Green.

Bonnici, Peter. *The Festival;* illus. by Lisa Kopper. Minneapolis: Carolrhoda, 1985. *48 Indian Festival.

Bonnici, Peter. *The First Rains;* illus. by Lisa Kopper. Minneapolis: Carolrhoda, 1985. #48 Indian Festival.

Brandenberg, Franz. *What's Wrong with a Van?;* illus. by Aliki. New York: Greenwillow, 1987. #24 Use It Again.

Bright, Robert. *My Red Umbrella.* New York: Morrow, 1959. #73 What Can You Do with an Umbrella?

Brillhart, Julie. *Story Hour—Starring Megan.* Morton Grove, Ill.: Whitman, 1992. *53 What Is a Library?

Bring a Torch, Jeanette Isabella! A Provençal carol attributed to Nicholas Saboly, 17th century; illus. by Adrienne Adams. New York: Scribner's, 1963. *68 Light a Candle.

Brimner, Larry Dane. *Country Bear's Good Neighbor;* illus. by Ruth Tietjen Councel. New York: Orchard, 1988. *60 A Fruitful Harvest; #66 Holiday Cake Tales.

Brown, Anthony. *I Like Books.* #52 What Is a Book?

Brown, Anthony. *Willy the Champ.* New York: Knopf, 1986. #39 Small Creatures Meet Big Bullies.

Brown, Anthony. *Willy the Wimp.* New York: Knopf, 1985. #39 Small Creatures Make Big Bullies.

Brown, Judy. *Peter's Pocket;* illus. by Julia Noonan. New York: Atheneum, 1974. #31 Families, Families, and More Families.

Brown, Marc. *Arthur's April Fool's Day.* New York: Little, Brown, 1983. #55 Trick an April Fool.

Brown, Marc. *Arthur's Tooth.* Boston: Little, Brown, 1985. *#76 A Tooth!, A Tooth!

Brown, Marc. *The True Francine*. Boston: Little, Brown, 1981. #34 Whoops!

Brown, Marc and Stephen Krensky. *Dinosaurs, Beware: A Safety Guide*. Boston: Little, Brown, 1982. #34 Whoops!

Brown, Marcia. *How Hippo!* New York, Scribner's, 1969. *#90 Happy Hippos.

Brown, Margaret Wise. *The Golden Egg Book*; illus. by Leonard Weisgard. New York: Golden, 1976. *54 Cra-a-ack!

Brown, Margaret Wise. *Goodnight Moon;* illus. by Clement Hurd. New York: Harper & Row, 1947. *33 Lullaby; #78 Bedtime.

Brown, Margaret Wise. *Quiet Noisy Book;* illus. by Leonard Weisgard. New York: Harper, 1950. #84 The Quiet Storytime.

Brown, Palmer. *Something for Christmas*. New York: Harper & Row, 1958. #71 Christmas Sharing. #69 Youngest One at Christmas.

Browne, Anthony. *I Like Books*. New York: Knopf, 1988. *52 What Is a Book?

Bruna, Dick. *Miffy's Bicycle*. New York: Price, Stern, Sloan, 1984. #13 Safe Biker!

Budbill, David. *Christmas Tree Farm*; illus. by Donald Carrick. New York: Macmillan, 1974. *70 Christmas Tree.

Buff, Mary and Conrad. *Dash and Dart*. New York: Viking, 1942. #88 The Timid Deer.

Bunting, Eve. *Night Tree*; illus. by Ted Rand. San Diego: Harcourt Brace Jovanovich, 1991. #70 Christmas Tree.

Burl Ives Sings Little White Duck. New York: Columbia, 1974. #20 Freaky Frog Day.

Burningham, John. *Mr. Gumpy's Motor Car*. New York: Crowell, 1973. *12 On the Road.

Burningham, John. *Mr. Gumpy's Outing*. New York: Holt, Rinehart & Winston, 1970. *34 Whoops!

Burningham, John. *Wobble Pop: Noisy Words*. New York: Viking, 1984. #74 What Can You Do with a Broom?

Byars, Betsy. *Go and Hush the Baby;* illus. by Emily Arnold McCully. New York: Viking, 1971. #8 Bad Babies.

Byrne, David. *Stay Up Late*; illus. by Maria Kalmar. New York: Viking Kestrel, 1987. #5 Here Comes the Babysitter!

Caines, Jeannette. *I Need a Lunch Box;* illus. by Pat Cummings. New York: Harper & Row, 1988. #75 What Can You Do with a Box?

Cannon, Janell. *Stellaluna*. San Diego: Harcourt Brace Jovanovich, 1993. *86 Bats, Bats, Bats.

Carle, Eric. *The Grouchy Ladybug*. New York: Crowell, 1977. *39 Small Creatures Meet Big Bullies; *93 Whale Song.

Carle, Eric. *The Mixed-up Chameleon*. New York: Crowell, 1984. #89 Crafty Chameleons.

Carle, Eric. *The Very Hungry Caterpillar*. New York: Philomel, 1979. *7 Greedy Glutton.

Carlson, Nancy. *Harriet's Halloween Candy*. Minneapolis: Carolrhoda, 1982. *38 I Want to Share with You Today.

Carlson, Nancy. *Loud Mouth George and the Sixth Grade Bully*. Minneapolis: Carol-rhoda, 1983. #39 Small Creatures Meet Big Bullies.

Carlson, Nancy. *A Visit to Grandma's*. New York: Viking, 1991. *25 Dinner at Grandma's House.

Carlstrom, Nancy White. *Baby-O*; illus. by Sucie Stevenson. Boston: Little, Brown, 1992. #31 Families, Families, and More Families.

Carlstrom, Nancy. *Poor Carl*. New York: Viking Kestrel, 1989. *8 Bad Babies; #41 Youngest One.

Carrick, Carol. *Dark and Full of Secrets*; illus. by Donald Carrick. New York: Clarion/Ticknor & Fields, 1984. *32 Gone Fishing.

Carrick, Carol. *The Highest Balloon on the Common*; illus. by Donald Carrick. New York: Greenwillow, 1977. #72 What Can You Do with a Balloon?

Carrick, Carol. *In the Moonlight, Waiting*; illus. by Donald Carrick. New York: Clarion, 1990. #1 A Walk in the Moonlight.

Casely, Judith. *When Grandpa Came to Stay*. New York: Greenwillow, 1986. #28 Grandpa and Me.

Chalmers, Mary. *Be Good, Harry*. New York: Harper & Row, 1967. #5 Here Comes the Babysitter!

Chalmers, Mary. *A Christmas Story*. New York: Harper & Row, 1956. #65 Holiday Stars.

Chalmers, Mary. *Throw a Kiss, Harry*. New York: Harper & Row, 1958. *37 Don't Be Shy.

Chapin, Tom and John Forster. *Sing a Whale Song;* illus. by Jerry Smath. New York: Random House, 1993. #93 Whale Song.

Charlip, Remy and Lilian Moore. *Hooray for Me!;* illus. by Vera B. Williams. New York: Parents, 1975. #35 I'm Proud to Be Me!

Chenery, Janet. *Wolfie*; illus. by Marc Simont. New York: Harper & Row, 1969. #87 Spiders.

Child, Lydia Maria. *Over the River and Through the Woods;* illus. by Brinton Turkle. New York: Coward, McCann & Geoghegan, 1979. *25 Dinner at Grandma's House. *67 Company's Coming.

Chönz, Selina. *Florina and the Wild Birds*. New York: Walck, 1953. #64 Winter Birds.

Claverie, Jean. *The Picnic*. New York: Crown, 1986. #27 Picnic!

Cleary, Beverly. *Lucky Chuck;* illus. by J. Winslow Higginbottom. New York: Morrow, 1984. #13 Safe Biker!; #34 Whoops!

Cleveland, David. *The April Rabbits*; illus. by Nurit Karlin. New York: Coward, McCann & Geoghegan, 1978. *55 Trick an April Fool.

Coatsworth, Elizabeth. *Good Night*; illus. by Jose Aruego. New York: Macmillan, 1972. *65 Holiday Stars.

Coatsworth, Elizabeth. *Under the Greenwillow*; illus. by Janina Domanska, New York: Macmillan, 1971. *83 Green.

Cobb, Vicki. *Writing It Down*; illus. by Marilyn Hafner. New York: Lippincott, 1989. #51 What Is Paper?

Coerr, Eleanor. *The Josephina Storyquilt*; illus. by Bruce Degen. New York: Harper & Row, 1986. #29 Quilts to Remember.

Cohen, Carol. *Wake Up, Groundhog*. New York: Crown, 1975. #56 Groundhog Day.

Cohen, Caron Lee. *Three Yellow Dogs!*; illus. by Peter Sis. New York: Greenwillow, 1986. #80 Three.

Cohen, Caron Lee. *Whiffle Squeek!*; illus. by Ted Rand. New York: Dodd, Mead, 1987. *62 Across the Bright Blue Sea. *#97 Whiffle Squeek!

Cole, Barbara Hancock. *Texas Star*; illus. by Barbara Minton. New York: Orchard, 1990. #29 Quilts to Remember.

Cole, Joanna. *A Calf Is Born*. Photos by Jerome Wexler. New York: Morrow, 1975. #91 Cow, Bull, Ox.

Cole, William. *Poem Stew*; illus. by Karen Ann Weinhaus. New York: Lippincott, 1981. *7 Greedy Gluttons.

Cone, Molly. *Louella and the Yellow Balloon*. New York: Crowell, 1988. *72 What Can You Do with a Balloon?

Cooney, Nancy Evans. *The Umbrella Day*; illus. by Melissa Bay Mathis. New York: Philomel, 1989. *73 What Can You Do with an Umbrella?

Cosner, Shaaron. *"Paper" Through the Ages*; illus. by Priscilla Kiedrowski. Minneapolis: Carolrhoda, 1984. #51 What Is Paper?

Cowicher, Helen. *Rain Forest*. New York: Farrar, Straus & Giroux, 1988. #4 Into the Rain Forest.

Craft, Ruth and Erik Blegvad. *The Winter Bear*. New York: Macmillan, 1974. *24 Use It Again.

Crews, Donald. *Bicycle Race*. New York: Greenwillow, 1985. #13 Safe Biker!

Crews, Donald. *Freight Train*. New York: Greenwillow, 1978. *12 On the Road.

Cristini, Ermanno, and Luigi Puricelli. *In the Pond*. Natick, Mass.: Picture Book Studio, 1984. *2 At the Bottom of the Pond.

Daly, Niki. *Not So Fast, Songololo*. New York: Atheneum, 1986. *49 South African Sing-Along.

Damrell, Liz. *Ride with the Wind*; illus. by Stephen Marchesi. New York: Orchard, 1991. *15 Ride Away!

Daugherty, James. *Andy and the Lion*. New York: Viking, 1979. *40 Gentle Giants. *53 What Is a Library?

David, Marguerite W. *The Heart of Wood*; illus. by Sheila Hamanaka. New York: Simon & Schuster, 1992. #23 Good Wood.

Day, Alexandra. *Carl's Masquerade*. New York: Farrar, Straus & Giroux, 1992. #63 Parties!

Day, Alexandra. *River Parade*. New York: Viking Penguin, 1990. *32 Gone Fishing.

Defty, Jeff. *Creative Fingerplays and Action Rhymes: An Index and Guide to Their Use*; illus. by Ellen Kae Hester. Phoenix, Ariz: Oryx, 1992.

Degen, Bruce. *Jamberry*. New York: Harper & Row, 1983. #60 A Fruitful Harvest.

Dennis, Wesley. *Flip and the Cows*. Hamden, Ct.: Linnet Books, 1989. #91 Cow, Bull, Ox.

Denslow, Sharon Phillips. *At Taylor's Place;* illus. by Nancy Carpenter. New York: Bradbury, 1990. *23 Good Wood.

De Paola, Tomie. *An Early American Christmas.* New York: Holiday House, 1987. *68 Light a Candle.

De Paola, Tomie. *The Art Lesson.* New York: Putnam's, 1989. *22 If I Were a Painter.

De Paola, Tomie. *The Cat on the Dovrefell.* New York: Putnam's, 1979. *63 Parties.

De Paola, Tomie. *Mother Goose.* New York: Putnam's, 1985.

De Paola, Tomie. *The Story of the Three Wise Kings.* New York: Putnam's, 1983. *65 Holiday Stars.

De Paola, Tomie. *Tom.* New York: Putnam's, 1993. #28 Grandpa and Me. #55 Trick an April Fool.

De Regniers, Beatrice Schenk. *May I Bring a Friend?* New York: Atheneum, 1964. *63 Parties.

Demi. *The Leaky Umbrella.* Englewood Cliffs, N.J.: Prentice-Hall, 1980. #74 What Can You Do with a Broom?

Dewey, Jennifer Owings. *At the Edge of the Pond.* Boston: Little, Brown, 1987. #2 At the Bottom of the Pond.

Domanska, Janina. *Din Dan Don It's Christmas.* New York: Greenwillow, 1975. *64 Winter Birds; #65 Holiday Stars.

Domanska, Janina. *I Saw a Ship A-Sailing.* New York: Macmillan, 1972. #62 Across the Bright Blue Sea.

Domanska, Janina. *What Do You See?* New York: Macmillan, 1974. *83 Green; *87 Spiders.

Dorros, Arthur. *Rain Forest Secrets.* New York: Scholastic, 1990. #4 Into the Rain Forest.

Douglass, Barbara. *Good As New;* illus. by Patience Brewster. New York: Lothrop, Lee & Shepard, 1982. #24 Use It Again.

Dubanavich, Arlene. *Pig William.* New York: Bradbury, 1985. #27 Picnic!

Dubanavich, Arlene. *Pigs at Christmas.* New York: Bradbury, 1986. *#70 Christmas Tree.

Du Bois, William Pène. *Bear Party.* New York: Viking, 1951. *63 Parties.

Duke, Kate. *Seven Froggies Went to School.* New York: Dutton, 1985. *#20 Freaky Frog Day.

Dunbar, Joyce. *A Cake for Barney.* New York: Orchard, 1987. #66 Holiday Cake Tales.

Du Quette, Keith. *A Ripping Day for a Picnic.* New York: Viking, 1990. #27 Picnic!

Duvoisin, Roger. *Petunia.* New York: Knopf, 1950. #52 What Is a Book?

Duvoisin, Roger. *Petunia's Christmas.* New York: Knopf, 1952. *#64 Winter Birds.

Eberle, Irmengarde. *Fawn in the Woods;* photos by Lilo Hess. New York: Crowell, 1962. #88 The Timid Deer.

Economakis, Olga. *Oasis of the Stars;* illus. by Blair Lent. New York: Coward, McCann, 1965. *46 To Grandad Abdullah's.

Edens, Cooper. *Santa Cows;* illus. by Daniel Lane. New York: Green Tiger, 1991. #91 Cow, Bull, Ox.

Edwards, Michelle. *Dora's Book*. Minneapolis: Carolrhoda, 1990. #52 What Is a Book?

Ehlert, Lois. *Growing Vegetable Soup*. New York: Harcourt Brace Jovanovich, 1987. #59 The Enormous Vegetable Harvest.

Ekoomiak, Normee. *Arctic Memories*. New York: Holt, 1988. #45 Northern Memories.

Elzbieta. *Dikou and the Baby Star*. New York: Crowell, 1988. *65 Holiday Stars.

Ets, Marie Hall. *Elephant in a Well*. New York: Viking, 1972. *36 Too Proud to Ask for Help.

Ets, Marie Hall and Aurora Labastida. *Nine Days to Christmas: A Story of Mexico*. New York: Viking, 1959. #65 Holiday Stars.

Ets, Marie Hall. *Play with Me*. New York: Viking, 1955. *37 Don't Be Shy. *84 The Quiet Storytime. *88 The Timid Deer.

Evans, Mari. *Jim Flying High;* illus. by Ashley Bryan. Garden City, N. Y.: Doubleday, 1979. *36 Too Proud to Ask for Help!

Everitt, Betsy. *Frida the Wondercat*. New York: Harcourt Brace Jovanovich, 1990. *79 Plain and Fancy; *95 Frida the Wondercat.

Field, Eugene. *Wynken, Blynken, and Nod;* illus. by Barbara Cooney. New York: Hastings House, 1964. *80 Three.

Field, Rachel. *A Road Might Lead to Anywhere;* illus. by Giles Laroche. Boston: Little, Brown, 1990. #17 Ride-a-Path.

Fischer, Hans. *The Birthday*. New York: Harcourt, Brace, and World, 1954. *63 Parties; *66 Holiday Cake Tales.

Fischetto, Laura. *All Pigs on Deck: Christopher Columbus' Second Marvelous Voyage;* illus. by Letizia Galli. New York: Delacorte, 1991. #62 Across the Bright Blue Sea.

Fisher, Leonard Everett. *Boxes! Boxes!* New York: Viking, 1984. *75 What Can You Do with a Box?

Fitzgerald, Rick. *Helen and the Great Quiet;* illus. by Marilyn MacGregor. New York: Morrow, 1989. #84 The Quiet Storytime.

Flack, Marjorie. *Angus and the Ducks*. New York: Doubleday, 1930. #57 Ducklings Dawdle; *94 The Goose Got Loose.

Flanders, Michael, and Donald Swan. *The Hippopotamus Song;* illus. by Nadine Bernard Westcott. Boston: Little, Brown, 1991. #90 Happy Hippos.

Fleischman, Paul. *Time Train;* illus. by Claire Ewart. New York: HarperCollins, 1991. #14 Out the Train Window.

Fleischman, Sid. *The Scarebird;* illus. by Peter Sis. New York: Greenwillow, 1988. #61 Scarecrows.

Fleming, Denise. *In the Small, Small Pond*. New York: Henry Holt, 1993. #2 At the Bottom of the Pond.

Florian, Douglas. *A Carpenter*. New York: Greenwillow, 1988. #23 Good Wood.

Florian, Douglas. *A Painter*. New York: Greenwillow, 1993. #22 If I Were a Painter.

Flournoy, Valerie. *The Patchwork Quilt;* illus. by Jerry Pinkney. New York: Dial, 1985. *29 Quilts to Remember.

Fox, Mem. *Possum Magic;* illus. by Julie Vivas. Nashville: Abingdon, 1987. #47 Koala, Kangaroo, and Kookaburra.

Fox, Mem. *Wilfrid Gordon McDonald Partridge;* illus. by Julie Vivas. Brooklyn, N.Y.: Kane/Miller, 1984. #38 I Want to Share with You Today.

Françoise. *Nöel for Jeanne-Marie.* New York: Scribner's, 1953. *69 Youngest One at Christmas.

Françoise. *Springtime for Jeanne-Marie.* New York: Scribner's, 1955. #94 The Goose Got Loose.

Frankel, Julie E. *Hare and Bear Go Shopping;* illus. by Ted Smith. St. Louis: Milliken, 1990. #43 To the Grocery Store.

Freeman, Don. *Corduroy.* New York: Puffin, 1968. *42 Policeman to the Rescue.

Freeman, Don. *Dandelion.* New York: Viking, 1964. *18 Dress Up.

Freeman, Don. *Hattie the Backstage Bat.* New York: Viking, 1970. *86 Bats, Bats, Bats.

Freeman, Don. *Quiet! There's a Canary in the Library.* San Carlos, Calif.: Golden Gate, 1969. *53 What Is a Library?

Frost, Robert. *Stopping by Woods on a Snowy Evening;* illus. by Susan Jeffers. New York: Dutton, 1978. *3 Winter Wonderland. *15 Ride Away! #70 Christmas Tree.

Gage, Wilson. *Cully Cully and the Bear;* illus. by James Stevenson. New York: Greenwillow, 1983. #85 Bears in Their Den.

Galdone, Paul. *The Gingerbread Boy.* New York: Clarion, 1975. *44 Bakers at Work

Galdone, Paul. *What's in Fox's Sack?* New York: Ticknor & Fields, 1988. *92 Watching Foxes.

Gantos, Jack. *Rotten Ralph's Rotten Christmas;* illus. by Nicol Rubel. Boston: Houghton Mifflin, 1984. *69 Youngest One at Christmas; *70 Christmas Tree.

Gantschev, Ivan. *The Christmas Train.* Boston: Little, Brown, 1982. #14 Out the Train Window.

Garelick, May. *Just My Size;* illus. by William Pène du Bois. New York: Harper & Row, 1990. *24 Use It Again.

Garland, Sarah. *Billy and Belle.* New York: Reinhardt Books in association with Viking, 1992. #41 Youngest One.

Garland, Sarah. *Going Shopping.* Boston: Atlantic Monthly, 1982. #43 To the Grocery.

Garland, Sarah. *Having a Picnic.* Boston: Atlantic Monthly, 1984. *27 Picnic!

Garland, Sarah. *Oh, No!* New York: Viking Kestrel, 1989. #30 Oh No, Baby!; #34 Whoops!

Gaspard de la Nuit: Part One, Ondine by Maurice Ravel. Vladimir Ashkenazy, piano. London 410255–1. *15 Ride Away!

Gay, Michael. *Night Ride.* New York: Morrow, 1987. #12 On the Road.

George, William T. *Christmas at Long Pond;* illus. by Lindsay Barrett George. New York: Greenwillow, 1982. #70 Christmas Tree!

George, William T. *Fishing at Long Pond;* illus. by Lindsay Barrett George. New York: Greenwillow, 1991. *2 At the Bottom of the Pond. #32 Gone Fishing.

George, William T. and Lindsay Barrett George. *Beaver at Long Pond.* New York: Greenwillow, 1988. #2 At the Bottom of the Pond.

George, William T. and Lindsay Barrett George. *Box Turtle at Long Pond.* New York: Greenwillow, 1989. #2 At the Bottom of the Pond.

Getz, Arthur. *Hamilton Duck*. New York: Golden, 1972. *64 Winter Birds.

Gibbons, Gail. *Check It Out! A Book About Libraries*. San Diego: Harcourt Brace Jovanovich, 1985. #53 What Is a Library?

Gibbons, Gail. *Paper, Paper, Everywhere*. New York: Harcourt Brace Jovanovich, 1983. *51 What Is Paper?

Gibbons, Gail. *The Seasons of Arnold's Apple Tree*. New York: Harcourt, 1988. #60 A Fruitful Harvest.

Giblin, James, and Dale Ferguson. *The Scarecrow Book*. New York: Crown, 1980. *61 Scarecrows.

Giesel, Theodor. *See* Seuss, Dr.

Gilman, Phoebe. *Something from Nothing: Adapted from a Jewish Folktale*. New York: Scholastic, 1992. #24 Use It Again!

Ginsburg, Mirra. *Across the Stream*; illus. by Nancy Tafuri. New York: Greenwillow, 1982. #57 Duckings Dawdle.

Ginsburg, Mirra. *The Chick and the Duckling*; illus. by Jose Aruego and Ariane Aruego; trans. from the Russian of V. Suteyev. New York: Macmillan, 1972. *36 Too Proud to Ask for Help; *54 Cra-a-ak!

Ginsburg, Mirra. *Good Morning Chick*; illus. by Byron Barton. Adapted from a story by Korney Chukovsky. New York: Greenwillow, 1980. *54 Cra-a-ack!; #57 Ducklings Dawdle.

Ginsburg, Mirra. *Mushroom in the Rain*; illus. by Jose Aruego & Ariane Dewey. Adapted from the Russian of V. Suteyev. New York: Collier, 1974. *82 Inside, Outside, Upside Down!

Ginsburg, Mirra. *The Sun's Asleep Behind the Hill*; illus. by Paul O. Zelinsky. New York: Greenwillow, 1982. *33 Lullaby.

Ginsburg, Mirra. *Three Kittens*; illus. by Giulio Maestro. Trans. from the Russian of V. Suteyev. New York: Crown, 1973. *82 Inside, Outside, Upside Down!; *80 Three.

Gleeson, Lilly. *The Great Big Scary Dog*; illus. by Armin Greder. New York: Tambourine, 1991. #40 Gentle Giants.

Glennon, Karen M. *Miss Eva and the Red Balloon*; illus. by Hans Poppel. New York: Simon & Schuster, 1990. *72 What Can You Do with a Ballon?

Goble, Paul. *The Girl Who Loved Wild Horses*. New York: Bradbury, 1978. *15 Ride Away!

Goble, Paul. *Iktomi and the Ducks: A Plains Indian Story*. New York: Orchard, 1990. #94 The Goose Got Loose.

Goffstein, M. B. *Artists' Helpers Enjoy the Evening*. New York: Harper & Row, 1987. #22 If I Were a Painter.

Goodall, John S. *Paddy's New Hat*. New York: Atheneum, 1980. *42 Policeman to the Rescue.

Graham, Bob. *Grandad's Magic*. Boston: Little, Brown, 1989. #28 Grandad and Me.

Graham, Margaret Bloy. *Be Nice to Spiders*. New York: Harper & Row, 1967. #87 Spiders.

Gray, Nigel. *A Balloon for Grandad*; illus. by Jane Ray. New York: Orchard, 1988.

*28 Grandpa and Me; *46 To Grandad Abdullah's; *72 What Can You Do with a Balloon?

Green, Nancy. *Abu Kassim's Shoes: An Arabian Tale*; illus. by W. T. Mars. Chicago: Follett, 1963. #46 To Grandad Abdullah's

Greenblat, Rodney A. *Aunt Ippy's Museum of Junk*. New York: HarperCollins, 1991. *24 Use It Again!

Greenblat, Rodney A. *Uncle Wizzmo's New Used Car*. New York: Harper & Row, 1990. *11 Toothgnasher Superflash.

Greenfield, Eloise. *Grandpa's Face*; illus. by Floyd Cooper. New York: Philomel, 1988. #28 Grandpa and Me.

Gretz, Susanna. *It's Your Turn, Roger*. New York: Dial, 1985. #38 I Want to Share with You Today.

Gretz, Susanna. *Roger Loses His Marbles*. New York: Dial, 1988. *26 The Relatives Came.

Gretz, Susanna. *Roger Takes Charge!* New York: Dial, 1987. #39 Small Creatures Meet Big Bullies.

Gretz, Susanna. *Teddy Bears Go Shopping*. New York: Four Winds, 1982. #43 To the Grocery Store.

Gretz, Susanna. *Teddy Bears Take the Train*. New York: Four Winds, 1987. #14 Out the Train Window.

Gretz, Susanna, and Alison Sage. *Teddy Bears Cookbook*; illus. by Susanna Gretz. New York: Doubleday, 1978. #6 Kitchen! Kitchen!

Grossman, Bill. *Tommy at the Grocery*; illus. by Victoria Chess. New York: Harper & Row, 1989. *43 To the Grocery Store.

Grover, Eulalie Osgood. *Mother Goose: The Classic Volland Edition*; illus. by Frederick Richardson. #99 The House That Jack Built.

Guback, Georgina. *Luka's Quilt*. New York: Greenwillow, 1994. #29 Quilts to Remember.

Guilfoile, Elizabeth. *Nobody Listens to Andrew*; illus. by Mary Stevenson. Chicago: Follett, 1957. #85 Bears in Their Dens.

Hadithi, Mwenye. *Crafty Chameleon;* illus. by Adrienne Kennaway. Boston: Little, Brown, 1987. *89 Crafty Chameleons.

Hadithi, Mwenye, and Adrienne Kennaway. *Hot Hippo*. Boston: Little, Brown, 1986. *90 Happy Hippos.

Hale, Irina. *Boxman*. New York: Viking, 1992. #75 What Can You Do with a Box?

Halloween. Golden LP242. Port Washington, N.Y.: Den-Lan Music, 1964. *74 What Can You Do with a Broom?

Hampton, Janie. *Come Home Soon, Baba*; illus. by Jenny Bent. New York: Bedrick/Blackie, 1993. #49 Shoes and Songs.

Happy Birthday by Sharon, Lois and Bram. EC0309. Toronto: Elephant Records, 1988.

Hardendorff, Jeanne R. *The Bed Just So*; illus. by Lisl Weil. New York: Four Winds, 1975. *78 Bedtime.

Harley, Rex. *Mary's Tiger*; illus. by Sue Porter. San Diego: Harcourt Brace Jovanovich, 1990. #22 If I Were a Painter.

Harlow, Joan Hiatt. *Shadow Bear*; illus. by Jim Arnosky. Garden City, N.Y.: Doubleday, 1981. #85 Bears in Their Dens.

Harper, Wilhelmina. *The Gunniwolf*. New York: Dutton, 1967. *17 Dance-a-Path.

Harrison, Ted. *O Canada*. Toronto: Kids Can Press, 1992. #45 Northern Winter.

Hartman, Wendy. *All the Magic in the World*; illus. by Niki Daly. New York: Dutton, 1993. #49 Shoes and Songs.

Havill, Juanita. *Jamaica's Find*; illus. by Anne Sibley O'Brien. Boston: Houghton Mifflin, 1986. *24 Use It Again.

Hawes, Judy. *My Daddy Longlegs;* illus. by Walter Lorraine. New York: Crowell, 1972. #87 Spiders.

Hawkins, Colin, y Jaqui Hawkins. *Donde Esta Mi Mama?* Madrid: Ediciones Altea, 1986. *54 Cra-a-ack!

Hawkins, Colin and Jacqui Hawkins. *Where's My Mommy?* New York: Crown, 1986. *54 Cra-a-ack!

Hayes, Sarah. *Bad Egg: The True Story of Humpty Dumpty*; illus. by Charlotte Voak. Boston: Little, Brown, 1957. #34 Whoops!

Hayes, Sarah. *Eat Up, Gemma*; illus. by Jan Ormerod. New York: Lothrop, Lee & Shepard, 1988. *8 Bad Babies; *25 Dinner at Grandma's House. *30 Oh No, Baby!; *60 A Fruitful Harvest.

Hayes, Sarah. *Happy Christmas Gemma*; illus. by Jan Ormerod. New York: Lothrop, Lee & Shepard, 1986. *66 Holiday Cake Tales; *69 Youngest One at Christmas; *70 Christmas Tree!

Hayes, Sarah. *This Is the Bear and the Picnic Lunch*; illus. by Helen Craig. Boston: Little, Brown, 1988. *27 Picnic!

Heath, Amy. *Sofie's Role*; illus. by Sheila Hamanaka. New York: Four Winds, 1992. #44 Bakers at Work.

Hedderwick, Mairi. *Katie Morag and the Big Boy Cousins*. Boston: Little, Brown, 1987. #26 The Relatives Came.

Heide, Florence Parry, and Judith Heide Gilliland. *The Day of Ahmed's Secret;* illus. by Ted Lewin. New York: Lothrop, Lee & Shepard, 1990. #46 To Grandad Abdullah's.

Hellard, Susan. *Eleanor and the Babysitter*. Boston: Little, Brown, 1991. #5 Here Comes the Babysitter!

Heller, Ruth. *How to Hide a Tree Frog and Other Amphibians*. New York: Grosset & Dunlap, 1986. #89 Crafty Chameleons.

Henkes, Kevin. *Chrysanthemum*. New York: Greenwillow, 1991. #35 I'm Proud to Be Me!

Hertz, Ole. *Tobias Catches a Trout*. Trans. by Tobi Tobias. Minneapolis: Carolrhoda, 1981. #32 Gone Fishing; #45 Northern Winter.

Hertz, Ole. *Tobias Goes Ice Fishing*. Minneapolis: Carolrhoda, 1981. #32 Gone Fishing; #45 Northern Winter.

Hertz, Ole. *Tobias Goes Seal Hunting.* Minneapolis: Carolrhoda, 1984. #45 Northern Winter.

Hertz, Ole. *Tobias Has a Birthday.* Minneapolis: Carolrhoda, 1984. #45 Northern Winter.

Hest, Amy. *Crack-of-Dawn Walkers;* illus. by Amy Schwartz. New York: Macmillan, 1984. #28 Grandpa and Me.

Hest, Amy. *The Purple Coat;* illus. by Amy Schwartz. New York: Four Winds, 1986. #28 Grandpa and Me.

Hildebrandt, Greg. *Treasures of Chanukah.* New Jersey: Unicorn Publishing, 1987. #68 Light a Candle.

Hines, Anna Grossnickle. *Grandma Gets Grumpy.* New York: Clarion /Ticknor & Fields, 1988. #25 Dinner at Grandma's House.

Hirsh, Marilyn. *I Love Hanukkah.* New York: Holiday House, 1984. *68 Light a Candle.

Hirsh, Marilyn, and Maya Narayan. *Leela and the Watermelon;* illus. by Marilyn Hirsh. New York: Crown, 1971. #48 Indian Festival.

Hirst, Robin and Sally. *My Place in Space;* illus. by Roland Harvey with Joe Levine. New York: Orchard, 1988. #21 Space Place.

Hoban, Lillian. *Arthur's Christmas Cookies.* New York: Harper & Row, 1972. #44 Bakers at Work.

Hoban, Russell. *A Bargain for Frances;* illus. by Lillian Hoban. New York: Harper & Row, 1970. #79 Plain and Fancy.

Hoffman, Phyllis. *Meatball;* illus. by Emily Arnold McCully. New York: HarperCollins, 1991. *41 Youngest One.

Hogan, Paula Z. *The Life Cycle of the Whale;* illus. by Karen Halt. Milwaukee: Raintree, 1979. *#90 Whale Song.

Holabird, Katherine. *Angelina's Christmas;* illus. by Helen Craig. New York: Clarkson N. Potter, 1985. *#71 Christmas Sharing.

Hong, Lily Toy. *How the Ox Star Fell From Heaven.* Morton Grove, Ill.: Whitman, 1991. *#91 Cow, Bull, Ox.

Hood, Flora. *One Luminaria for Antonio;* illus. by Ann Kirn. New York: Putnam's, 1966. *68 Light a Candle.

Hoopes, Lyn Littlefield. *Wing-a-ding;* illus. by Stephen Gammell. Boston: Little, Brown, 1990. *74 What Can You Do with a Broom?

Hopkins, Lee Bennett. *Good Books, Good Times!;* illus. by Harvey Stevenson. New York: Harper & Row, 1990. *52 What Is a Book?

Hopkins, Lee Bennett. *Side by Side: Poems to Read Together;* illus. by Hilary Knight. New York: Simon & Schuster, 1988. *94 The Goose Got Loose.

Horowitz, Ruth. *Bat Time;* illus. by Susan Avishai. New York: Four Winds, 1991. *86 Bats, Bats, Bats.

Horvath, Betty. *The Cheerful Quiet;* illus. by Jo Ann Stover. New York: Watts, 1969. #84 The Quiet Storytime.

Horwitz, Elinor Lander. *When the Sky Is Like Lace;* illus. by Barbara Cooney. Philadelphia: Lippincott, 1975. *A Walk in the Moonlight.

Howard, Elizabeth Fitzgerald. *Chita's Christmas Tree;* illus. by Floyd Cooper. New York: Bradbury, 1989. *67 Company's Coming.

Howard, Elizabeth Fitzgerald. *The Train to Lulu's;* illus. by Robert Casilla. New York: Bradbury, 1988. *14 Out the Train Window.

Howell, Lynn and Richard. *Winifred's New Bed.* New York: Knopf, 1985. *78 Bedtime.

Hudson, Wade. *Pass It On: African-American Poetry for Children;* illus. by Floyd Cooper. New York: Scholastic, 1993. *30 Oh No, Baby!; *41 Youngest One.

Hughes, Shirley. *George the Babysitter.* Englewood Cliffs, N.J.: Prentice-Hall, 1978. #5 Here Comes the Babysitter!

Hurd, Thacher. *Mamma Don't Allow.* New York: Harper & Row, 1984. #1 A Walk in the Moonlight.

Hurd, Thacher. *Mystery on the Docks.* New York: Harper & Row, 1983. #42 Policeman to the Rescue.

Hurd, Thacher. *The Pea Patch Jig.* New York: Crown, 1986. *59 The Enormous Vegetable Harvest.

Hutchins, Pat. *Don't Forget the Bacon.* New York: Greenwillow, 1976. *43 To the Grocery Store.

Hutchins, Pat. *The Doorbell Rang.* New York: Greenwillow, 1986. #26 The Relatives Came; *38 I Want to Share with You Today; *44 Bakers at Work; *71 Christmas Sharing.

Hutchins, Pat. *Happy Birthday Sam.* New York: Greenwillow, 1978. *41 Youngest One; *81 Small and Tall.

Hutchins, Pat. *Rosie's Walk.* New York: Macmillan, 1968. *39 Small Creatures Meet Big Bullies; *82 Inside, Outside, Upside Down!

Hutchins, Pat. *Silly Billy.* New York: Greenwillow, 1992. #8 Bad Babies.

Hutchins, Pat. *The Silver Christmas Tree.* New York: Macmillan, 1974. *65 Holiday Stars.

Hutchins, Pat. *The Surprise Party.* New York: Macmillan, 1986, 1969. #63 Parties.

Hutchins, Pat. *Where's the Baby?* New York: Greenwillow, 1988. *30 Oh No, Baby!

Hyman, Trina Schart. *Little Red Ridinghood.* New York: Holiday House, 1983. *17 Dance-a-Path.

I'm Not Small. Songs by Patty Zeitlin and Marcia Berman. AC547. Freeport, N.Y.: Educational Activities, 1973. Audiocassette with book. *37 Don't Be Shy; *39 Small Creatures Meet Big Bullies; *81 Small and Tall.

Irvine, Joan. *Build It with Boxes;* illus. by Linda Hendry. New York: Morrow, 1993. #75 What Can You Do with a Box?

Isadora, Rachel. *At the Crossroads.* New York: Greenwillow, 1991. *49 Shoes and Songs.

Isadora, Rachel. *Over the Green Hills.* New York: Greenwillow, 1992. *49 Shoes and Songs.

Isenbart, Hans-Heinrich. *A Duckling Is Born*; trans. by Catherine Edwards Sadler; photos by Othmar Baumli. New York: Putnam's, 1981. #57 Ducklings Dawdle.

Iwamura, Kazuo. *Ton and Pon: Big and Little*. New York: Bradbury, 1980. *81 Small and Tall.

Janice. *Little Bear Marches in the St. Patrick's Day Parade*; illus. by Mariana. New York: Lothrop, Lee & Shepard, 1967. #73 What Can You Do with an Umbrella?

Janice. *Little Bear's Pancake Party*; illus. by Mariana. New York: Lothrop, Lee & Shepard, 1960. #63 Parties.

Janosch. *The Magic Auto*. New York: Crown, 1971. #11 Toothgnasher Superflash.

Jarrell, Randall. *A Bat Is Born*; illus. by John Schoenherr. New York: Macmillan, 1964. *86 Bats, Bats, Bats.

Jarrell, Randall. *The Bat Poet*; illus. by Maurice Sendak. New York: Macmillan, 1964. #86 Bats, Bats, Bats.

Jaye, Mary Tinnin. *Making Music Your Own*. Parkridge, Ill.: Silver Burdett, 1971. *14 Out the Train Window.

Jeffers, Susan. *All the Pretty Horses*. New York: Macmillan, 1974. *15 Ride Away!

Johnston, Tony. *Grandpa's Song;* illus. by Brad Snead. New York: Dial, 1991. #28 Grandpa and Me.

Johnston, Tony. *The Quilt Story;* illus. by Tomie de Paola. New York: Putnam's, 1985. *29 Quilts to Remember.

Johnston, Tony, and Tomie de Paola. *The Badger and the Magic Fan*. New York: Putnam's, 1990. *50 Reaching the Sky.

Jonas, Ann. *Round Trip*. New York: Greenwillow, 1983. #9 Upside Down Day.

Jonas, Ann. *The Quilt*. New York: Greenwillow, 1984. #29 Quilts to Remember.

Joose, Barbara M. *Spiders in the Fruit Cellar;* illus. by Kay Chorao. New York: Knopf, 1983. #87 Spiders.

Jordan, E. L. *Animal Atlas of the World*. Maplewood, N.J.: Hammond, 1969. #47 Koala, Kangaroo, and Kookaburra.

Joyce, William. *George Shrinks*. New York: Harper, 1985. #81 Small and Tall.

Kahl, Virginia. *The Duchess Bakes a Cake*. New York: Scribner's, 1955. #66 Holiday Cakes.

Kalan, Robert. *Blue Sea;* illus. by Donald Crews. New York: Greenwillow, 1979. *#81 Small and Tall.

Karlin, Bernie & Mati. *Night Ride;* illus. by Berni Karlin. New York: Simon & Schuster, 1988. *26 The Relatives Came.

Keats, Ezra Jack. *Regards to the Man in the Moon*. New York: Four Winds, 1981. #21 Space Place.

Keats, Ezra Jack. *The Snowy Day*. New York: Viking, 1962. *3 Winter Wonderland.

Keats, Ezra Jack. *Whistle for Willie*. New York: Viking, 1964. *55 Trick an April Fool.

Kent, Jack. *The Egg Book*. New York: Macmillan, 1975. #54 Cra-a-ack!

Kent, Jack. *The Fat Cat*. New York: Parents, 1971. #7 Greedy Gluttons.

Kerr, Judith. *Mog's Christmas*. New York: Collins, 1976. *70 Christmas Tree.

Kesselman, Wendy. *Emma*; illus. by Barbara Cooney. New York: Doubleday, 1980. *22 If I Were a Painter.

Kesselman, Wendy. *There's a Train Going By My Window*; illus. by Tony Chen. New York: Doubleday, 1982. #14 Out the Train Window.

Kessler, Leonard. *The Silly Mother Goose*. Champaign, Ill.: Garrard, 1980. #34 Whoops!

Khalsa, Dayal Kaur. *Tales of a Gambling Grandma*. New York: Clarkson N. Potter, 1986. #25 Dinner at Grandma's House.

Kimmelman, Leslie. *Frannie's Fruits*; illus. by Petra Mathers. New York: Harper & Row, 1989. #60 A Fruitful Harvest.

Kimmelman, Leslie. *Me & Nana*; illus. by Marilee Robin Burton. New York: Harper & Row, 1990. #25 Dinner at Grandma's House.

Kimura, Yuriko. *Christmas Present from a Friend*; illus. by Masako Matsumura. Nashville: Abingdon, 1984. *71 Christmas Sharing.

Kingman, Lee. *Catch the Baby!*; illus. by Susanna Natti. New York: Viking, 1990. *30 Oh No, Baby!

Kirn, Ann. *Nine in a Line*. New York: Norton, 1966. #46 To Grandad Abdullah's.

Kitamura, Satoshi. *UFO Diary*. New York: Farrar, Straus and Giroux, 1989. #21 Space Place.

Kline, Suzy. *Ooops!*; illus. by Dora Leder. Niles, Ill.: Whitman, 1988. #34 Whoops!

Krasilovsky, Phyllis. *The Cow Who Fell in the Canal*; illus. by Peter Spier. Garden City, N. Y.: Doubleday, 1953. *91 Cow, Bull, Ox.

Krasilovsky, Phyllis. *The Shy Little Girl*; illus. by Trina Schart Hyman. Boston: Houghton Mifflin, 1970. *37 Don't Be Shy.

Kraus, Robert. *Whose Mouse Are You?*; illus. by Jose Aruego. New York: Macmillan, 1970. *35 I'm Proud to Be Me; #41 Youngest One.

Krauss, Ruth. *The Carrot Seed*; illus. by Crockett Johnson. New York: Harper & Row, 1945. *35 I'm Proud to Be Me!; *59 The Enormous Vegetable Harvest.

Krauss, Ruth. *Charlotte and the White Horse*; illus. by Maurice Sendak. New York: Harper, 1955. #15 Ride Away!

Krauss, Ruth. *The Happy Egg*; illus. by Crockett Johnson. New York: O'Hara, 1967. #54 Cra-a-ack!

Krauss, Ruth. *A Very Special House*; illus. by Maurice Sendak. New York: Harper & Row, 1953. #99 The House That Jack Built.

Kruss, James. *3 × 3: Three by Three*; illus. by Eva Johanna Rubin. New York: Macmillan, 1963. *80 Three.

Kudrna, C. Imbior. *To Bathe a Boa*. Minneapolis: Carolrhoda, 1986.*#77 Bathtime.

Kuskin, Karla. *The Philharmonic Gets Dressed*. New York: Harper, 1982. #18 Dress Up!

Kuskin, Karla. *Which Horse Is William?* New York: Harper & Row, 1959. #*55 Trick an April Fool.

Kwitz, Mary DeBall. *Little Chick's Story*; illus. by Cyndy Szekeres. New York: Harper & Row, 1978. *57 Ducklings Dawdle.

La Fontaine, Jean de. *The Hare and the Tortoise*; illus. by Brian Wildsmith. New York: Oxford, 1966. *35 I'm Proud to Be Me.

La Fontaine, Jean de. *The Lion and the Rat*; illus. by Brian Wildsmith. Oxford, England: Oxford University Press, 1963. *35 I'm Proud to Be Me. *#40 Gentle Giants.

Langstaff, John. *Frog Went A-Courtin'*; illus. by Feodor Rojankovsky. San Diego: Harcourt Brace Jovanovich, 1955. *20 Freaky Frog Day.

Larrick, Nancy. *Mice Are Nice*; illus. by Ed Young. New York: Philomel, 1990. *21 Space Place.

Larrick, Nancy. *When the Dark Comes Dancing: A Bedtime Poetry Book;* illus. by John Wallner. New York: Philomel, 1983. #33 Lullaby.

Lavies, Bianca. *Lily Pad Pond.* New York: Dutton, 1989. #2 At the Bottom of the Pond.

Leaf, Munro. *The Story of Ferdinand*; illus. by Robert Lawson. New York: Viking, 1936. #91 Cow, Bull, Ox.

Lear, Edward. *The Jumblies*; illus. by Ted Rand. New York: Putnam's, 1989. *101 The Jumblies.

Lee, Jeanne M. *The Legend of the Milky Way.* New York: Holt, Rinehart and Winston, 1983. *50 Reaching the Sky.

Lent, Blair. *From King Bogan's Hall to Nothing at All.* Boston: Little, Brown, 1967. *86 Bats, Bats, Bats.

Lent, Blair. *John Tabor's Ride.* Boston: Little, Brown, 1966. #93 Whale Song.

Le Tord, Bijou. *A Brown Cow.* Boston: Little, Brown, 1989. *91 Cow, Bull, Ox.

Le Tord, Bijou. *Good Wood Bear.* New York: Bradbury, 1985. *23 Good Wood.

Le Tord, Bijou. *My Grandma Lioni.* New York: Bradbury, 1987. #25 Dinner at Grandma's House.

Levinson, Nancy Smiler. *Clara and the Bookwagon*; illus. by Carolyn Croll. New York: Harper & Row, 1988. #53 What Is a Library?

Levinson, Riki. *I Go With My Family to Grandma's*; illus. by Diane Goode. New York: Dutton, 1986. *26 The Relatives Came.

Levy, Elizabeth. *Something Queer at the Library;* illus. by Mordicai Gerstein. New York: Delacorte, 1977. #53 What Is a Library?

Lewin, Hugh. *Jafta's Father;* illus. by Lisa Kopper. Minneapolis: Carolrhoda, 1983. *49 Shoes and Songs.

Lewin, Ted. *Amazon Boy.* New York: Macmillan, 1993. #4 Into the Rain Forest.

Lewis, J. Patrick. *Earth Verse and Water Rhymes*; illus. by Robert Sabuda. New York: Atheneum, 1991. *92 Watching Foxes.

Lewis, Richard. *In a Spring Garden*; illus. by Ezra Jack Keats. New York: Dial, 1965. *50 Reaching the Sky.

Lewison, Wendy Cheyett. *Shy Vi;* illus. by Stephen John Smith. New York: Simon & Schuster, 1993. #37 Don't Be Shy.

Lifton, Betty Jean. *Joji and the Amanojaku*; illus. by Eiichi Mitsui. New York: Norton, 1965. #61 Scarecrows.

Lifton, Betty Jean. *Joji and the Dragon*; illus. by Eiichi Mitsui. Hamden, Conn.: Linnet, 1989. #61 Scarecrows.

Lille, Patricia. *Everything Has a Place*; illus. by Nancy Tafuri.

Lillegard, Dee. *Sitting in My Box*; illus. by Jon Agee. New York: Dutton, 1989. *75 What Can You Do with a Box?

Lillie, Patricia. *Everything Has a Place;* illus. by Nancy Tafuri. New York: Greenwillow, 1993. #82 Inside, Outside, Upside Down!

Lindbergh, Reeve. *The Day the Goose Got Loose*; illus. by Steven Kellogg. New York: Dial, 1990. *42 Policeman to the Rescue; *94 The Goose Got Loose.

Lindbloom, Steven. *Let's Give Kitty a Bath*; illus. by True Kelley. New York: Addison-Wesley, 1982. #77 Bathtime.

Lindgren, Astrid. *Christmas in Noisy Village*. New York: Viking, 1963. *67 Company's Coming.

Lindgren, Astrid. *The Tomten*; illus. by Harald Wiberg. New York: Coward-McCann, 1967. #3 Winter Wonderland.

Lindgren, Astrid. *The Tomten and the Fox;* illus. by Harald Wiberg. Adapted from a poem by Karl-Erik Forsslun. New York: Coward-McCann, 1966. #1 A Walk in the Moonlight; *3 Winter Wonderland; *65 Holiday Stars; *92 Watching Foxes.

Lindgren, Barbro. *Sam's Wagon*; illus. by Eva Eriksson. New York: Morrow, 1986. *34 Whoops!

Lindgren, Barbro and Eva Eriksson. *The Wild Baby Goes to Sea;* trans. by Jack Prelutsky. New York: Greenwillow, 1982. #8 Bad Babies.

Lionni, Leo. *A Color of His Own*. New York: Pantheon, 1975. *89 Crafty Chameleons.

Lionni, Leo. *Inch by Inch*. New York: Astor-Honor, 1960. #83 Green.

Lionni, Leo. *Little Blue and Little Yellow*. New York: Astor-Honor, 1959. #83 Green.

Lionni, Leo. *Matthew's Dream*. New York: Knopf, 1991. #22 If I Were a Painter.

Lionni, Leo. *Swimmy*. New York: Pantheon, 1968. #39 Small Creatures Meet Big Bullies; *55 Trick an April Fool.

Lionni, Leo. *Tico and the Golden Wings*. New York: Pantheon, 1964. #64 Winter Birds.

Lloyd, Errol. *Nini at Carnival*. New York: Crowell, 1979. #18 Dress Up!

Lobel, Arnold. *On Market Street*; illus. by Anita Lobel. New York: Greenwillow, 1981. #43 To the Grocery Store.

Lobel, Arnold. *The Turnaround Wind*. New York: Harper & Row, 1988. #9 Upside Down Day.

Lobel, Arnold. *A Zoo for Mister Muster*. New York: Harper & Row, 1962. #42 Policeman to the Rescue.

London, Jonathan. *The Owl Who Became the Moon*; illus. by Ted Rand. New York: Dutton, 1993. #14 Out the Train Window.

Lubin, Leonard B. *This Little Pig*. New York: Lothrop, Lee & Shepard, 1985. *79 Plain and Fancy.

Macaulay, David. *Black and White*. Boston: Houghton Mifflin, 1990. #14 Out the Train Window; #91 Cow, Bull, Ox.

MacDonald, Elizabeth. *John's Picture;* illus. by David McTaggert. New York: Viking, 1990. #22 If I Were a Painter.

MacDonald, Margaret Read. *Booksharing: 101 Programs to Use with Preschoolers.* Hamden, Conn.: Library Professional Publications, 1988. #54 Cra-a-ack!

MacDonald, Margaret Read. *Look Back and See: Twenty Lively Tales for Gentle Tellers.* New York: H.W. Wilson, 1991. *46 To Grandad Abdullah's; *47 Koala, Kangaroo, and Kookaburra; *74 What Can You Do with a Broom?; #85 Bears in Their Dens.

MacDonald, Margaret Read. *A Parent's Guide to Storytelling.* New York: HarperCollins, 1995. *80 Three; *85 Bears in Their Dens.

MacDonald, Margaret Read. *Twenty Tellable Tales.* New York: H. W. Wilson, 1986. *45 Northern Winter.

Maestro, Betsy and Giulio. *Where Is My Friend?* New York: Crown, 1976. * 34 Whoops!; *82 Inside, Outside, Upside Down!

Mahy, Margaret. *The Boy Who Was Followed Home*; illus. by Steven Kellogg. New York: Watts, 1975. #90 Happy Hippos.

Mahy, Margaret. *The Horrendous Hullabaloo*; illus. by Patricia MacCarthy. New York: Viking, 1992. *10 Parrot Parties.

Markun, Patricia Maloney. *The Little Painter of Sabana Grande*; illus. by Robert Casilla. New York: Bradbury, 1993. #22 If I Were a Painter.

Martin, Bill, Jr. *Barn Dance;* illus. by Ted Rand. New York: Holt, 1986. #61 Scarecrows.

Martin, Bill, Jr. *The Happy Hippopatami;* illus. by Betsy Everett. San Diego: Harcourt Brace Jovanovich, 1991. *90 Happy Hippos.

Martin, Jacqueline Briggs. *Good Times on Grandfather Mountain*; illus. by Susan Gaber. New York: Orchard, 1992. #23 Good Wood.

Marshall, James. *George and Martha One Fine Day.* Boston: Houghton Mifflin, 1978. *55 Trick an April Fool; *90 Happy Hippos.

Marzollo, Jean. *In 1492;* illus. by Steve Bjorkman. New York: Scholastic, 1991. #62 Across the Bright Blue Sea.

Masha. *Three Little Kittens.* Racine, Wisc.: Golden, 1974. *77 Bathtime; *80 Three.

Massie, Diane Redfield. *The Baby Beebee Bird.* New York: Harper & Row, 1963. *16 Where Is the Green Parrot?

Mathers, Petra. *Sophie and Lou.* New York: HarperCollins, 1991. #37 Don't Be Shy.

Matsuno, Masako. *Taro and the Bamboo Shoot: A Japanese Tale.* New York: Pantheon, 1964. *50 Reaching the Sky.

Matsuoka, Kyoka. *There's a Hippo in My Bath!*; illus. by Akiko Hayashi. New York: Doubleday, 1982. *77 Bathtime; *90 Happy Hippos.

Mayer, Marianna. *Marcel the Pastry Chef;* illus. by Gerald McDermott. New York: Bantam, 1991. #44 Bakers at Work.

Mayer, Mercer. *A Boy, a Dog, and a Frog.* New York: Dial, 1962. #2 At the Bottom of the Pond.

Mayer, Mercer. *Merry Christmas Mom and Dad.* New York: Golden, 1982. #71 Christmas Sharing.

Mazer, Anne. *The Salamander Room;* illus. by Steve Johnson. New York: Knopf, 1991. *19 If a Forest Grew in Your Room.

McCarthy, Bobette. *Ten Little Hippos: A Counting Book.* New York: Bradbury, 1992. #90 Happy Hippos.

McCleod, Emilie Warren. *The Bear's Bicycle;* illus. by David McPhail. Boston: Little, Brown, 1974. *13 Safe Biker!

McCloskey, Robert. *Blueberries for Sal.* New York: Viking, 1948. #85 Bears in Their Dens.

McCloskey, Robert. *Burt Dow, Deep-Water Man.* New York: Viking, 1963. #93 Whale Song.

McCloskey, Robert. *Make Way for Ducklings.* New York: Viking, 1989. *42 Policeman to the Rescue; *57 Ducklings Dawdle.

McCloskey, Robert. *One Morning in Maine.* New York: Viking, 1952. *76 A Tooth! A Tooth!

McCully, Emily Arnold. *The Grandma Mix-up.* New York: Harper & Row, 1988. #25 Dinner at Grandma's House.

McCully, Emily Arnold. *New Baby.* New York: Harper & Row, 1988. #30 Oh No, Baby!

McDermott, Gerald. *Papagayo the Mischief Maker.* San Diego: Harcourt Brace Jovanovich, 1992. *10 Parrot Parties; #16 Where Is the Green Parrot?

McDermott, Gerald. *Raven: A Trickster Tale from the Pacific Northwest.* San Diego: Harcourt Brace Jovanovich, 1993. #55 Trick an April Fool.

McDermott, Gerald. *Zomo the Rabbit.* San Diego: Harcourt Brace Jovanovich, 1992. #55 Trick an April Fool.

McKee, David. *Two Can Toucan.* New York: Abelard-Schuman, 1964. #16 Where Is the Green Parrot?

McNulty, Faith. *The Lady and the Spider;* illus. by Bob Marstall. New York: Harper & Row, 1986. #87 Spiders.

McPhail, David. *The Bear's Toothache.* Boston: Little, Brown, 1972. *76 A Tooth! A Tooth!

McPhail, David. *Captain Toad and the Motorbikes.* New York: Atheneum, 1978. #20 Freaky Frog Day.

McPhail, David. *Fix-It.* New York: Dutton, 1984. #24 Use It Again.

McPhail, David. *The Train.* Boston: Little, Brown, 1977. #14 Out the Train Window.

Meyers, Odette. *The Enchanted Umbrella;* illus. by Margot Zemach. San Diego: Harcourt Brace Jovanovich, 1988. #73 What Can You Do with an Umbrella?

Miller, Edna. *Mousekin's Golden House.* Englewood Cliffs, N. J.: Prentice-Hall, 1964. *59 The Enormous Vegetable Harvest.

Miller, Edna. *Pebbles, a Pack Rat.* Englewood Cliffs, N.J.: Prentice-Hall, 1976. #61 Scarecrows.

Minarik, Else Holmelund. *Little Bear;* illus. by Maurice Sendak. New York: Harper & Row, 1957. *21 Space Place; #67 Company's Coming.

Modern Tunes for Rhythms and Instruments by Hap Palmer. Freeport, N.Y.: Educational Activities, 1978.

Monsel, Helen A. *Paddy's Christmas*. New York: Knopf, 1942. *71 Christmas Sharing.

Moore, Elaine. *Grandma's Promise*; illus. by Elise Primavera. New York: Lothrop, Lee & Shepard, 1988. #25 Dinner at Grandma's House.

Moore, Inga. *Oh, Little Jack*. Cambridge, Mass.: Candlewick, 1992. *41 Youngest One.

Moore, Lillian. *Sunflakes: Poems for Children*; illus. by Jan Ormerod. New York: Clarion, 1992. *8 Bad Babies; *9 Upside Down Day; *28 Grandpa and Me; *30 Oh No, Baby!

Morrison, Eve. *The Christmas Box*; illus. by David Small. New York: Morrow, 1985. #75 What Can You Do with a Box?

Morris, Winifred. *Just Listen*; illus. by Patricia Cullen-Clark. New York: Atheneum, 1990. #25 Dinner at Grandma's House.

Moss, Marissa. *Regina's Big Mistake*. Boston: Houghton Mifflin, 1990. #22 If I Were a Painter.

Murphy, Jim. *Backyard Bear*; illus. by Jeffrey Greene. New York: Scholastic, 1993. #85 Bears in Their Dens.

Newton, Laura P. *William the Vehicle King*; illus. by Jacqueline Rogers. New York: Bradbury, 1987. #11 Toothgnasher Superflash.

Nichol, bp. *Once: A Lullaby;* illus. by Anita Lobel. New York: Greenwillow, 1983. #33 Lullaby.

Numeroff, Laura Joffe. *If You Give a Mouse a Cookie*; illus. by Felicia Bond. New York: Harper & Row, 1985. *6 Kitchen! Kitchen!; *74 What Can You Do with a Broom?

O'Brien, Anne Sibley. *It Hurts!* New York: Holt, 1986. *34 Whoops!

O'Callahan, Jay. *Tulips*; illus. by Debrah Santini. Saxonville, Mass.: Picture Book Studio, 1992. #55 Trick an April Fool.

Olschewski, Alfred. *Winterbird*. Boston: Houghton Mifflin, 1969. #64 Winter Birds.

O'Neil, Mary. *Hailstones and Halibut Bones*. New York: Doubleday, 1961. *83 Green.

Orbach, Ruth. *Apple Pigs*. New York: Philomel, 1976. *60 A Fruitful Harvest.

Ormerod, Jan. *Messy Baby*. New York: Lothrop, Lee & Shepard, 1985. #34 Whoops!

Ormerod, Jan. *101 Things to Do with a Baby*. New York: Lothrop, Lee & Shepard, 1984. #8 Bad Babies.

Otsuka, Yuzo. *Suho and the White Horse*; trans. by Ann Herring; illus. by Suekichi Akaba. New York: Viking, 1981. #15 Ride Away!

Parenteau, Shirley. *I'll Bet You Thought I Was Lost*; illus. by Lorna Tomei. New York: Lothrop, Lee & Shepard, 1981. #43 To the Grocery Store.

Parker, Dorothy O. *Liam's Catch;* illus. by Robert Andrew Parker. New York: Viking, 1972. #32 Gone Fishing.

Parker, Nancy Winslow. *General Store*. New York: Greenwillow, 1988. *43 To the Grocery Store.

Parker, Nancy Winslow. *Love from Aunt Betty*. New York: Dodd, Mead, 1983. #6 Kitchen! Kitchen!

Parker, Nancy Winslow. *Poofy Loves Company*. New York: Dodd, Mead, 1980. #34 Whoops!

Parnall, Peter. *Quiet*; illus. by Byrd Baylor. New York: Morrow, 1989. *84 The Quiet Storytime.

Pavey, Peter. *I'm Taggerty Toad*. New York: Bradbury, 1980. #20 Freaky Frog Day.

Pellowski, Anne. *The Family Storytelling Handbook*. New York: Macmillan, 1987. #29 Quilts to Remember.

Petersham, Maud and Mishka. *The Circus Baby*. New York: Macmillan, 1950. #34 Whoops!

Petroski, Catherine. *Beautiful My Mane in the Wind;* illus. by Robert Andrew Parker. Boston: Houghton Mifflin, 1983. #15 Ride Away!

Pienkowski, Jan. *Dinner Time*; text by Ann Carter; paper engineering by Marcin Stajewski and James Roger Diaz. Los Angeles: Price/Stern/Sloan, 1991. *52 What Is a Book?

Pienkowski, Jan. *Haunted House*. New York: Dutton, 1979. #86 Bats, Bats, Bats.

Pinkwater, Daniel. *Bear's Picture*. New York: Dutton, 1972. #22 If I Were a Painter.

Pinkwater, Daniel. *Ducks*. Boston: Little, Brown, 1984. *94 The Goose Got Loose.

Pinkwater, Daniel. *Guys from Space*. New York: Macmillan, 1989. *21 Space Place.

Pinkwater, Daniel. *Roger's Umbrella*; illus. by James Marshall. New York: Dutton, 1982. *73 What Can You Do with an Umbrella?

Pinkwater, Daniel. *Toothgnasher Superflash*. New York: Four Winds, 1981. *11 Toothgnasher Superflash.

Plath, Sylvia. *The Bed Book*; illus. by Emily McCully. New York: Harper & Row, 1976. #78 Bedtime.

Polacco, Patricia. *Just Plain Fancy*. New York: Bantam Books, 1990. #79 Plain and Fancy.

Polacco, Patricia. *The Keeping Quilt*. New York: Simon & Schuster, 1988. #29 Quilts to Remember.

Polushkin, Maria. *Big Brother Blues*; illus. by Ellen Weiss. New York: Bradbury, 1987. *30 Oh No, Baby!

Polushkin, Maria. *Mama's Secret*; illus. by Felicia Bond. New York: Four Winds, 1984. *60 A Fruitful Harvest.

Porter, Sue. *My Clothes*. England: Bedrick/Blackie, 1982. *52 What Is a Book?

Potter, Beatrix. *The Story of a Fierce Bad Rabbit*. New York: Warne, 1906. #58 Beatrix Potter Day.

Potter, Beatrix. *The Tale of Benjamin Bunny*. New York: Warne, 1902. *58 Beatrix Potter Day.

Potter, Beatrix. *Tale of Mr. Jeremy Fisher*. New York: Warne, 1906. #20 Freaky Frog Day; *58 Beatrix Potter Day.

Potter, Beatrix. *The Tale of Mrs. Tiggy Winkle*. New York: Warne, 1905. *58 Beatrix Potter Day.

Potter, Beatrix. *The Tale of Peter Rabbit*. New York: Warne, 1902. *58 Beatrix Potter Day.

Potter, Beatrix. *The Tale of the Flopsy Bunnies.* New York: Warne, 1909. #58 Beatrix Potter Day.

Prater, John. *The Gift.* New York: Viking Kestrel, 1986. #75 What Can You Do with a Box?

Price, Matthew, and Jean Claveria. *Peekaboo!* New York: Knopf, 1985. *52 What Is a Book?

Quindlen, Anna. *The Tree That Came to Stay;* illus. by Nancy Carpenter. New York: Crown, 1992. *70 Christmas Tree.

Rand, Gloria. *Salty Dog;* illus. by Ted Rand. New York: Holt, 1989. #62 Across the Bright Blue Sea.

Raynor, Mary. *Mr. and Mrs. Pig's Evening Out.* New York: Atheneum, 1976. #5 Here Comes the Babysitter!

Reiss, John S. *Colors.* New York: Bradbury, 1969. *83 Green.

Rey, H. A. *Curious George Rides a Bike.* Boston: Houghton Mifflin, 1952. #13 Safe Biker!; #51 What Is Paper?

Rey, H. A. *Elizabite, Adventures of a Carniverous Plant.* Hamden, Conn.: Linnet, 1990. #19 If a Forest Grew.

Reyher, Becky. *My Mother Is the Most Beautiful Woman in the World;* illus. by Ruth Gannett. New York: Lothrop, Lee & Shepard, 1945. *61 Scarecrows.

Rice, Eve. *At Grammy's House;* illus. by Nancy Winslow Parker. New York: Greenwillow, 1990. *25 Dinner at Grandma's House.

Rice, Eve. *Benny Bakes a Cake.* New York: Greenwillow, 1981. *#6 Kitchen! Kitchen! *66 Holiday Cake Tales.

Richardson, Frederick. *Mother Goose: The Classic Volland Edition.* Chicago: Rand McNally, 1971. #99 The House That Jack Built.

Rinard, Judith. *Creatures of the Night.* Washington, D. C.: National Geographic, 1977. #86 Bats, Bats, Bats.

Robart, Rose. *The Cake That Mack Ate;* illus. by Maryann Kovalski. Boston: Atlantic Monthly, 1986. *66 Holiday Cake Tales.

Rockwell, Anne. *Bikes.* New York: Dutton, 1987. #13 Safe Biker!

Rockwell, Anne. *I Like the Library.* New York: Dutton, 1977. #53 What Is a Library?

Rockwell, Anne. *Pots and Pans;* illus. by Lizzy Rockwell. New York: Macmillan, 1993. #6 Kitchen! Kitchen!

Rockwell, Anne F. *The Supermarket.* New York: Macmillan, 1979. #43 To the Grocery Store.

Rockwell, Anne and Harlow. *My Babysitter.* New York: Macmillan, 1988. *5 Here Comes the Babysitter!

Rockwell, Harlow. *My Dentist.* New York: Greenwillow, 1975. #76 A Tooth! A Tooth!

Roe, Eileen. *Staying with Grandma;* illus. by Jacqueline Rogers. New York: Bradbury, 1989. *25 Dinner at Grandma's House

Rogers, Jean. *King Island Christmas;* illus. by Rie Munoz. New York: Greenwillow, 1985. *45 Northern Winter; *68 Light a Candle.

Rogow, Zach. *Oranges*; illus. by Mary Szilagyi. New York: Orchard, 1988. *60 A Fruitful Harvest.

Root, Phyllis. *The Old Red Rocking Chair;* illus. by John Sandford. New York: Arcade/ Little, Brown, 1992. #24 Use It Again!

Ross, Pat. *M & M and the Bad News Babies*; illus. by Marilyn Hafner. New York: Pantheon, 1987. #5 Here Comes the Babysitter!

Roy, Ron. *Three Ducks Went Wandering*; illus. by Paul Galdone. New York: Seabury, 1979. *57 Ducklings Dawdle.

Rupert, Rona. *Straw Sense*; illus. by Mike Dooling. New York: Simon & Schuster, 1993. #61 Scarecrows; #49 Shoes and Songs.

Ryder, Joanne. *Catching the Wind;* illus. by Michael Rothman. New York: Morrow, 1989. *94 The Goose Got Loose.

Ryder, Joanne. *Chipmunk Song;* illus. by Lynne Cherry. New York: Dutton, 1987. *56 Groundhog Day.

Ryder, Joanne. *Lizard in the Sun;* illus. by Michael Rothman. New York: Morrow, 1990. #89 Crafty Chameleon.

Ryder, Joanne. *The Spiders Dance;* illus. by Robert J. Blake. New York: Harper, 1981. #87 Spiders.

Ryder, Joanne. *White Bear, Ice Bear*; illus. by Michael Rothman. New York: Morrow, 1989. #1 A Walk in the Moonlight; #3 Winter Wonderland.

Ryder, Joanne. *Winter Whale*; illus. by Michael Rothman. New York: Morrow, 1991. *93 Whale Song.

Rylant, Cynthia. *The Relatives Came*; illus. by Stephen Gammell. New York: Bradbury, 1985. *26 The Relatives Came; #67 Company's Coming.

Rylant, Cynthia. *When I Was Young in the Mountains*; illus. by Diane Goode. New York: Dutton, 1982. *28 Grandpa and Me; *31 Families, Families, and More Families.

Sadler, Marilyn. *Alistair in Outer Space;* illus. by Roger Bollen. New York: Simon & Schuster, 1984. #21 Space Place.

Sandburg, Carl. *The Wedding Procession of the Rag Doll and the Broom Handle and Who Was in It;* illus. by Harriet Pincus. New York: Harcourt Brace & World, 1967. *6 Kitchen! Kitchen! *#61 Scarecrows; *74 What Can You Do with a Broom?

Sasaki, Isao. *Snow*. New York: Viking, 1980. #3 Winter Wonderland.

Sauer, Julia L. *Mike's House;* illus. by Don Freeman. New York: Viking, 1954. #53 What Is a Library?

Scheidl, Gerda Marie. *Four Candles for Simon;* illus. by Marcus Pfister. New York: North-South Books, 1987. #68 Light a Candle.

Schertle, Alice. *William and Grandpa*; illus. by Lydia Dabcovich. New York: Lothrop, Lee & Shepard, 1989. *28 Grandpa and Me.

Schertle, Alice. *Witch Hazel*; illus. by Margot Tomes. New York: HarperCollins, 1991. #61 Scarecrows.

Schlein, Miriam. *Deer in the Snow;* illus. by Leonard P. Kessler. New York: Abelard-Schuman, 1956. #88 The Timid Deer.

Schneider, Rex. *The Wide-Mouthed Frog*. Owings Mills, Md.: Stemmer House, 1980. *20 Freaky Frog Day.

Schoenherr, John. *Bear*. New York: Philomel, 1991. #85 Bears in Their Dens.

Schram, Penninah. *The Big Sukkah*; illus. by Jacqueline Kahane. Rockville, Md.: Kar-Ben Copies, 1986. #67 Company's Coming.

Scott, Ann Herbert. *On Mother's Lap;* illus. by Glo Coalson. New York: McGraw-Hill, 1972. *33 Lullaby; *38 I Want to Share with You Today; *45 Northern Winter.

Scott, Ann Herbert. *On Mother's Lap;* illus. by Glo Coalson. New York: Clarion, 1992. See above.

Seeger, Pete and Charles Seeger. *The Foolish Frog*; illus. by Miloslav Jagr. New York: Macmillan, 1973. *20 Freaky Frog Day.

Segal, Lore. *Tell Me a Mitzi*; illus. by Harriet Pincus. New York: Farrar, Straus and Giroux, 1970. *5 Here Comes the Babysitter!

Selig, Sylvie. *Kangaroo*. London: Jonathan Cape, 1980. *53 What Is a Book?

Sendak, Maurice. *In the Night Kitchen*. New York: Harper & Row, 1970. *6 Kitchen! Kitchen! *#44 Bakers at Work.

Sendak, Maurice. *Where the Wild Things Are*. New York: Harper & Row, 1963. *19 If a Forest Grew in Your Room.

Seuss, Dr. *I Had Trouble in Getting to Solla Sollew*. New York: Random House, 1971. #12 On the Road.

Seuss, Dr. *Horton Hatches the Egg*. New York: Random House, 1940. *54 Cra-a-ack!

Shannon, George. *The Surprise;* illus. by Jose Aruego and Ariane Dewey. New York: Greenwillow, 1983. *75 What Can You Do with a Box. *66 Holiday Cake Tales.

Sharmat, Marjorie Weinman. *I'm Terrific!;* illus. by Vera B. Williams. New York: Holiday House, 1977. #35 I'm Proud to Be Me!

Sheldon, Dyan. *The Whale's Song;* illus. by Gary Blythe. New York: Dial, 1991. #93 Whale Song.

Sherman, Ivan. *I Do Not Like It When My Friend Comes to Visit*. New York: Harcourt Brace Jovanovich, 1973. #38 I Want to Share with You Today.

Showers, Paul. *The Listening Walk*; illus. by Aliki. New York: HarperCollins, 1991. *84 The Quiet Storytime.

Shulevitz, Uri. *Dawn*. New York: Farrar, Straus and Giroux, 1974. #32 Gone Fishing.

Siberell, Anne. *Whale in the Sky*. New York: Dutton, 1982. #93 Whale Song.

Siebert, Diane. *Trucksong;* illus. by Byron Barton. New York: Crowell, 1983. *12 On the Road.

Simple Pleasure by Bobby McFerrin. Hollywood, Calif.: EMI Manhattan, 1988. CD or cassette. *17 Dance-a-Path.

Singer, Marilyn. *Turtle in July*; illus. by Jerry Pinkney. New York: Macmillan, 1989. *2 At the Bottom of the Pond; *#23 Good Wood.

Sis, Peter. *Follow the Dream! The Story of Christopher Columbus*. New York: Knopf, 1991. #62 Across the Bright Blue Sea.

Sloat, Teri. *The Eye of the Needle*. New York: Dutton, 1990. #7 Greedy Gluttons.

Slote, Joseph. *The Star Rocker;* illus. by Dirk Zimmer. New York: Harper & Row, 1982. #33 Lullaby.

Small, David. *Paper John.* New York: Farrar, Straus, and Giroux, 1987. #51 What Is Paper?

Smith, Barry. *Tom and Annie Go Shopping: A Can You Find? Book.* Boston: Houghton Mifflin, 1988. #43 To the Grocery Store.

Smith, Lane. *The Big Pets.* New York: Viking, 1991. *40 Gentle Giants.

Soya, Kiyoshi. *A House of Leaves;* illus. by Akiko Hayashi. New York: Philomel, 1987. *83 Green; *84 The Quiet Storytime.

Spier, Peter. *The Fox Went Out on a Chilly Night.* Garden City, N. Y.: Doubleday, 1961. *92 Watching Foxes.

Spohn, David. *Winter Wood.* New York: Lothrop, Lee & Shepard, 1991. #23 Good Wood.

Spohn, Kate. *Ruth's Bake Shop.* New York: Orchard, 1990. *44 Bakers at Work; #66 Holiday Cake Tales.

Standiford, Natalie. *The Best Little Monkeys in the World;* illus. by Hilary Knight. New York: Random House, 1987. #5 Here Comes the Babysitter!

Steig, William. *Doctor de Soto.* New York: Farrar, Straus and Giroux, 1982. *76 A Tooth! A Tooth!

Steig, William. *Gorky Rises.* New York: Farrar, Straus and Giroux, 1980. #20 Freaky Frog Day.

Steig, William. *Tiffky Doofky;* New York: Farrar, Straus, and Giroux, 1978. #24 Use It Again!

Steig, William. *The Zabajaba Jungle.* New York: Farrar, Straus, and Giroux, 1987. #4 Into the Rain Forest.

Stevens, Kathleen. *The Beast in the Bathtub;* illus. by Ray Bowler. Minneapolis: Gareth Stevens, 1985. #77 Bathtime.

Stock, Catherine. *Where Are You Going, Manyoni?* New York: Morrow, 1993. #49 Shoes and Songs.

Stott, Dorothy. *Little Duck's Bicycle Ride.* New York: Dutton, 1991. *9 Upside Down Day.

Street, Julia M. *Candle Love Feast;* illus. by Anna Marie Magagna. New York: Coward-McCann, Geoghegan, 1959. *68 Light a Candle.

Tafuri, Nancy. *Have You Seen My Duckling?* New York: Greenwillow, 1984. #57 Ducklings Dawdle.

Taylor, Judy. *Sophie and Jack;* illus. by Susan Gantner. New York: Philomel, 1982. *27 Picnic!

Teague, Mark. *Frog Medicine.* New York: Scholastic, 1991. #20 Freaky Frog Day.

Teague, Mark. *Moog-Moog, Space Barber.* New York: Scholastic, 1990. *20 Space Place.

Tejima, Keizaburo. *Fox's Dream.* New York: Philomel, 1987. #92 Watching Foxes.

Testa, Fulvio. *The Paper Airplane.* New York: Holt, 1988. #51 What Is Paper?

There Was an Old Woman Who Swallowed a Fly. Purton, Wiltshire, England: Child's Play, 1973. *7 Greedy Gluttons.

Thomas, Elizabeth. *Green Beans*; illus. by Vicki Jo Redenbaugh. Minneapolis: Carolrhoda, 1992. #25 Dinner at Grandma's House.

Thompson, Colin. *The Paper Bag Prince*. New York: Knopf, 1992. #24 Use It Again!

Titherington, Jeanne. *Baby's Boat*. New York: Greenwillow, 1992. *62 Across the Bright Blue Sea.

Titherington, Jeanne. *Where Are You Going, Emma?* New York: Greenwillow, 1988. *17 Dance-a-Path; *28 Grandpa and Me.

Tolstoy, Alexei. *The Great Big Enormous Turnip*; illus. by Helen Oxenbury. New York: Watts, 1968. *59 The Enormous Vegetable Harvest.

Tompert, Ann. *Little Fox Goes to the End of the World*; illus. by John Wallner. New York: Crown, 1976. #62 Across the Bright Blue Sea.

Tripp, Paul. *The Strawman Who Smiled by Mistake*; illus. by Wendy Watson. Garden City, N.Y.: Doubleday, 1967. #61 Scarecrows.

Tsutsui, Yoriko. *Before the Picnic*; illus. by Akiko Hayashi. New York: Philomel, 1987. #27 Picnic!

Tursky, Krystyna. *Coppelia: The Story of the Ballet*. Morristown, N.J.: Silver Burdett, 1986. *98 Dancing Puppets.

Tusa, Tricia. *The Family Reunion*. New York: Farrar, Straus and Giroux, 1993. #26 The Relatives Came.

Tusa, Tricia. *Stay Away from the Junkyard!* New York: Macmillan, 1988. #24 Use It Again!

Tworkov, Jack. *The Camel Who Took a Walk*; illus. by Roger Duvoisin. New York: Dutton, 1951. *#4 Into the Rain Forest; *#17 Dance-a-Path.

Tyron, Leslie. *Albert's Alphabet*. New York: Atheneum, 1991. #23 Good Wood.

Udry, Janice May. *The Moon Jumpers*; illus. by Maurice Sendak. New York: Harper & Row, 1959. #1 A Walk in the Moonlight.

Udry, Janice May. *What Mary Jo Shared*; illus. by Eleanor Mill. Chicago: Albert Whitman, 1966. *37 Don't Be Shy.

Ueno, Noriko. *Elephant Buttons*. New York: Harper & Row, 1973. *81 Small and Tall.

Ungerer, Tomi. *Rufus*. New York: Harper, 1961. #86 Bats, Bats, Bats.

Van Allsburg, Chris. *The Polar Express*. Boston: Houghton Mifflin, 1985. *14 Out the Train Window.

Vaughan, Marcia K. *Wombat Stew*; illus. by Pamela Lofts. Englewood Cliffs, N.J.: Silver Burdett, 1984. #47 Koala, Kangaroo, and Kookaburra.

Vernon, Tannis. *Adrienne and the Magic Clockwork Train*. New York: Crown, 1990. #14 Out the Train Window.

Vincent, Gabrielle. *Ernest and Celestine's Patchwork Quilt*. New York: Greenwillow, 1982. *29 Quilts to Remember.

Vincent, Gabrielle. *Ernest and Celestine's Picnic*. New York: Greenwillow, 1982. *27 Picnic!

Vincent, Gabrielle. *Merry Christmas Ernest and Celestine*. New York: Morrow, 1984. #63 Parties!; *67 Company's Coming; #69 Youngest One at Christmas.

Viorst, Judith. *The Goodbye Book*; illus. by Kay Chorao. New York: Atheneum, 1988. *5 Here Comes the Babysitter!

Vipont, Elfrida. *The Elephant and the Bad Baby*; illus. by Raymond Briggs. New York: Coward-McCann, 1969. *8 Bad Babies.

Wade, Alan. *I'm Flying*; illus. by Petra Mathers. *72 What Can You Do with a Balloon?

Waggoner, Karen. *The Lemonade Babysitter*; illus. by Dorothy Donohue. Boston: Little, Brown, 1992. #5 Here Comes the Babysitter!

Wagner, Jenny. *The Bunyip of Berkeley's Creek*; illus. by Ron Brooks. Scarsdale, N.Y.: Bradbury, 1973. #47 Koala, Kangaroo, and Kookaburra.

Wagner, Karen. *Chocolate Chip Cookies*; illus. by Leah Palmer Preiss. New York: Henry Holt, 1990. *44 Bakers at Work.

Ward, Lynd. *The Biggest Bear*. Boston: Houghton Mifflin, 1952. *40 Gentle Giants; *81 Small and Tall; #85 Bears in Their Dens.

Ward, Lynd. *The Silver Pony*. Boston: Houghton Mifflin, 1973. #15 Ride Away!

Watanabe, Shigeo. *How Do I Put It On?;* illus. by Yasuo Ohtomo. New York: Philomel, 1977. *35 I'm Proud to Be Me!

Watanabe, Shigeo. *I Can Build a House!;* illus. by Yasuo Ohtomo. New York: Philomel, 1982. *35 I'm Proud to Be Me!

Watanabe, Shigeo. *I Can Ride*; illus. by Yasuo Ohtomo. New York: Philomel, 1981. #34 Whoops!

Watanabe, Shigeo. *I Can Take a Bath*; illus. by Yasuo Ohtomo. New York: Philomel, 1986. #77 Bathtime.

Watanabe, Shigeo. *What a Good Lunch!*; illus. by Yasuo Ohtomo. New York: Philomel, 1980. *8 Bad Babies; *51 What Is Paper?

Watson, Clyde. *Father Fox's Pennyrhymes*; illus. by Wendy Watson. New York: Crowell, 1971. #92 Watching Foxes.

Watson, Wendy. *Has Winter Come?* New York: Collins & World, 1978. #56 Groundhog Day

Watson, Wendy. *Lollipop*. New York: Crowell, 1976. *43 To the Grocery Store.

Welber, Robert. *A Winter Picnic*; illus. by Deborah Ray. New York: Pantheon, 1970. *27 Picnic!

Weller, Frances Ward. *I Wonder If I'll See a Whale*; illus. by Ted Lewin. New York: Philomel, 1991. *93 Whale Song.

Wellington, Monica. *Mr. Cookie Baker*. New York: Dutton, 1992. #44 Bakers at Work.

Wells, Rosemary. *Max's Christmas*. New York: Dial, 1986. *69 Youngest One at Christmas.

Wells, Rosemary. *Morris's Disappearing Bag*. New York: Dial, 1975. *69 Youngest One at Christmas.

Wells, Rosemary. *Shy Charles*. New York: Dial, 1988. #5 Here Comes the Babysitter!; *37 Don't Be Shy; *42 Policeman to the Rescue.

Westcott, Nadine Bernard. *The Giant Vegetable Garden*. Boston: Little, Brown, 1980. #59 The Enormous Vegetable Harvest.

Westcott, Nadine Bernard. *I Know an Old Woman Who Swallowed a Fly.* Boston: Little, Brown, 1980. #87 Spiders.

Westcott, Nadine Bernard. *The Lady with the Alligator Purse.* Boston: Little, Brown, 1988. *5 Here Comes the Babysitter!

Westcott, Nadine Bernard. *Skip to My Lou.* Boston: Little, Brown, 1989. *100 Skip to My Lou.

Wezel, Peter. *The Good Bird.* New York: Harper & Row, 1964. *16 Where Is the Green Parrot?; *38 I Want to Share with You Today.

Wheeler, Cindy. *Marmalade's Picnic.* New York: Knopf, 1983. #27 Picnic!

Whittington, Mary K. *Carmina, Come Dance!*; illus. by Michael McDermott. New York: Atheneum, 1989. *15 Ride Away!

Whittington, Mary K. *The Patchwork Lady;* illus. by Jane Dyer. San Diego: Harcourt Brace Jovanovich, 1991. *67 Company's Coming; *79 Plain and Fancy.

Wideman, Christine. *Housekeeper of the Wind;* illus. by Lisa Disimini. New York: Harper & Row, 1990. #74 What Can You Do with a Broom?

Wiesner, David. *Tuesday.* New York: Clarion, 1991. *2 At the Bottom of the Pond; *20 Freaky Frog Day.

Wildsmith, Brian. *Daisy.* New York: Pantheon, 1984. #91 Cow, Bull, Ox.

Williams, Karen Lynn. *Galimoto.*; illus. by Catharine Stock. New York: Lothrop, Lee & Shepard, 1990. #36 Too Proud to Ask for Help.

Williams, Vera B. *More, More, More Said the Baby!* New York: Greenwillow, 1991. *31 Families, Families, and More Families.

Winn, Marie. *The Fireside Book of Children's Songs.* New York: Simon and Schuster, 1966. *28 Grandpa and Me.

Winter, Jeanette. *Come Out to Play.* New York: Knopf, 1986. *1 A Walk in the Moonlight; *18 Dress Up.

Winter, Jeanette. *Diego*; text by Jonah Winter. New York: Knopf, 1991. *22 If I Were a Painter.

Winthrop, Elizabeth. *Bear and Mrs. Duck*; illus. by Patience Brewster. New York: Holiday House, 1988. #5 Here Comes the Babysitter!

Wolff, Ashley. *A Year of Birds.* New York: Dodd, Mead, 1984. *64 Winter Birds.

Wolf, Janet. *The Rosy Fat Magenta Radish.* Boston: Little Brown, 1990. #59 The Enormous Vegetable Harvest.

Wolkstein, Diane. *Little Mouse's Painting;* illus. by Maryjane Begin. New York: Morrow, 1992. #22 If I Were a Painter.

Wood, Audrey. *King Bidgood's in the Bathtub;* illus. by Don Wood. San Diego: Harcourt Brace Jovanovich, 1985. #77 Bathtime.

Wood, Audrey. *The Napping House;* illus. by Don Wood. San Diego: Harcourt Brace Jovanovich, 1984. *5 Here Comes the Babysitter!; *78 Bedtime.

Wood, Audrey. *Oh My Baby Bear!* San Diego: Harcourt Brace Jovanovich, 1990. *Oh No, Baby!

Wood, Audrey. *Silly Sally.* San Diego: Harcourt Brace Jovanovich, 1992. *9 Upside Down Day.

Wood, Don and Audrey. *The Little Mouse, the Red Ripe Strawberry, and the Big Hungry Bear.* Purton, Wiltshire, England: Child's Play, 1984. *59 The Enormous Vegetable Harvest.

Xiong, Blia. *Nine-In-One Grrr Grrr*; illus. by Nancy Hom. Adapted by Cathy Spagnoli. San Francisco: Children's Book Press, 1989. *39 Small Creatures Meet Big Bullies.

Yashima, Taro. *Umbrella.* New York: Viking, 1958. *73 What Can You Do with an Umbrella?

Yashima, Taro. *Youngest One.* New York: Viking, 1962. *37 Don't Be Shy; *41 Youngest One.

Ylla. *Two Little Bears.* New York: Harper, 1954. #85 Bears in Their Dens.

Yolen, Jane. *Owl Moon*; illus. by John Schoenherr. New York: Philomel, 1987. *1 A Walk in the Moonlight; *3 A Winter Wonderland.

Yolen, Jane. *Picnic with Piggins*; illus. by Jane Dyer. San Diego: Harcourt Brace Jovanovich, 1988. #27 Picnic!

Yolen, Jane. *The Three Bears Rhyme Book*; illus. by Jane Dyer. San Diego: Harcourt Brace Jovanovich, 1987. *17 Dance-a-Path; *33 Lullaby; *53 What Is a Library?; *80 Three.

Yorinks, Arthur and Richard Egielski. *Hey, Al.* New York: Farrar, Straus and Giroux, 1986. #10 Parrot Parties; *16 Where Is the Green Parrot?; *9 Plain and Fancy.

Young, Ruth. *A Trip to Mars*; illus. by Cocca-Leffler. New York: Orchard, 1990. *21 Space Place.

Yulya. *Bears Are Sleeping*; illus. by Nonny Hogrogian. New York: Scribners, 1967. #85 Bears in Their Dens.

Zacharias, Thomas and Wanda. *But Where Is the Green Parrot?* New York: Delacorte, 1968. *10 Parrot Parties; *16 Where Is the Green Parrot?

Zemach, Harve. *Mommy, Buy Me a China Doll;* illus. by Margot Zemach. New York: Farrar, Straus, and Giroux, 1966. *31 Families, Families, and More Familes.

Ziefert, Harriet and Arnold Lobel. *Bear Goes Shopping: A Guessing Game Story.* New York: Harper & Row, 1986. #43 To the Grocery Store.

Zion, Gene. *Dear Garbage Man*; illus. by Margaret Bloy Graham. New York: Harper, 1957. *24 Use It Again.

Zion, Gene. *Harry the Dirty Dog;* illus. by Margaret Bloy Graham. New York: Harper & Row, 1956. *77 Bathtime.

Zion, Gene. *The Plant Sitter*; illus. by Margaret Bloy Graham. New York: Harper, 1959. *19 If a Forest Grew in Your Room.

Zolotow, Charlotte. *Mr. Rabbit and the Lovely Present*; illus. by Maurice Sendak. New York: Harper, 1962. #60 A Fruitful Harvest.

Zolotow, Charlotte. *My Grandson Lew*; illus. by William Pene du Bois. New York: Harper & Row, 1972. #28 Grandpa and Me.

Films and Videos

Alexander and the Car with the Missing Headlight. Weston, Conn.: Weston Woods, 1966. 16 mm film or video. #11 Toothgnasher Superflash.

Bats. Oley, Pa.: Bullfrog Films, 1986. 8 min. video. #86 Bats, Bats, Bats.

Bell on a Deer. Studio City, Calif.: Filmfair, 1987. 16 min. 16 mm film or video. *88 The Timid Deer.

A Boy, a Dog, and a Frog. New York: Phoenix Films/ BFA Films & Video, 1981. 9 min. 16 mm film or video. *2 At the Bottom of the Pond.

Burt Dow, Deep-Water Man. Weston, Conn.: Weston Woods, 1983. 10 min. 16 mm film or video. #90 Whale Song.

Dr. De Soto. Weston, Conn.: Weston Woods, 1984. 10 min. 16 mm film or video. *76 A Tooth! A Tooth!

Dream of the Wild Horses. (Le Sange Des Chevaux Sauvages.) Albert Lamorisse, director. New York: Contemporary Films, 1962. 9 min. 16 mm film. #15 Ride Away!

The Foolish Frog. Weston, Conn.: Weston Woods, 1971. 8 min. 16 mm film or video. *20 Freaky Frog Day.

The Greedy Cat. Seattle, Wa.: Sign-A-Vision, 1988. Video. *7 Greedy Gluttons.

Hot Hippo. Weston, Conn.: Weston Woods, 1989. 6 min. 16 mm film or video. *90 Happy Hippos.

The House That Jack Built. Seattle, Wa.: Sign-A-Vision, 1987. 15 min. Video. #99 The House That Jack Built.

Let's Give Kitty a Bath. New York: Phoenix/ BFA, 1986. 12 min. 16 mm film or video. #77 Bathtime.

Lullaby. International Film Bureau, 1975. 4 min. 16 mm film. #33 Lullaby.

Luxo, Jr. Pixar, 1988. Los Angeles: Direct Cinema. 3 min. 16 mm film or video. *34 Whoops!

Mole and the Green Star. New York: McGraw-Hill, 1970. 8 min. 16 mm film or video. *56 Groundhog Day; *65 Holiday Stars.

Mole and the Umbrella. Phoenix, 1982. 9 min. 16 mm film or video. *73 What Can You Do with an Umbrella?

The Napping House. Weston, Conn.: Weston Woods, 1985. 5 min. 16 mm film or video. #33 Lullaby.

The Owl Who Married a Goose. Celebrity Films, 1976. 8 min. 16 mm film. *45 Northern Winters.

The Red Balloon. Albert Lamorisse, director. Janus Films, 1956. 34 min. 16 mm film or video. *72 What Can You Do with a Balloon.

The Remarkable Riderless Runaway Tricycle. Phoenix, 1982. 11 min. 16 mm film or video. #13 Safe Biker!

Susie the Little Blue Coupe. Walt Disney, 1952. 8 min. 16 mm film or video. *11 Toothgnasher Superflash.

Tales of Beatrix Potter. EMI Film Productions. New York: HBO Cannon Video, 1971. 86 min. Video. #20 Freaky Frog Day; *58 Beatrix Potter Day.

Tin Toy. Pixar, Los Angeles: Direct Cinema, 1988. 4 min. 16 mm film or video. *8 Bad Babies.

The Ugly Duckling. Walt Disney Productions, 1939. 8 min. 16 mm film or video. *57 Ducklings Dawdle.

The Ugly Duckling. Weston, Conn.: Weston Woods, 1982. 15 min. 16 mm film or video. *57 Ducklings Dawdle.

Where the Wild Things Are. Weston, Conn.: Weston Woods, 1975. 8 min. 16 mm film or video. #19 If a Forest Grew.

Subject Index